IMAGES
of America

AROUND BRADFORD
VOLUME II

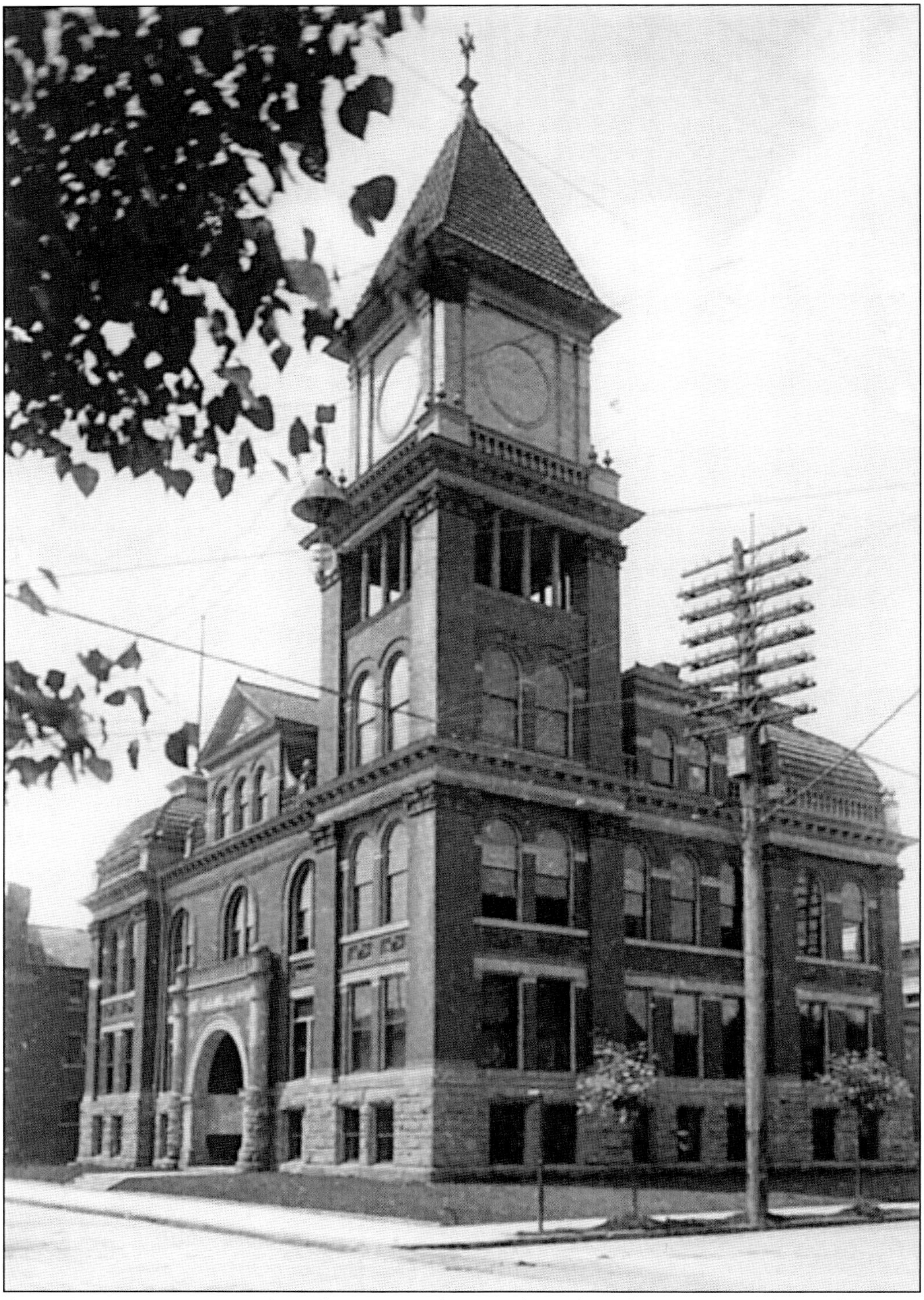

City Hall, 1900. Located on the corner of Kennedy and Boylston Streets, this well-known symbol of Bradford was built in 1898 by William Hanley. It was nearly destroyed by fire in 1901 but was rebuilt, and served as Bradford's city building for many more years. The structure is currently undergoing restoration.

Introduction

Shakespeare wrote, "When to the sessions of sweet silent thought, I summon up the remembrance of things past." Perhaps this remembrance of things past is what Louis Daguerre had in mind when he invented the daguerreotype in 1849. Nothing can bring back a memory like a photograph. In today's world of computers, television, and videotapes, a simple photograph seems almost old fashioned; a relic of a world that modern society has outgrown. It doesn't talk, move, change colors, or play games. It doesn't have to. It is said that a photograph is worth a thousand words. We at the Bradford Landmark Society have found that a photograph is worth a thousand memories.

In our first book, *Around Bradford*, we tried to gather a collection of photographs that answered many of the questions about the city that people often ask us. Why was that building built? Who was that man? What is that monument? When did that happen?

Events, people, places. . . all had their place in that first book. This time, though, we took a different approach. This time, we want people to remember. We chose photographs that reflected the times when they were taken: VJ Day on Main Street, the gangsters of the 1920s, the Derrick City School fire, Tommy Darcy, baseball, the trolleys, and the last steam train out of Bradford.

It was a pleasurable task and made researching *Around Bradford II* much easier. Anyone who entered the Herbig Bakery was pounced on and asked, "do you remember this picture?" And they usually did! It's funny, but whenever anyone holds an old photograph, they inevitably end up smiling. It's the power of remembrance.

Around Bradford II begins at the turn of the century. As we approach the end of this century, it is important to look back one hundred years and see how far we have traveled as a society and as a city. This year also marks the 100th anniversary of the Spanish-American War; the first war on foreign soil that this city had ever experienced. The patriotism of those Bradfordians in 1898 was remarkable.

Our second chapter covers the history of oil exploration in Bradford. We felt that it deserved a place of prominence, for oil shaped the growth of the city and made the name Bradford internationally known. Next, we explored that golden era in Bradford, the Age of Innocence as it is sometimes referred to, between 1900 and 1910 when the city was young, growing, and wealthy. The approaching war years of 1915–20 found Bradford losing its isolation as the automobile became popular, and soldiers brought back new and interesting ideas. The Roaring Twenties really roared in Bradford, with countless speakeasies, the KKK, gangsters, and Prohibition. Our chapter on sports will bring back memories of boxing, baseball, football, golf, the Valley Hunt, basketball, skiing, and the early days of horse racing. Our last chapter, "Memories are Made of This," is really the theme of the book. Many of the people who read this book will remember first hand the events pictured here, or will remember family or friends' experiences.

The Bradford Landmark Society is truly dedicated to helping people learn the history of the town and its people. The tremendous success of our first book has proven to us that Shakespeare was right—people want "the remembrance of things past." There is no better way than through photographs. A photograph can take you to a dance in 1890; it can send you marching down the street with World War I soldiers; it can stand you in a field next to a burning oil tank; it can take you to Luna Park in the summertime. Who said that they never invented the time machine? You're holding it in your hand.

One

Looking Backward, Moving Forward

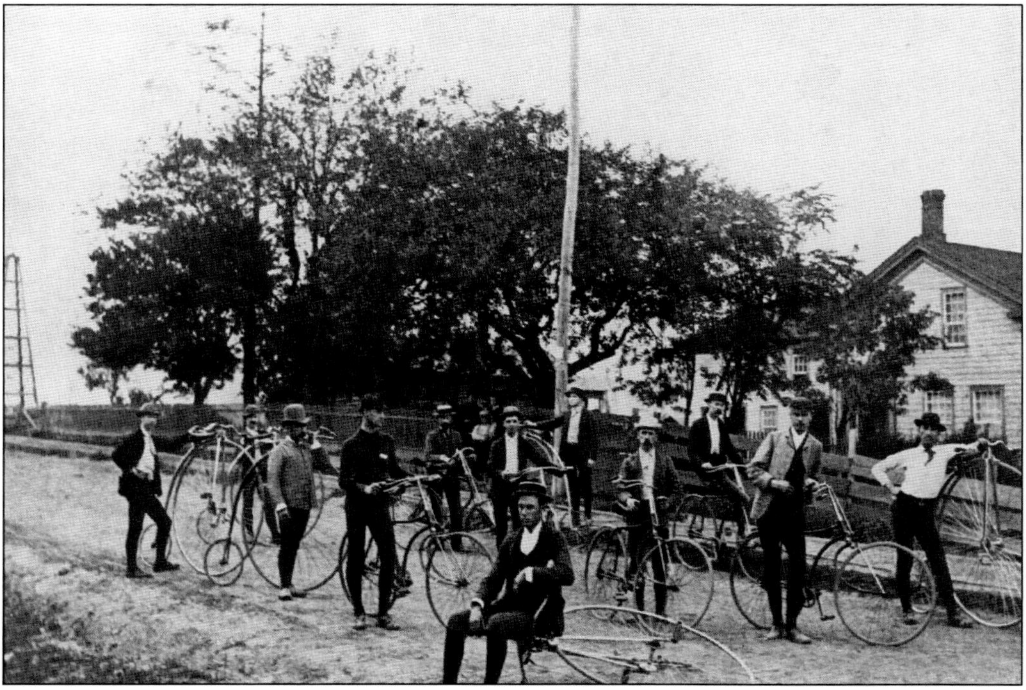

THE BICYCLE CLUB, C. 1888. These large-wheeled bikes (called "ordinaries") required strong individuals with long legs, for they were heavy and cumbersome. Here, members of the Bicycle Club stop for a breather in front of the Fisher Homestead on East Main Street. The man sitting on his bicycle is Harvey Haggerty, who later was the president of the Bradford National Bank.

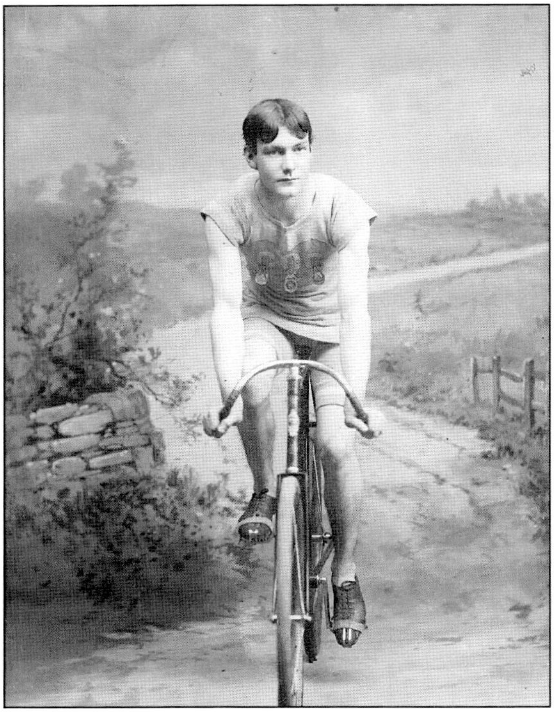

CLIFF BAUER, CYCLIST, 1898. By the 1880s, a "safety" bike—similar to today's version—had been invented, and bicycling became the rage in Bradford. Coaster brakes, however, were not invented until after 1900, and reports of pedestrians being run down were so prevalent that Bradford soon passed an ordinance requiring that all bikes must be equipped with a bell to warn those in the cyclist's path.

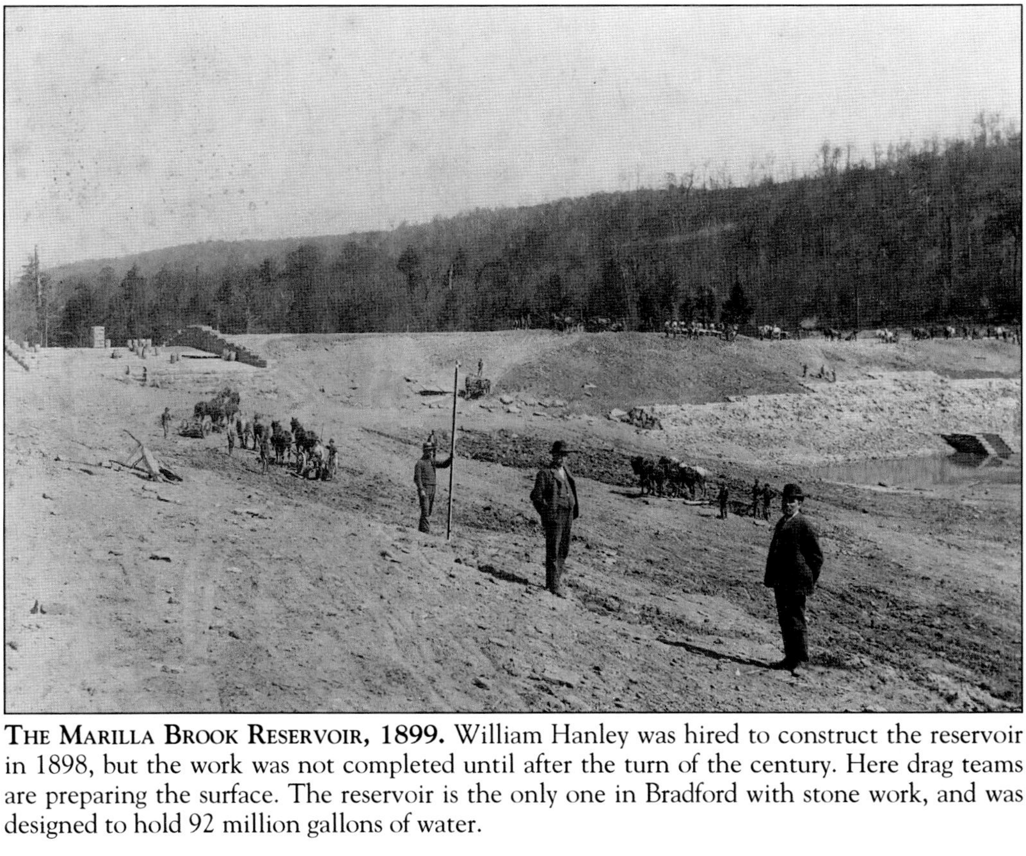

THE MARILLA BROOK RESERVOIR, 1899. William Hanley was hired to construct the reservoir in 1898, but the work was not completed until after the turn of the century. Here drag teams are preparing the surface. The reservoir is the only one in Bradford with stone work, and was designed to hold 92 million gallons of water.

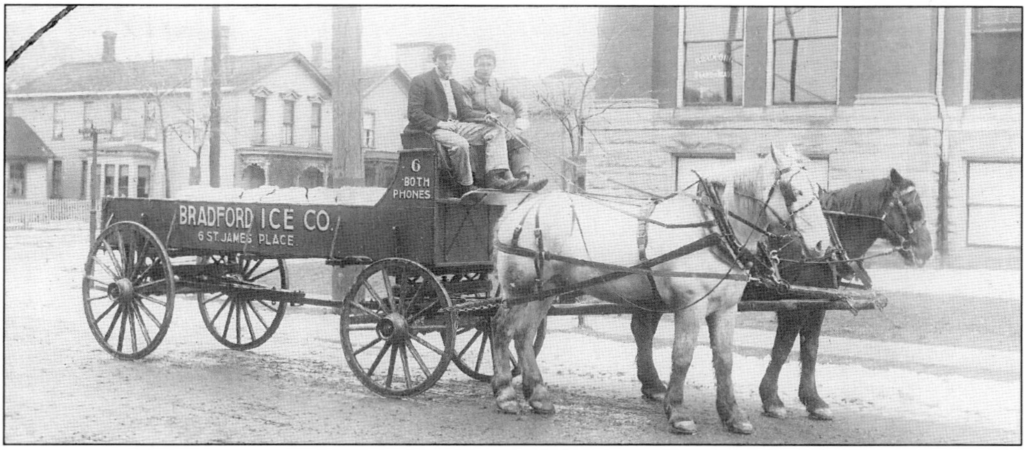

The Bradford Ice Company, 1900. Founded in 1882 by John Sheehy, this company met Bradford's need for ice, cutting over 20,000 tons of ice each year from Bennett Brook, and storing it in a dozen icehouses. A two-year supply was always kept on hand to avoid any possibility of an "ice famine."

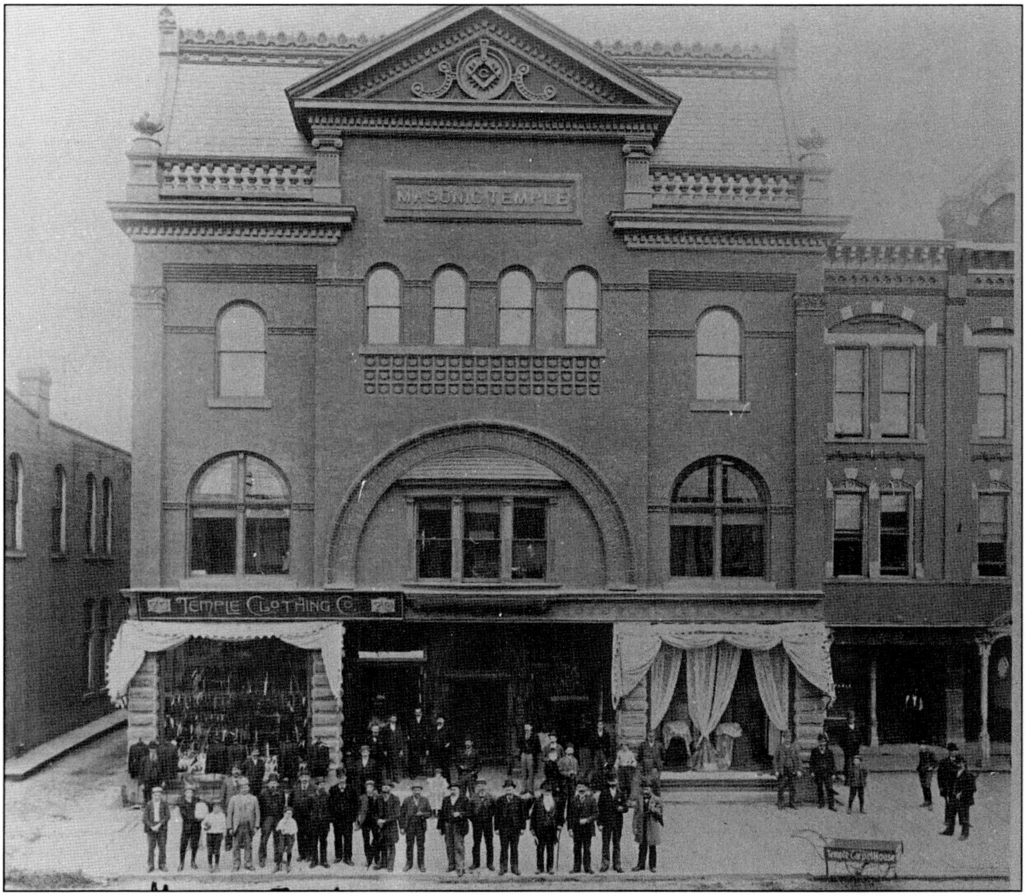

The Masonic Temple Building, 1890. Still standing today at 57 Main Street, this impressive brick building was home to the Masonic Lodge of Bradford. Notice the wide plank sidewalk in front of the building.

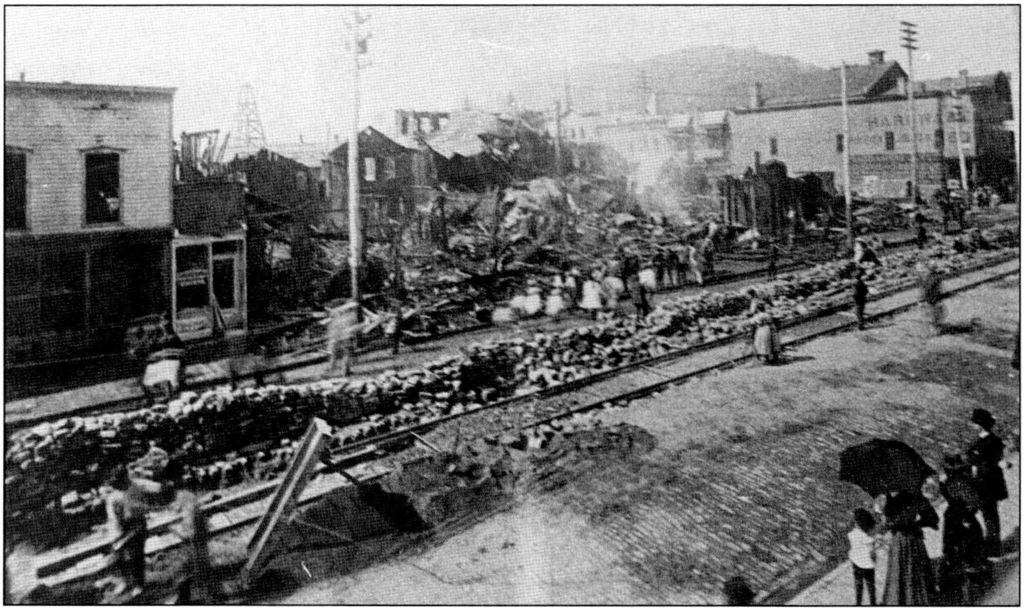

Fire on Main Street, 1879. This photograph shows two things very clearly: the ruins of a building destroyed by fire on the corner of Chestnut and Main Streets, and the paving of Main Street with cobblestones. The right-hand side of the street has been completed, which must have seemed like a luxury to Bradfordians used to dusty roads and mud holes.

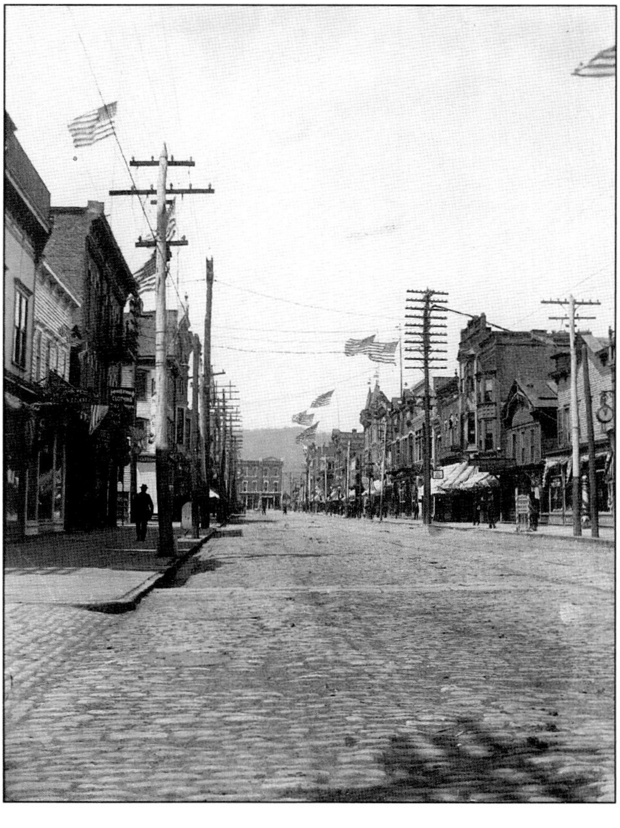

Looking Up Main Street, 1897. Main Street was originally paved with cobblestones. Paving with vitrified brick—a harder brick—was undertaken in the summer of 1899. The cobblestones were then reused in the construction of the retaining wall at the top of Pearl Street, near a grassy triangle called "Third Ward Park."

Warner's Business College, c. 1890. Bradford's first business college was founded in 1887 to teach the basics of business to both men and women. Located in Pompelon Hall, and later on Main Street, Wagner's Business College remained in existence until at least 1925. This building is still standing on the corner of South Avenue and Chautauqua Place.

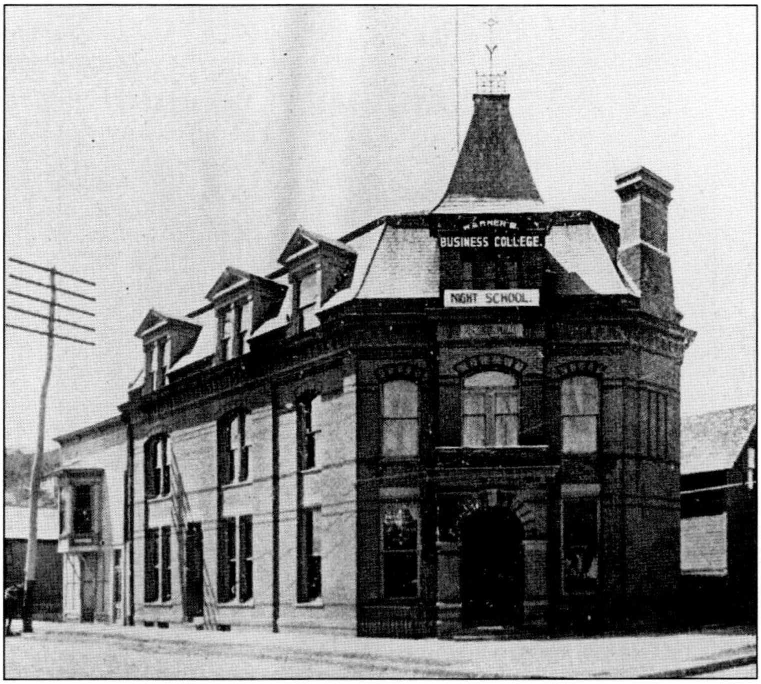

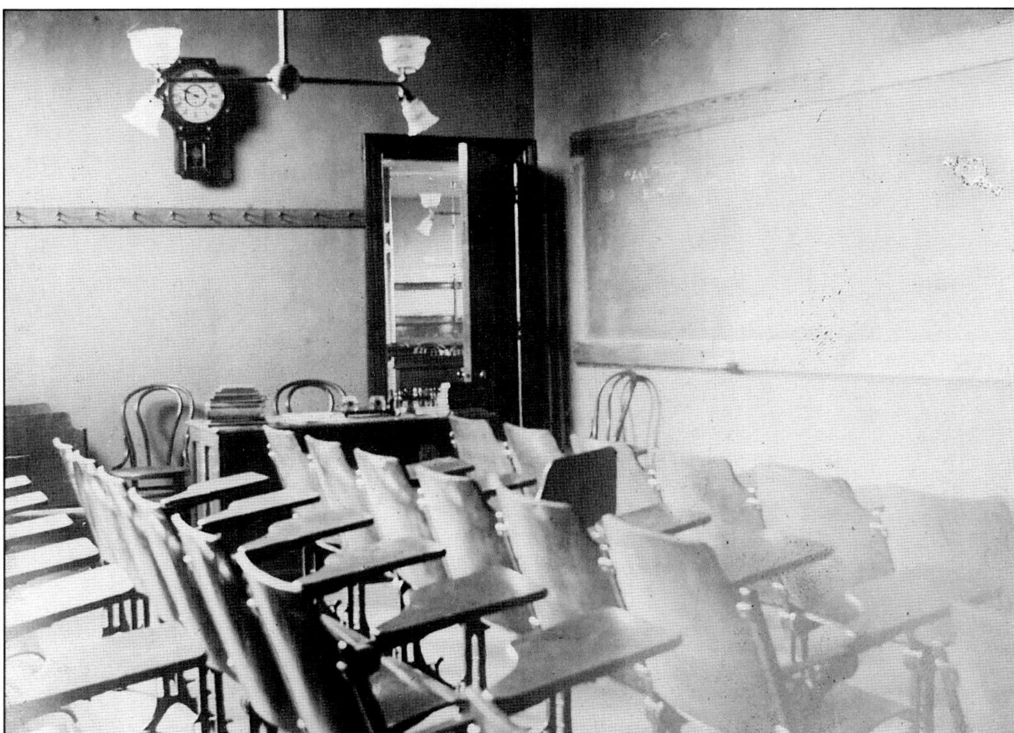

A Classroom in the Wagner Business College, c. 1890. Here, topics such as bookkeeping, typewriting, dictation, penmanship, rapid calculation, basic arithmetic, and other related subjects were taught. The school remained open year round and if a student applied himself, the basic course could be learned in four months.

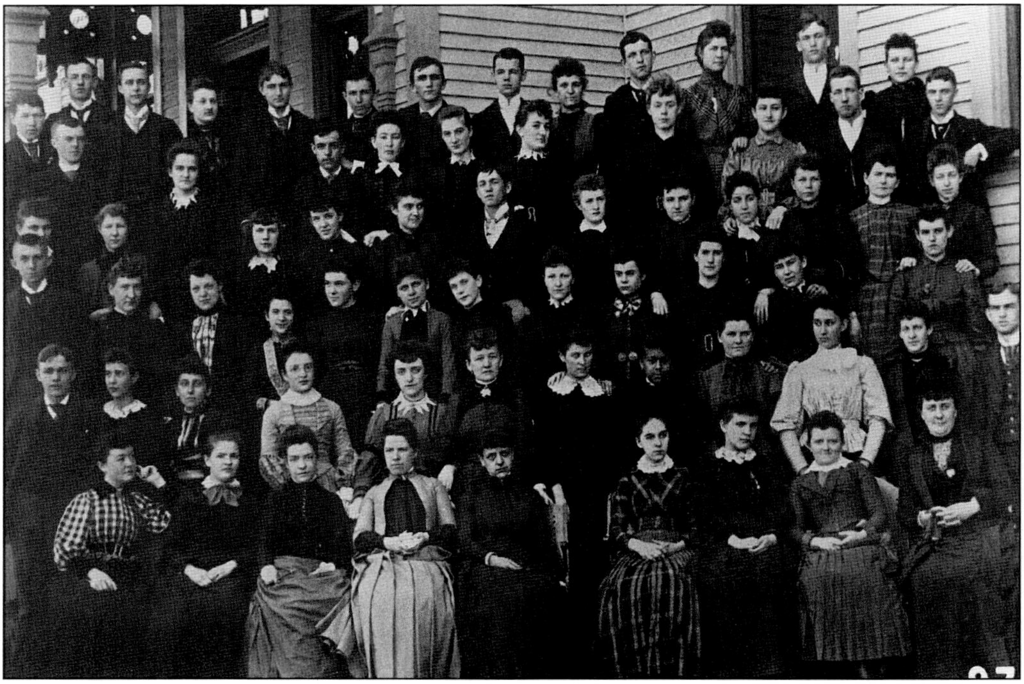

Ella Boyce Kirk, 1861(?)–1930. As a young teacher, her first assignment was in the Bradford city schools. In 1887 she was appointed superintendent of schools, marking her as the first woman to hold this distinction in the United States. She died of tuberculosis in 1930, at the home of her daughter in southern Pennsylvania. She is seen here in the lower right corner, with the senior class students.

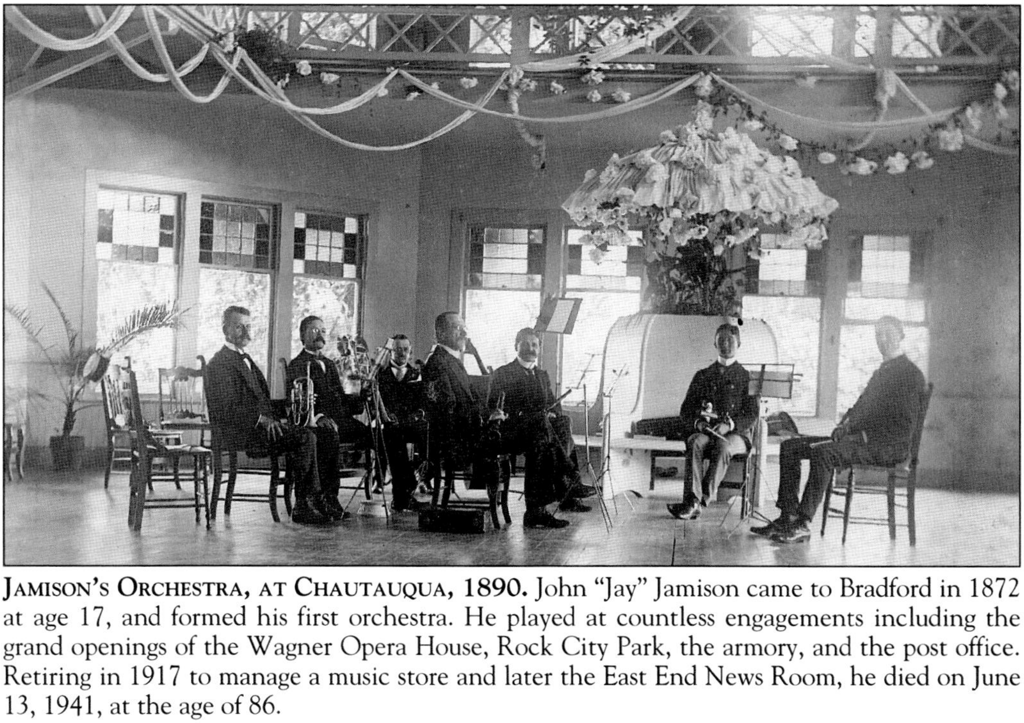

Jamison's Orchestra, at Chautauqua, 1890. John "Jay" Jamison came to Bradford in 1872 at age 17, and formed his first orchestra. He played at countless engagements including the grand openings of the Wagner Opera House, Rock City Park, the armory, and the post office. Retiring in 1917 to manage a music store and later the East End News Room, he died on June 13, 1941, at the age of 86.

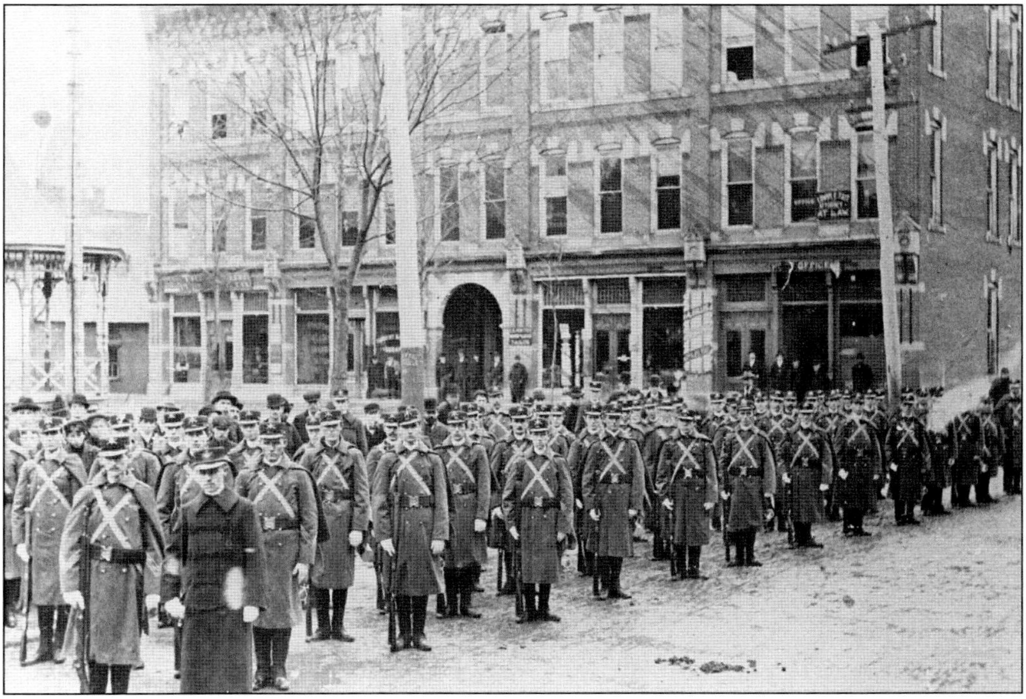

Sixteenth Regiment, Company C, 1898. These men are in formation at the head of Main Street, in front of the Public Square. The Odd Fellows Building can be seen behind them. In April, these men were sent to Puerto Rico to fight the Spanish-American War. This year marks the 100th anniversary of that war.

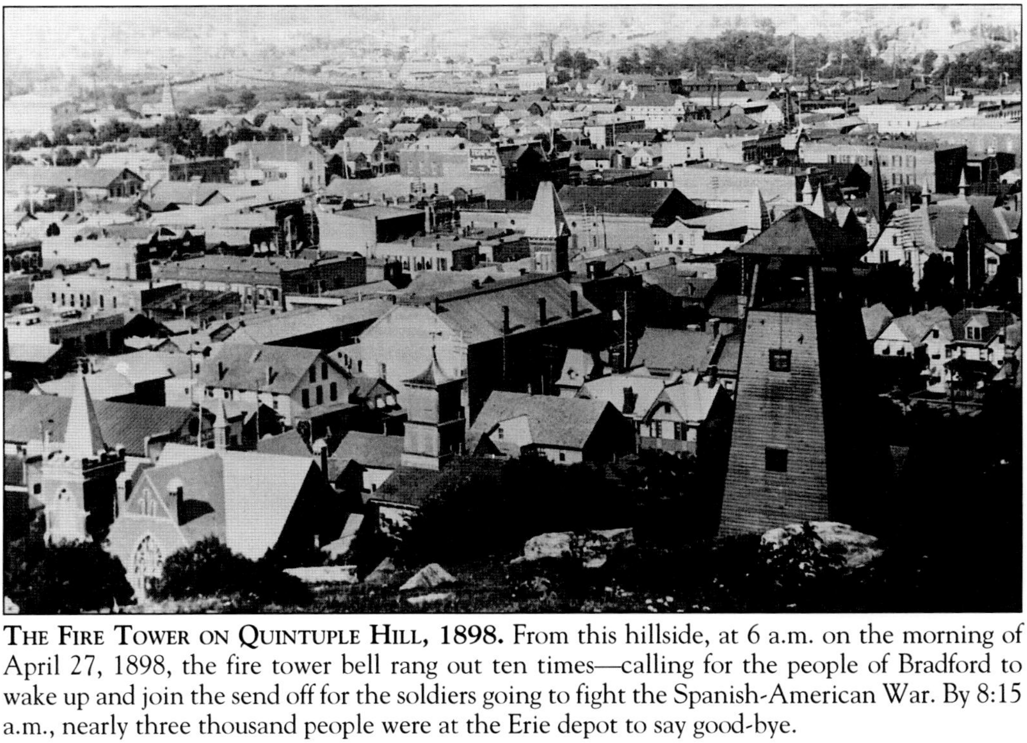

The Fire Tower on Quintuple Hill, 1898. From this hillside, at 6 a.m. on the morning of April 27, 1898, the fire tower bell rang out ten times—calling for the people of Bradford to wake up and join the send off for the soldiers going to fight the Spanish-American War. By 8:15 a.m., nearly three thousand people were at the Erie depot to say good-bye.

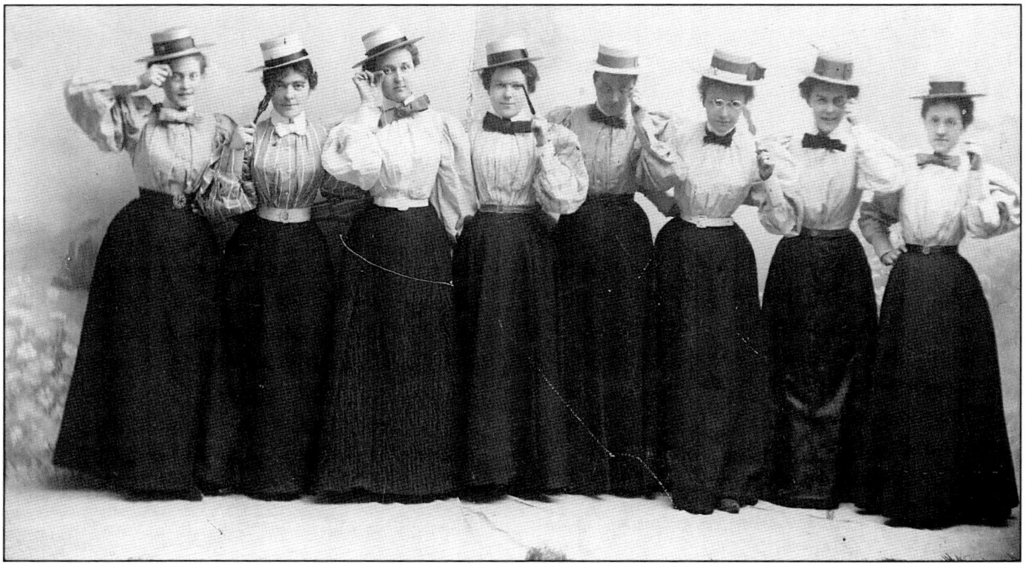

Pageant Season's Minuet, 1895. These young women were all contemporaries, and the daughters of affluent men. Listed from left to right are Lillian Cavanaugh, Flora McLean, Claudia Coffin, Flora Fleming, Grace Emery, Nell Mallory, Blanche Chapman, and Bey VanWormer.

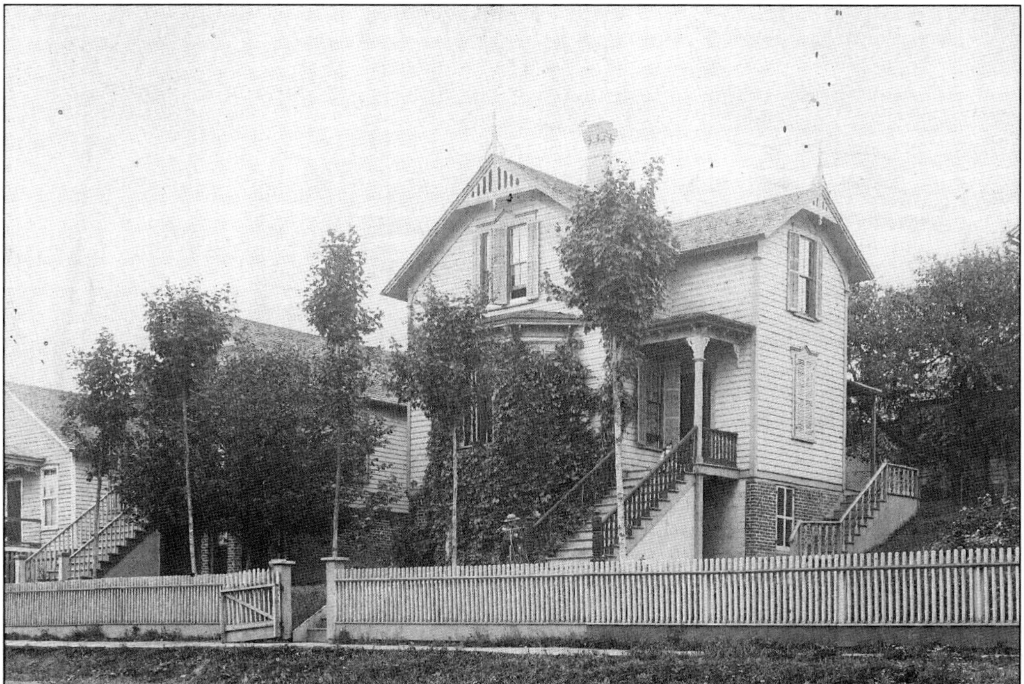

The Bird Home, c. 1880. This house, located at the corner of North Center and Summer Streets, was the childhood home of John "Jay" Bird and his sister, Cora Bird (Ball). Jay Bird, who died in 1974, was a successful oil man and co-founder of the Hanley-Bird Co. (oil and gas producers). The house is still standing today.

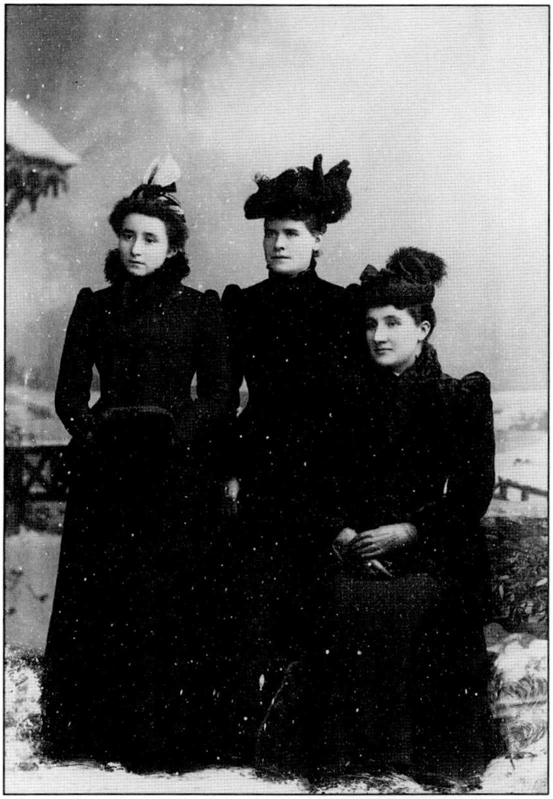

Hannah, Anna, and Mary Murphy, 1898. These sisters lived at 117 High Street. Each worked as a domestic servant in separate houses in Bradford.

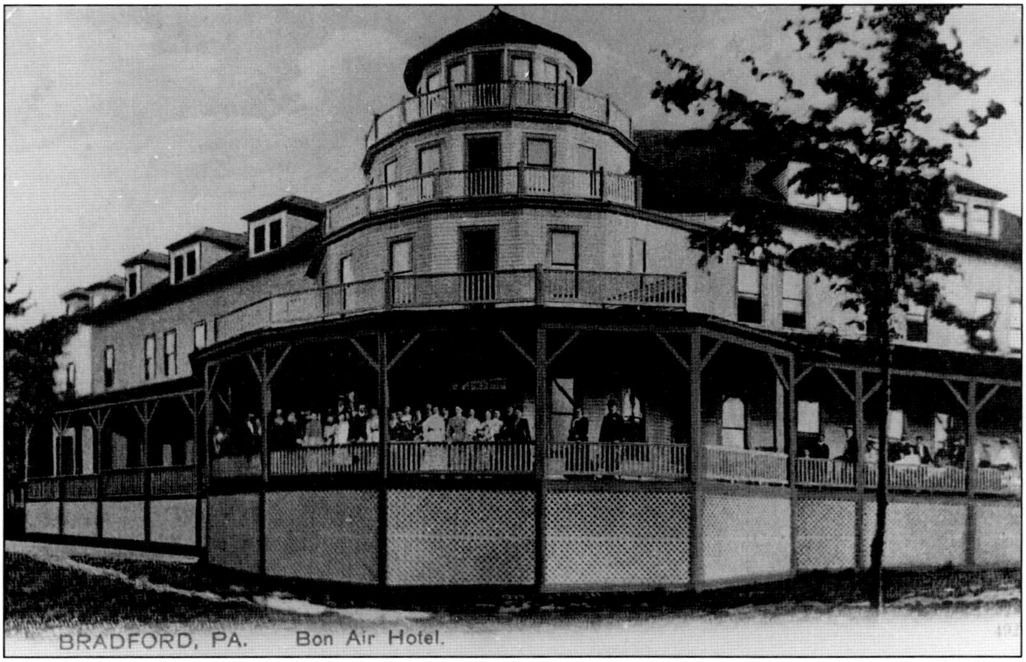

The Bon Air Hotel, Rock City, 1898. The Bon Air Hotel, built in 1896, was a popular resort at the end of the century. Located on the trolley line, it was easily accessible to Bradfordians, and its location near Rock City guaranteed cool summer entertainment.

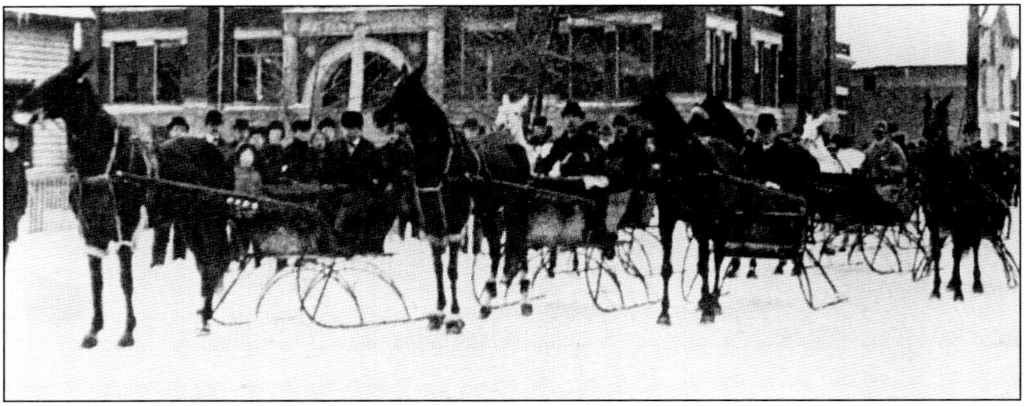

Sleigh Races on Boylston Street, December 28, 1897. Horse racing was popular in winter as sleighs replaced sulkies, and streets replaced the track. Many spectators had come to see Martha T, a fast pacer owned the Rev. Houghton of the Church of Eternal Hope. Houghton owned several trotters, and could be seen nearly every week—summer or winter—"at the races."

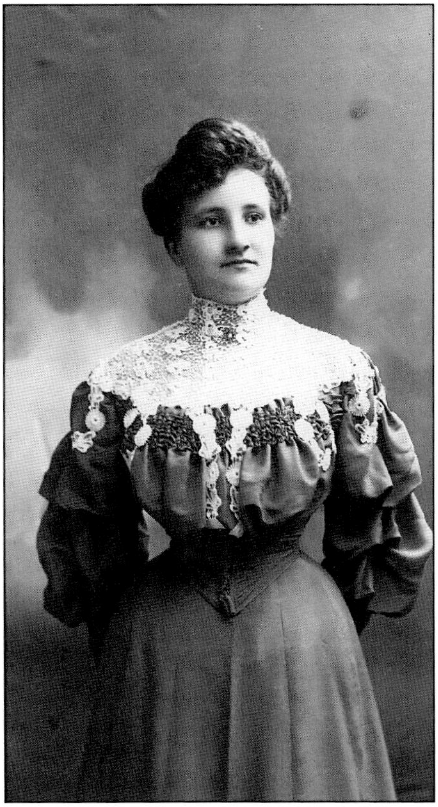

The Price of Fashion, 1900. Wearing a beautiful dress, and corseted to a 18-inch waist, this woman was the ideal fashion model at the turn of the century. Although a tiny waist was highly desired, such corseting could cause severe internal problems, back strain, and difficulty in childbirth.

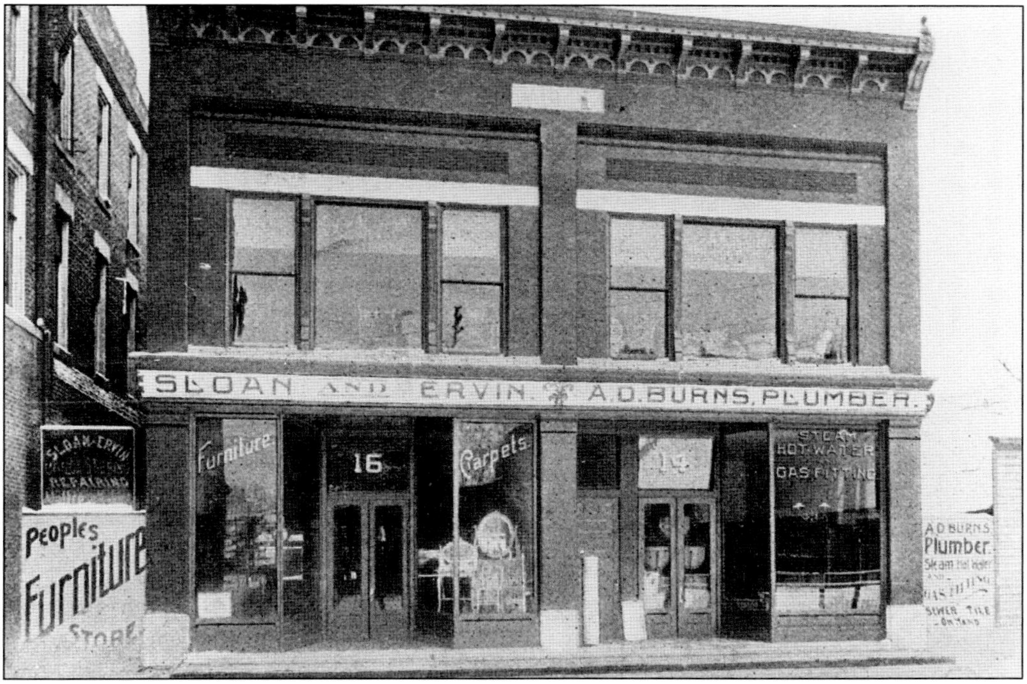

SLOAN AND ERVIN, 1898. This furniture and carpet store was tucked away in the corner of the Public Square. In 1898, it was awarded the contract to furnish all the furniture for the new city hall on Kennedy Street. This building is still standing.

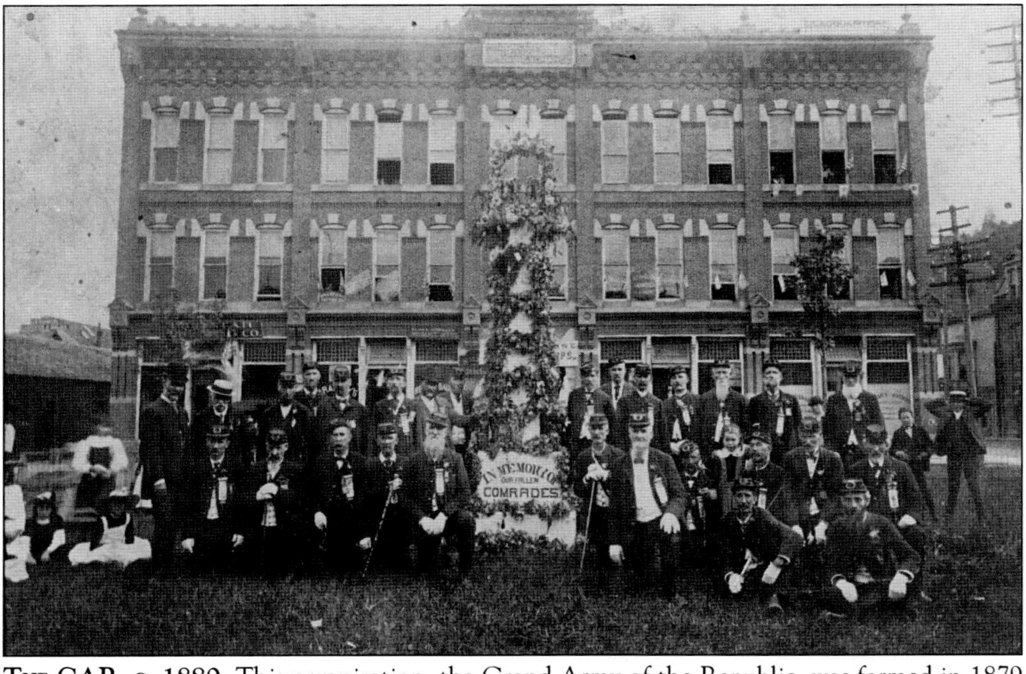

THE GAR, C. 1880. This organization, the Grand Army of the Republic, was formed in 1879 by veterans of the Civil War. Known as the John S. Melvin Post 141, it remained in existence until after the turn of the century. Here, members are honoring their comrades in the Public Square on Memorial Day.

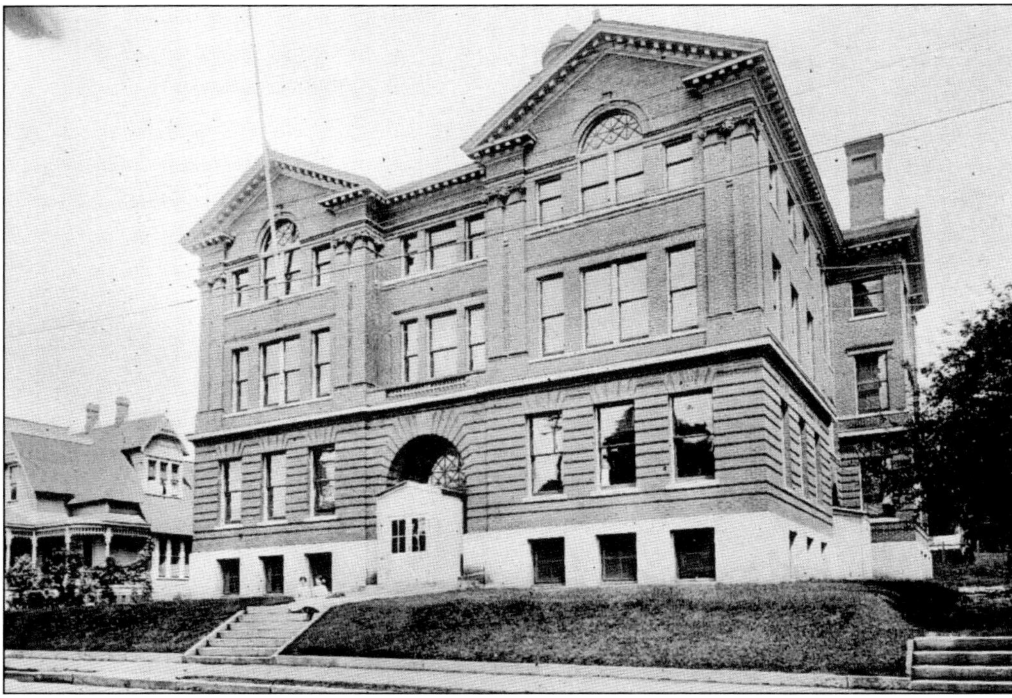

The New High School, 1898. Severe overcrowding in the existing schools (one teacher reportedly had 79 students, and it was estimated that on any day, over 50 students had no desks to sit at) forced the city council in 1897 to consider building a new high school. After much debate at council meetings, the new school was built at the head of Mechanic Street.

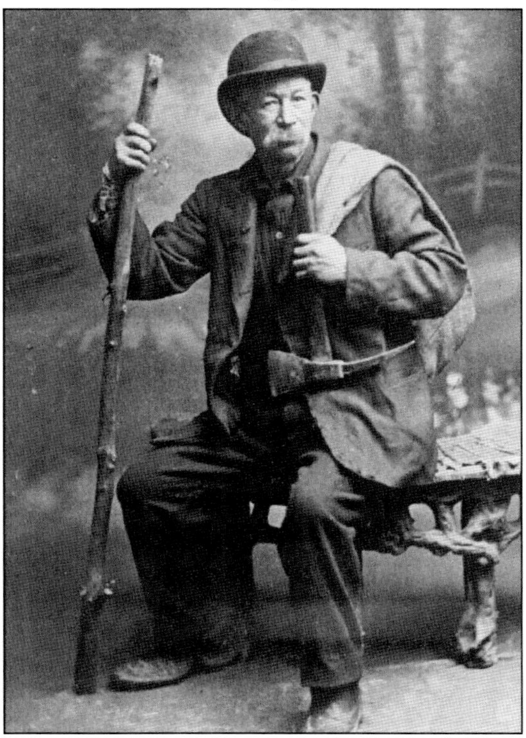

Tansy Jack, 1842(?)–1907. A colorful character about town whose real name was Fred Jones, Tansy was originally from England. He led a vagabond life, selling plants and herbs and doing odd jobs. Fond of drink and penniless, he nevertheless had many influential friends and was given an impressive funeral; his casket covered with wreaths and wild flowers picked by children. "Poor old Tansy Jack," wrote the *Bradford Era*, "he was a harmless chap and honest."

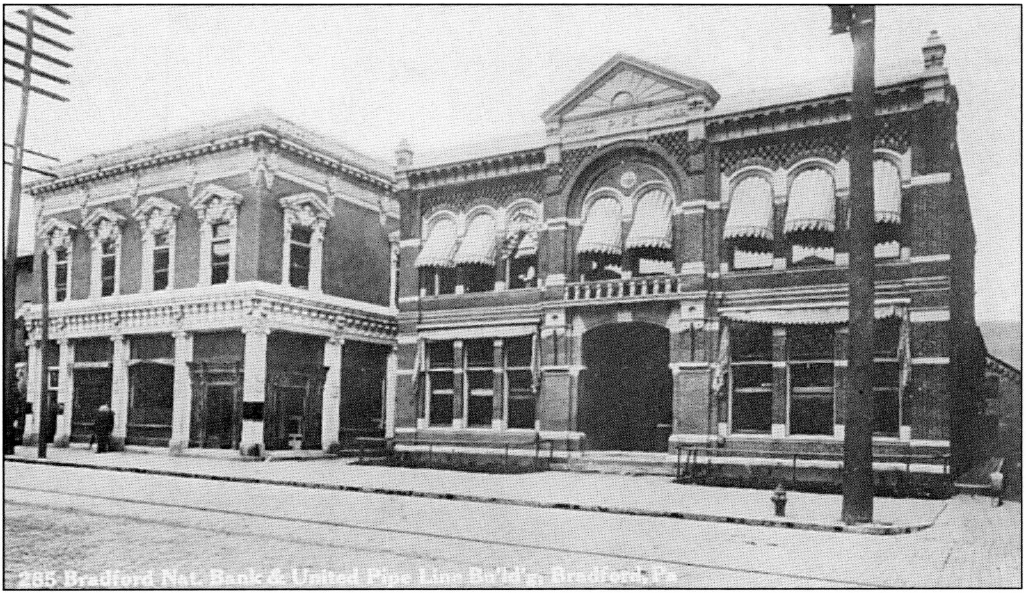

THE BRADFORD NATIONAL BANK, C. 1900. The bank is located next to the United Pipe Building on Main Street.

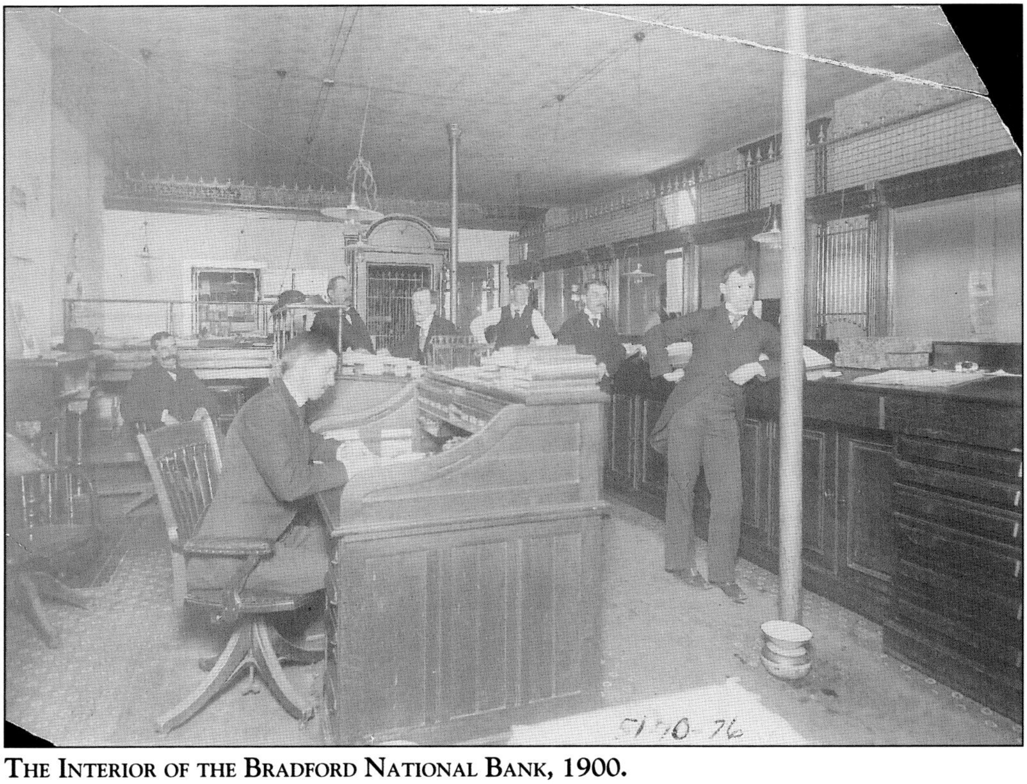

THE INTERIOR OF THE BRADFORD NATIONAL BANK, 1900.

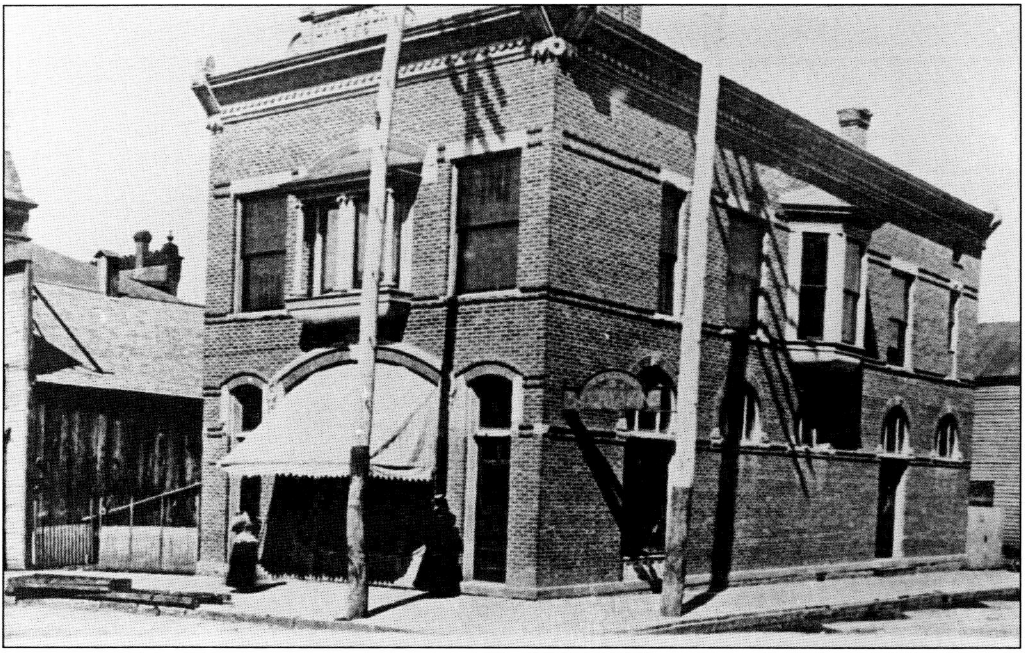

Koch's Undertaking Parlor, c. 1895. This building on the corner of Corydon Street and South Avenue was built by Otto Koch, who had come to Bradford from Dunkirk, New York, where he and his father ran a mortuary. In 1906, Koch joined Kendall Manufacturing, and the funeral business was run by Koch's brother Frederick.

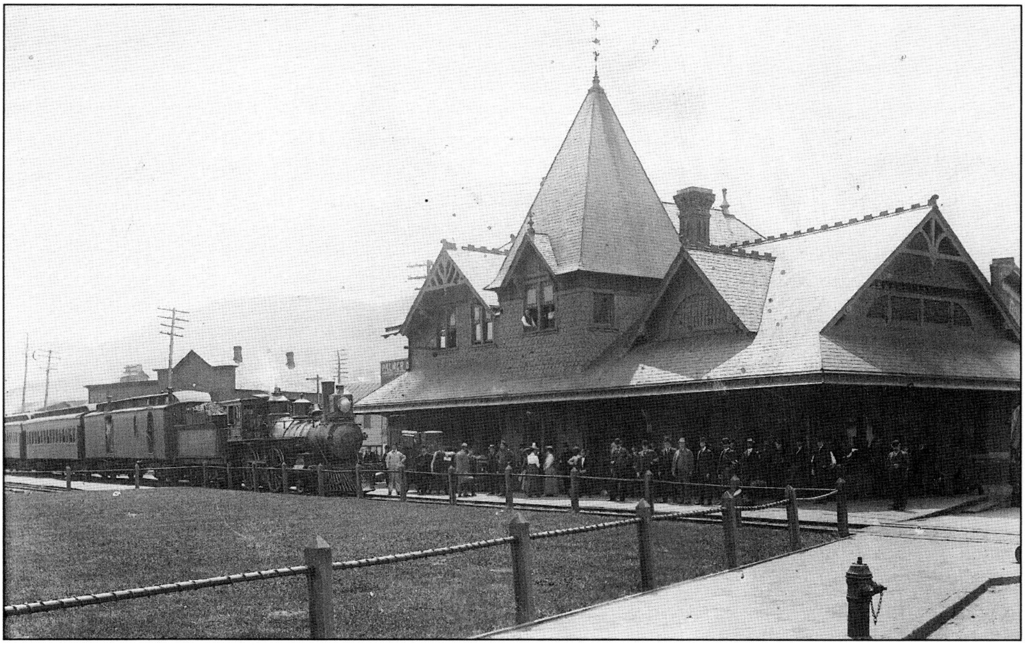

The Erie Railroad Station, c. 1895. This beautiful station was opened on April 6, 1898, and replaced the old union depot, which was demolished with one quick pull on a cable attached to a locomotive. The station was razed during Bradford's redevelopment phase.

Two

Oil, Men!

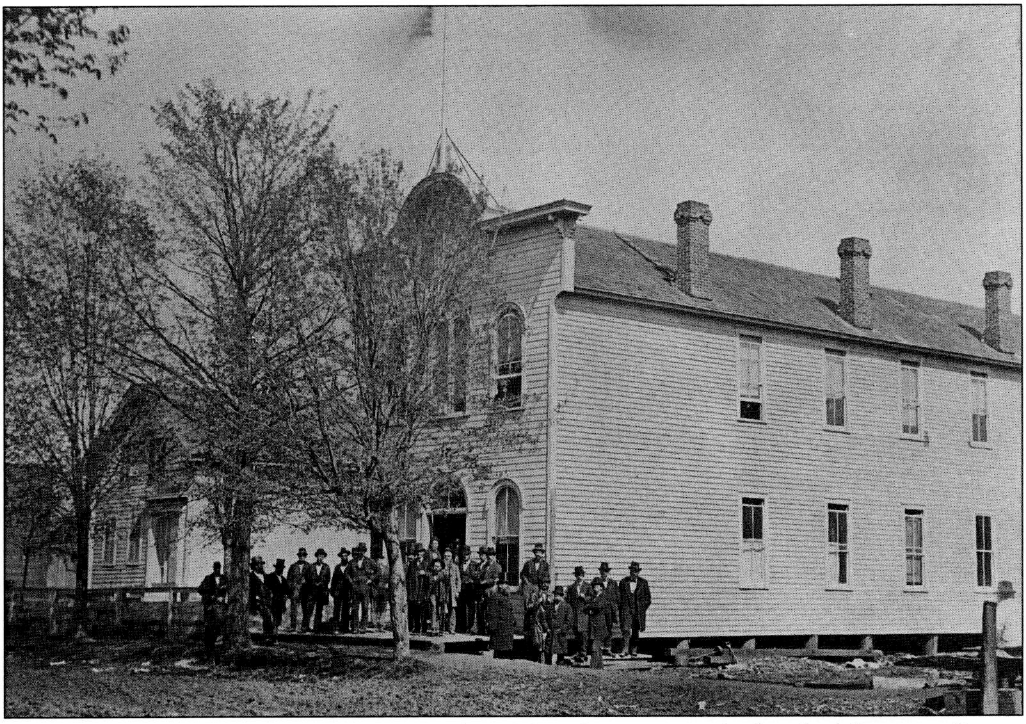

The First Oil Exchange, 1876. Located on Main Street, near the head of Congress Street, this was one of the first buildings in town to be dedicated to the oil industry. As oil production increased, a larger building was needed. Its replacement, the Bradford Oil Exchange, was built in the summer of 1878 at a cost of $44,000.

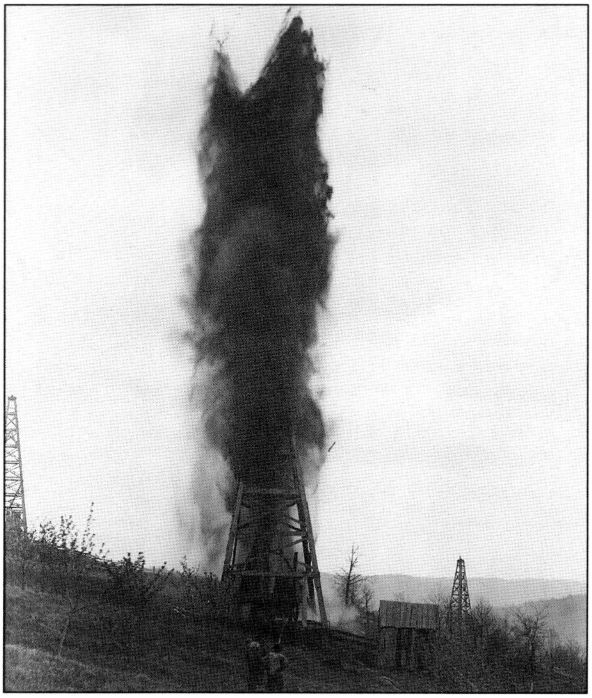

TORPEDOING AN OIL WELL, 1886. One of the earliest methods used to rejuvenate a well was through the use of nitroglycerin "torpedoes" that were dropped into a well and exploded. Results were gratifying, but the instability of nitroglycerin was responsible for many deaths on the oil fields. This well had just been torpedoed.

THE BRADFORD OIL EXCHANGE, c. 1890. A beautiful Victorian building, it served as the center of the oil industry when over a million dollars in stock were traded daily. Later known as the Lyceum, this building still stands, having undergone tremendous modifications over its lifetime including the removal of the third floor. It is known today as the Northwest Savings Bank Building.

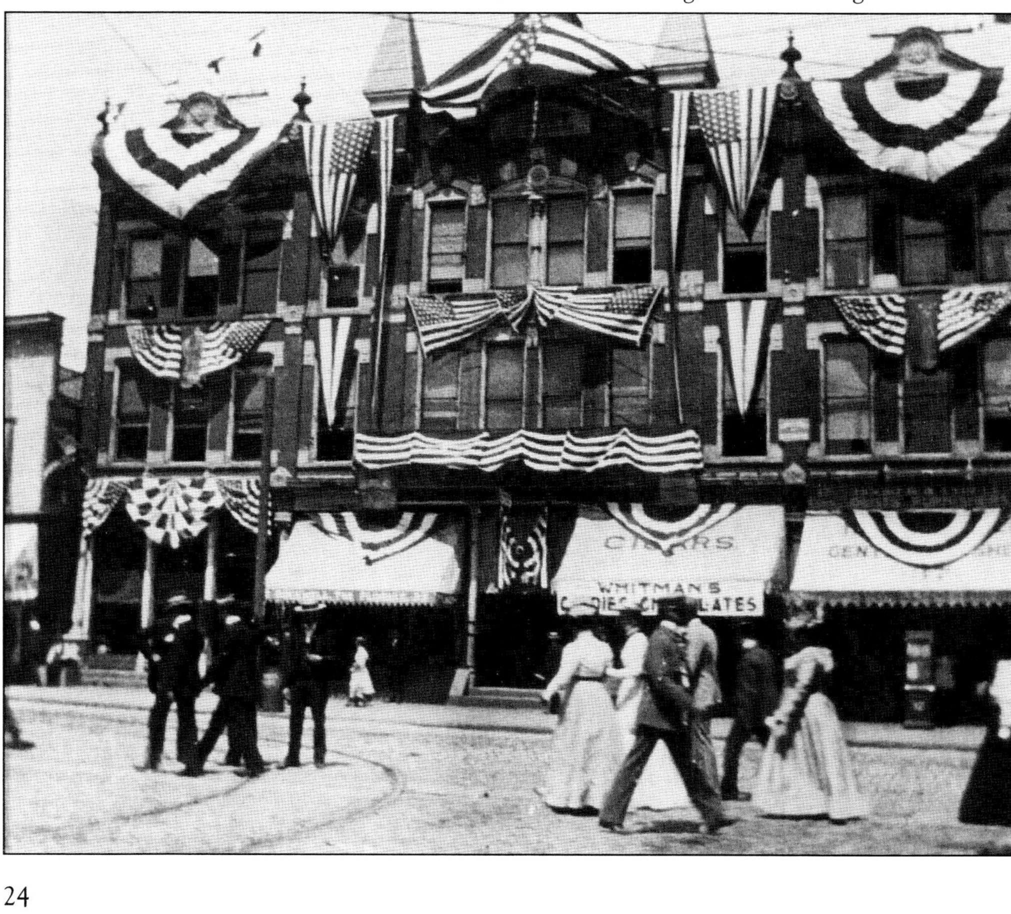

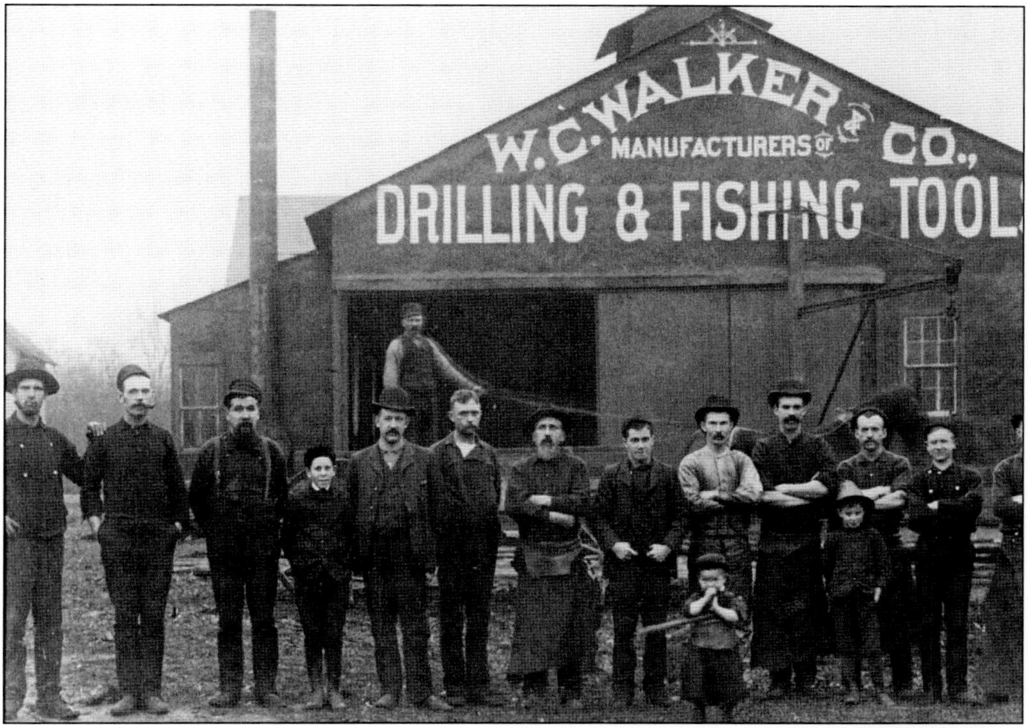

THE W.C. WALKER COMPANY, 1887. This company was located on Elm Street and forged iron tools for the oil fields.

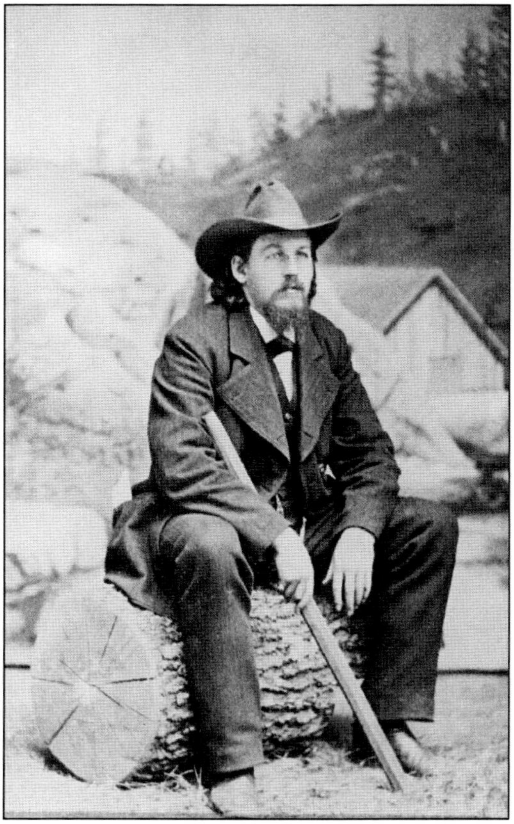

OWEN ROBERTS, C. 1880. Brother of Colonel A.E. Roberts, who invented and patented the nitroglycerin torpedo, Owen ran the family business on Main Street. The torpedo—a tin tube filled with "nitro," lowered into a well, and exploded—gave new life to old wells. Both brothers charged exorbitant prices for the invention, and soon "moonlighters" secretly shot wells at night to avoid their prices.

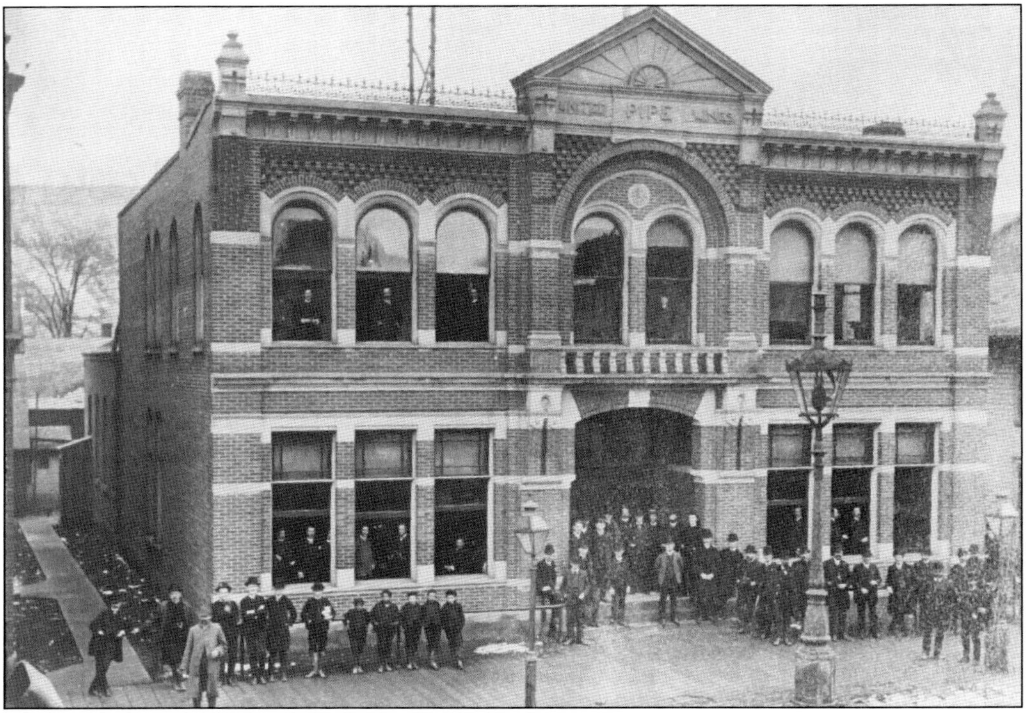

The United Pipe Line Company, c. 1895. This company, a division of Standard Trust Co., created one of the most important oil trunk lines in its time, piping oil to the seaboard. This Main Street building, built in 1884, later became the Bradford Club.

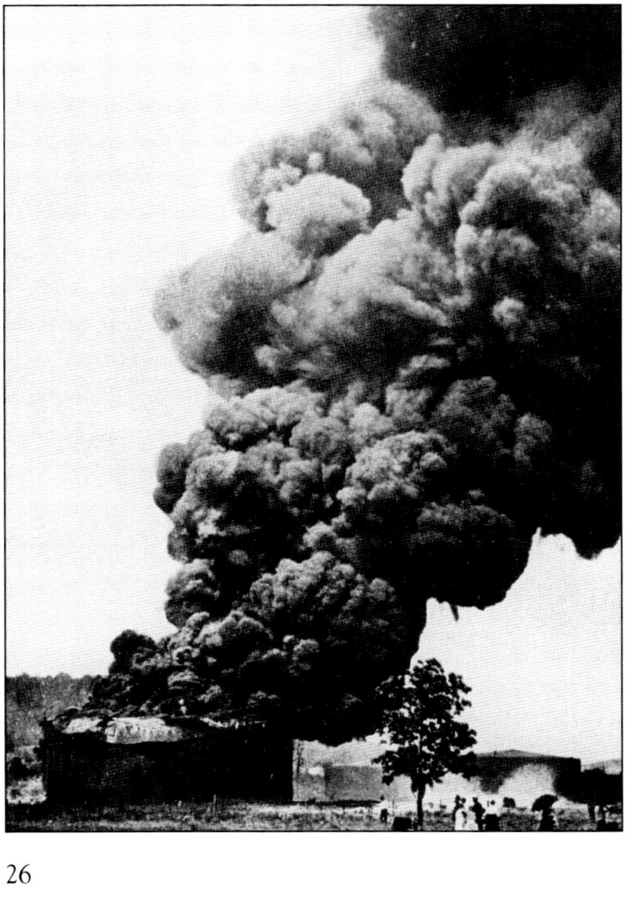

A Burning Oil Tank, c. 1890. Such fires were often uncontrollable—this fire burned 35,000 barrels of oil before being brought under control. One fire company, the United Hose Company, used a small rifle cannon to shoot holes in these big tanks to draw off the oil and thus control the fire.

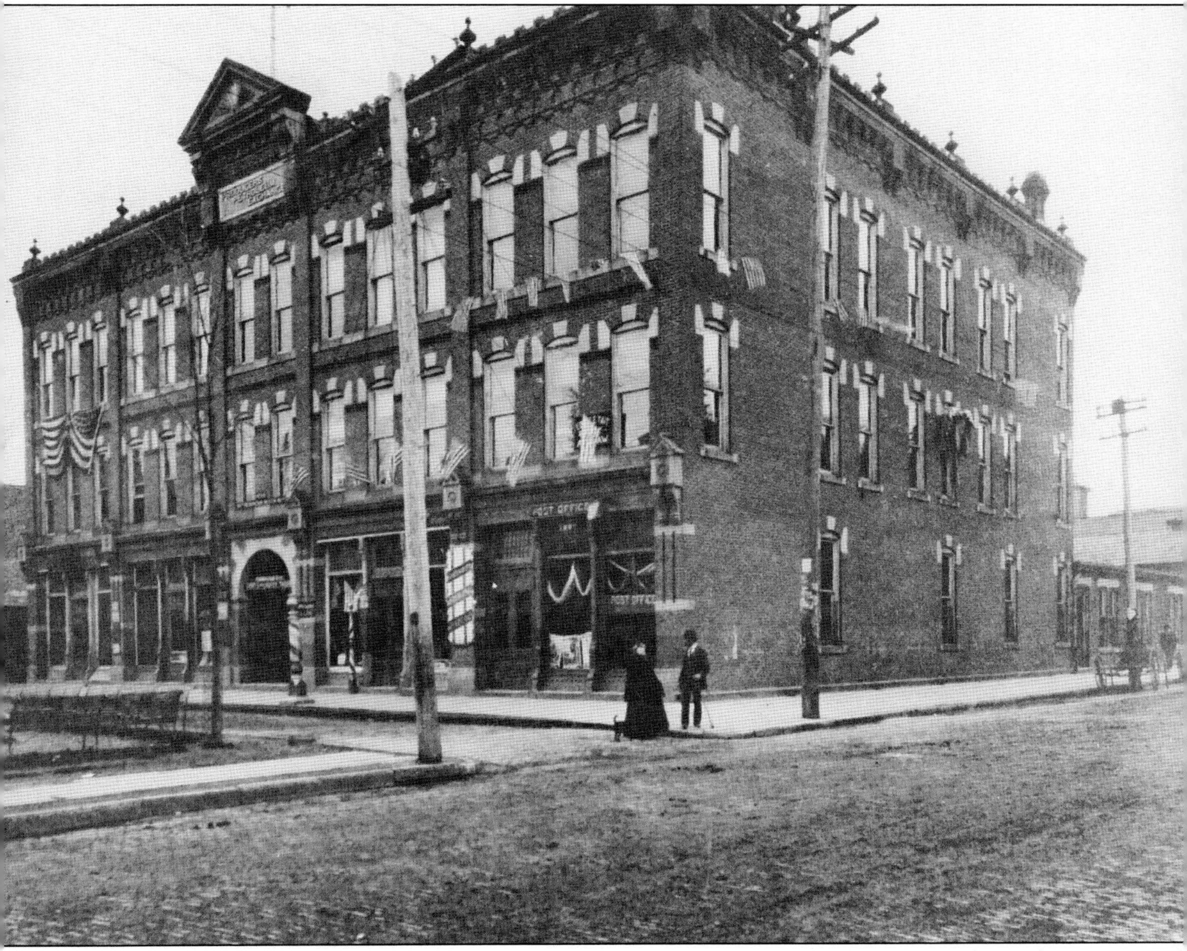

The Producers Petroleum Oil Exchange, c. 1900. A second oil exchange was formed in November 1882 with over 500 members. This building, on the corner of South Avenue and the Public Square, was built shortly thereafter in 1894. The organization lasted only a short time, and the building was sold to the International Order of Odd Fellows. It was destroyed by fire on December 23, 1902.

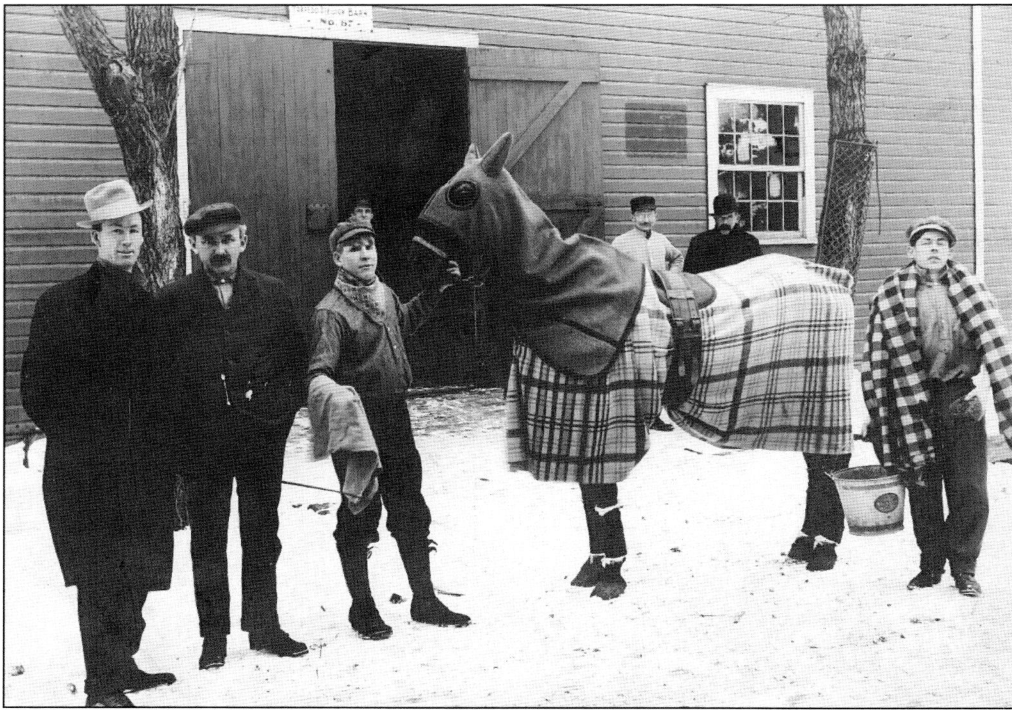

TORPEDO BARN, C. 1900. Oil exploration, drilling, and production went on daily, regardless of the weather. This horse, a valuable asset to a drilling site, is well protected against the frigid cold.

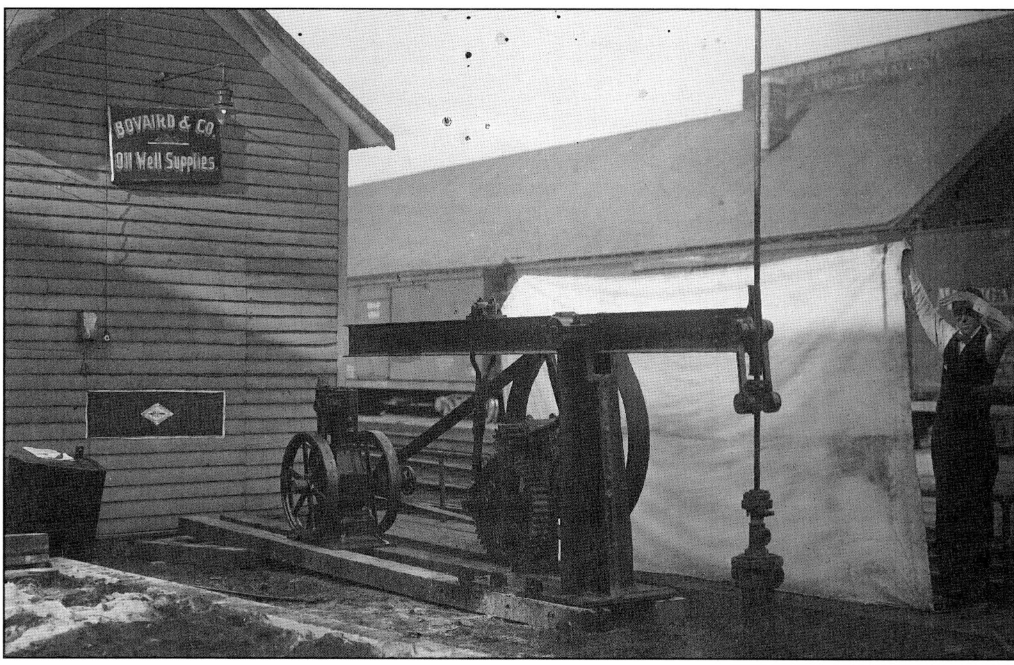

BOVAIRD & COMPANY'S OIL JACK, C. 1905. This photograph was taken outside the company's Bradford office (the man at the right is holding up a sheet to block out distractions). This pumping jack was a familiar site on the fields surrounding the town.

FILLING THE SHELL, C. 1910. These men are very carefully filling a torpedo at the top of the well.

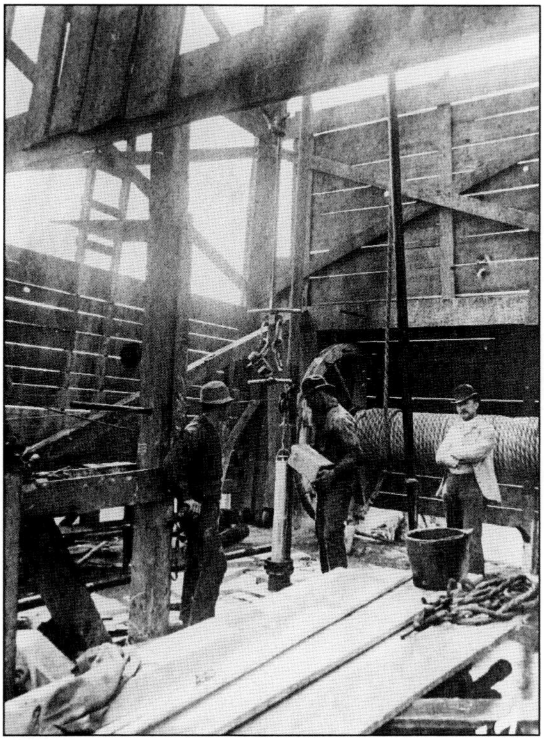

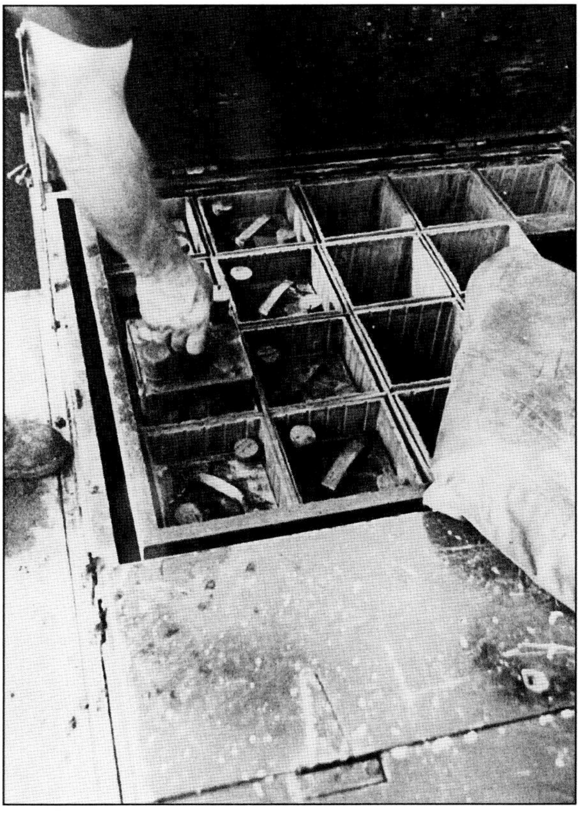

NITROGLYCERIN CARRYING CASE. Nitroglycerin was dangerous to transport, and every precaution was taken to assure that it would travel safely.

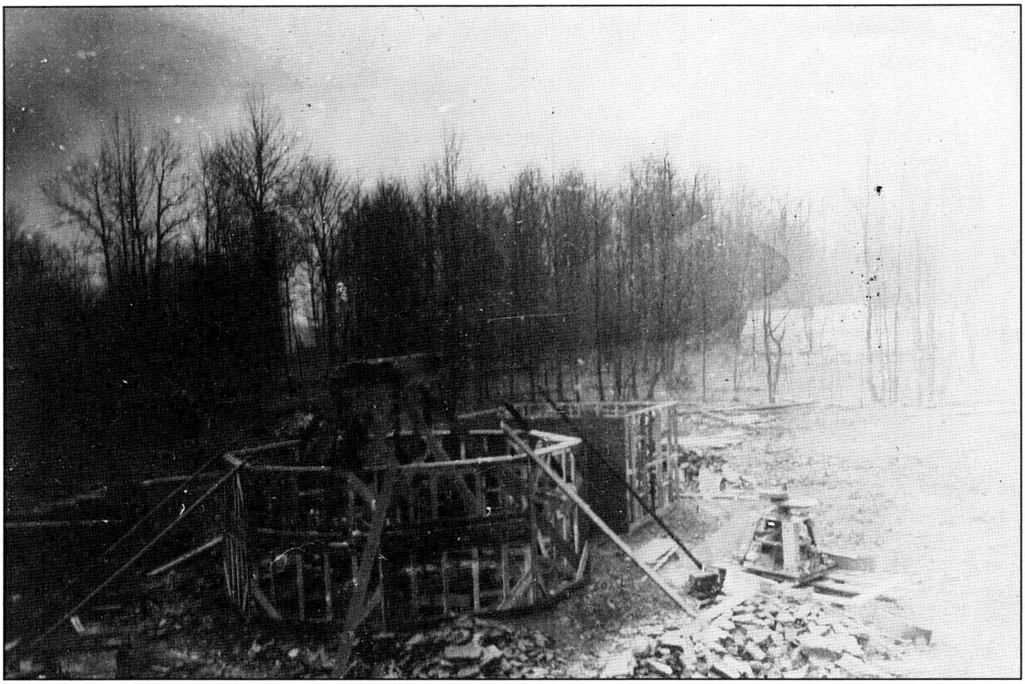

An Octagon-Shaped Powerhouse Under Construction, c. 1908. Built by the South Penn Oil Company near Cyclone (then Simpson), the eight-sided buildings were more expensive and time consuming to build than regular powerhouses. Only a handful were built, and few survive today.

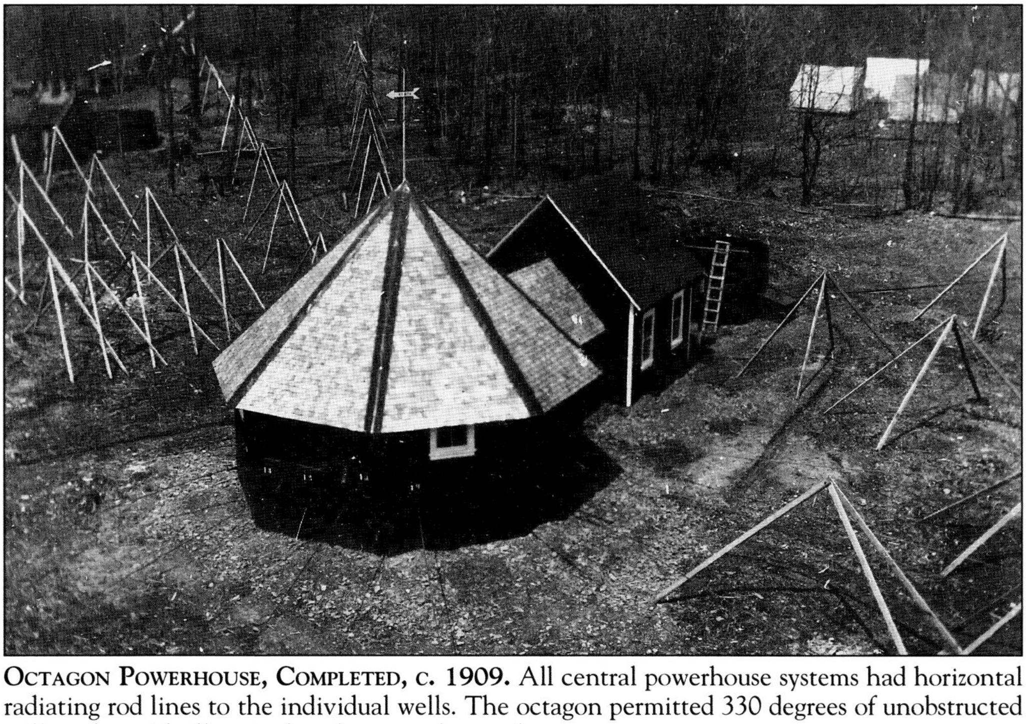

Octagon Powerhouse, Completed, c. 1909. All central powerhouse systems had horizontal radiating rod lines to the individual wells. The octagon permitted 330 degrees of unobstructed pull, and was ideally suited to the central powerhouse system.

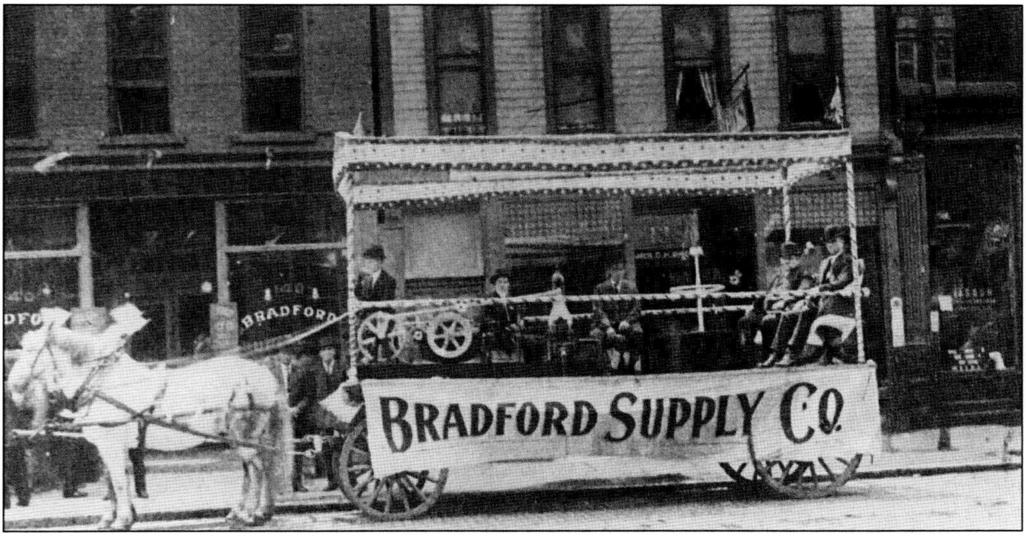

A Bradford Oil Supply Float, Old Home Week 1909. The industrial division parade was held on Wednesday that week. This float is passing in front of the company's original store at 140 Main Street. Founded in 1907, the Bradford Oil Supply advertised "a complete stock of all kinds of materials required by oil and natural gas contractors and producers."

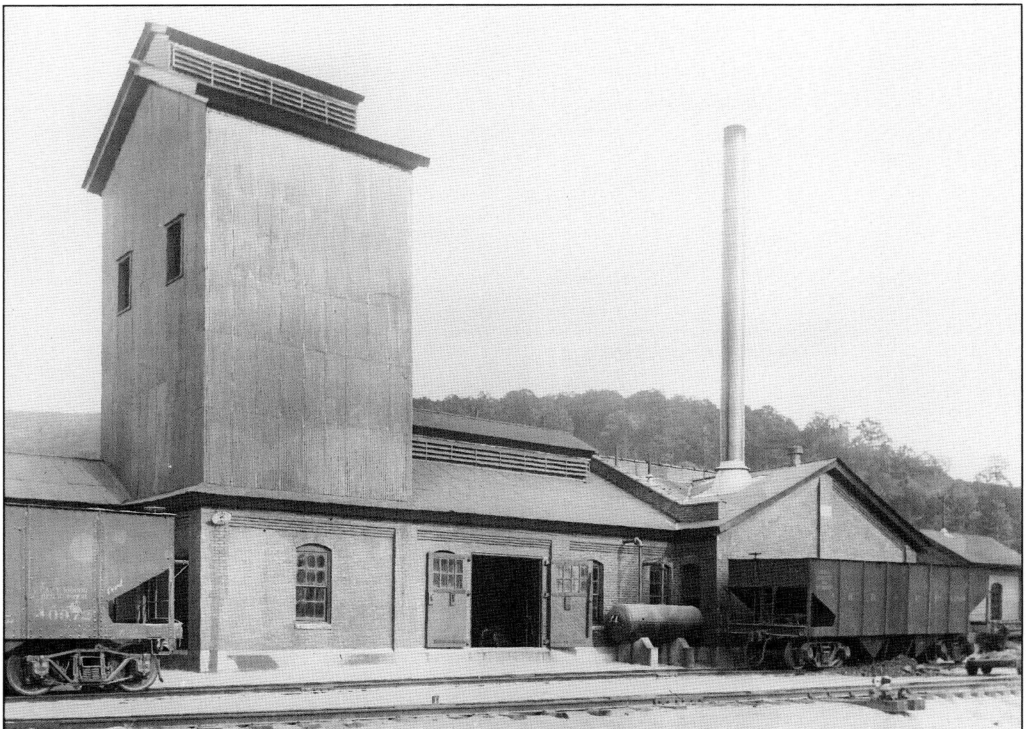

Creosote Production Plant, 1909. This plant was operated by the Buffalo, Rochester, & Pittsburgh Railroad and located at the end of Kinzua Street off High Street. Creosote, a timber preservative that is a by-product of the oil industry, was used to extend the life of railroad ties.

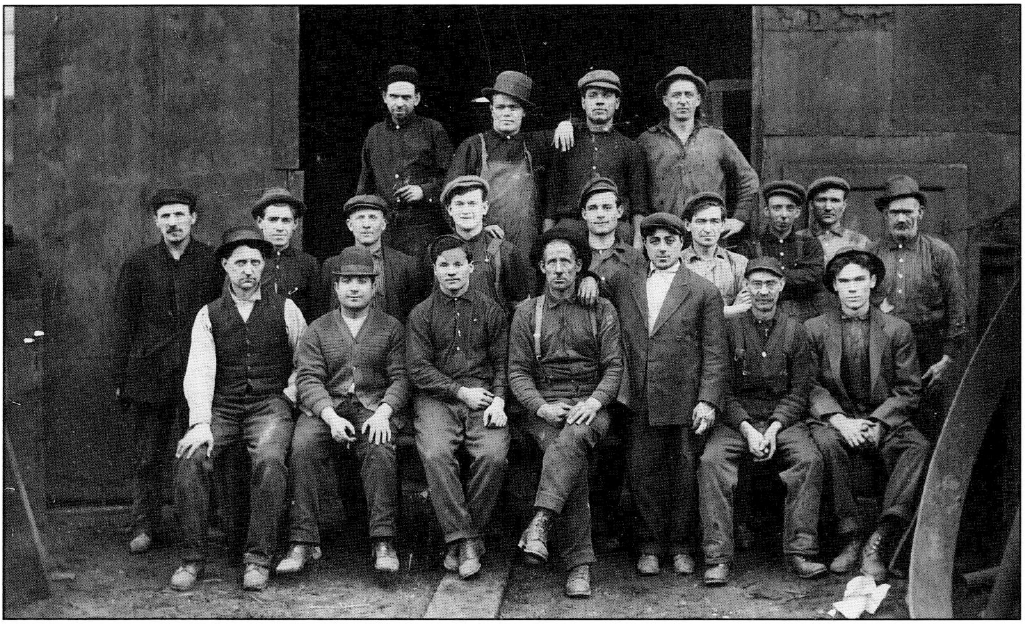

E.R. CALDWELL EMPLOYEES, c. 1905. E.R. Caldwell operated a general foundry and machine shop on Hilton Street. The shop was originally founded in 1896 and by 1900 was averaging 10 tons of castings daily, manufacturing steam pumps, gas engines, starting pumps, and hydraulic wheel presses for the oil industry. Sold to Earl Emery in 1918, it was considered one of the largest and most modern foundries between Buffalo and Pittsburgh and employed 250 workers.

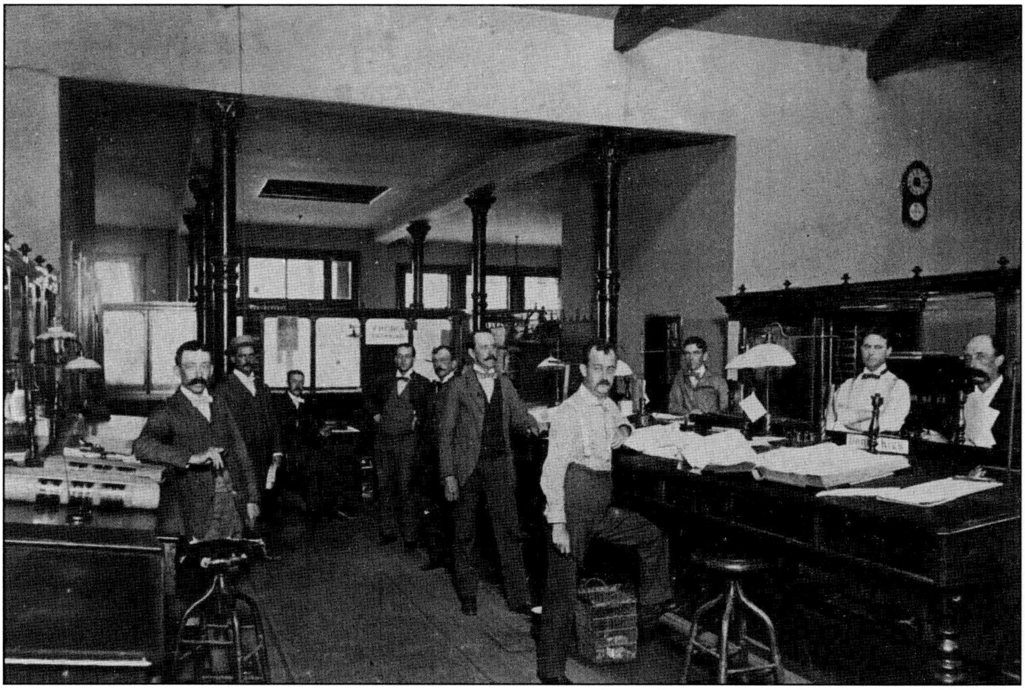

NATIONAL TRANSIT COMPANY, c. 1910. A division of Standard Oil Company, this company specialized in the transportation of oil from the Bradford fields to market. Here, employees pause in the middle of their transactions.

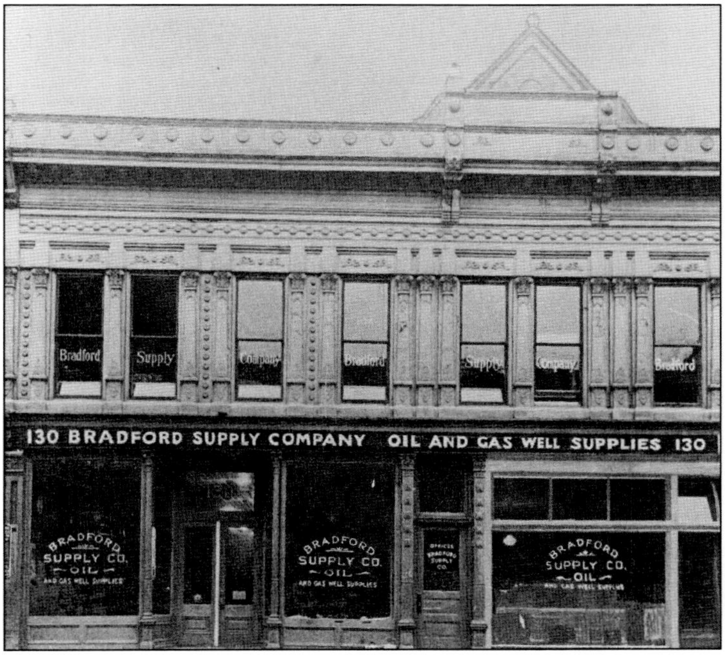

The Bradford Supply Company, 130 Main Street, c. 1920. By 1919, the company had moved to 130 Main Street, and had expanded to three other locations: Warren, PA; Robinson, IL; and Chanute, KA. Later it became Bradford Pipe & Supply, which is still in operation today. This building served as the city's municipal building in the 1960s, and was razed during the city's redevelopment phase.

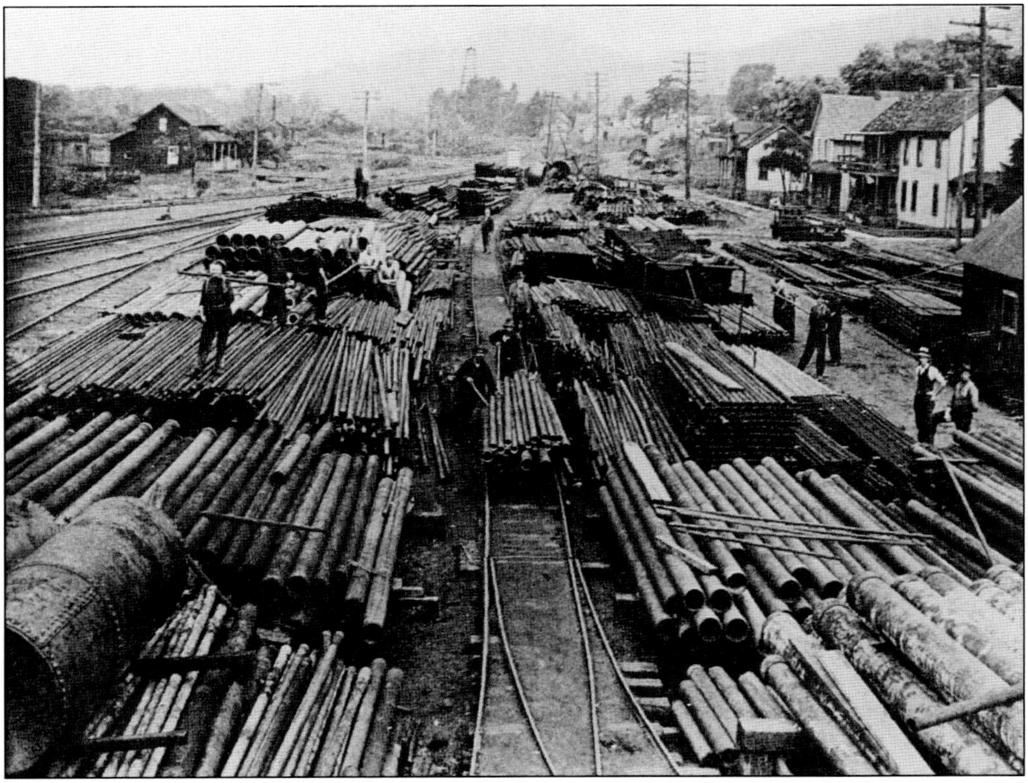

A Pipe Yard, c. 1912. Such pipe was essential to the success of the oil fields. This pipe yard was located south of the city along the railroad line.

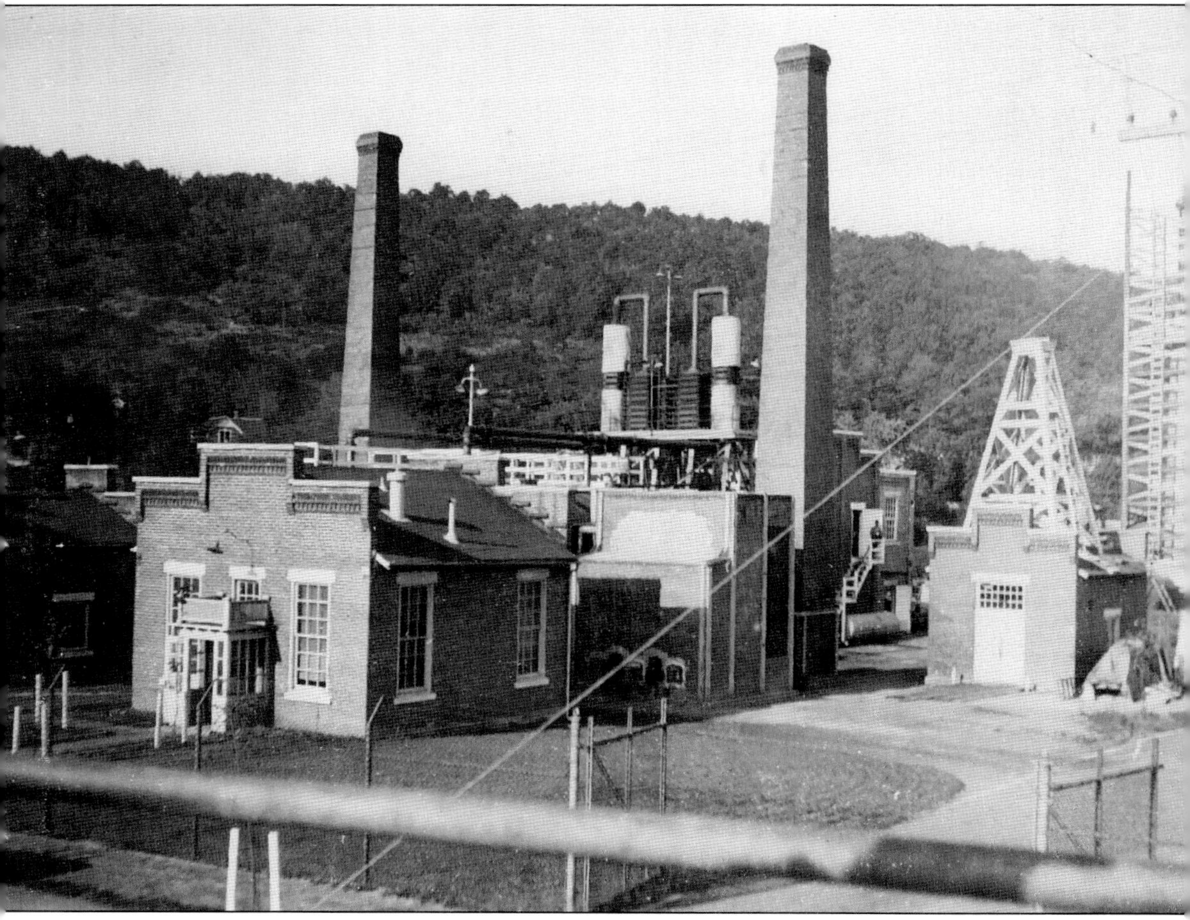

THE EMERY MANUFACTURING PLANT, 1921. Purchased from John Haggerty in 1888 by Lewis Emery, this plant became the largest oil refinery in Bradford, covering over 6 acres just north of the city. In 1925, it was producing 50,000 barrels of crude oil per month. In 1929 it was sold to South Penn Oil Company, and eventually resold to the Kendall Refinery.

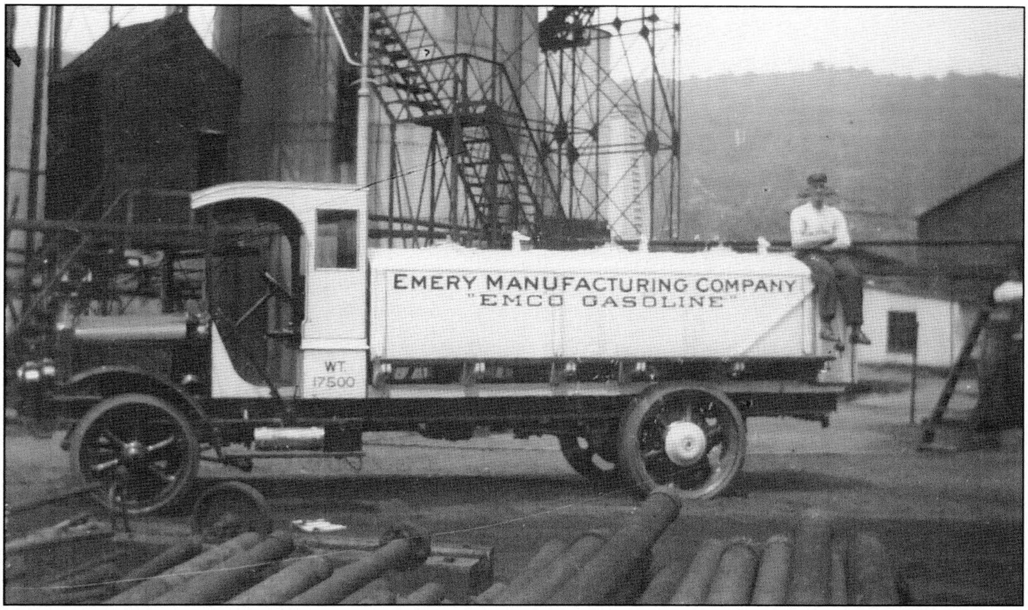

An EMCO Gasoline Truck, July 1921. The Emery Company trade logo, EMCO, was displayed on gasoline trucks, railroad tank cars, service stations, and gasoline pumps in all parts of the country. EMCO products included lubricating oils, automobile oils, gasoline, illuminating oils, wax, grease, and benzene.

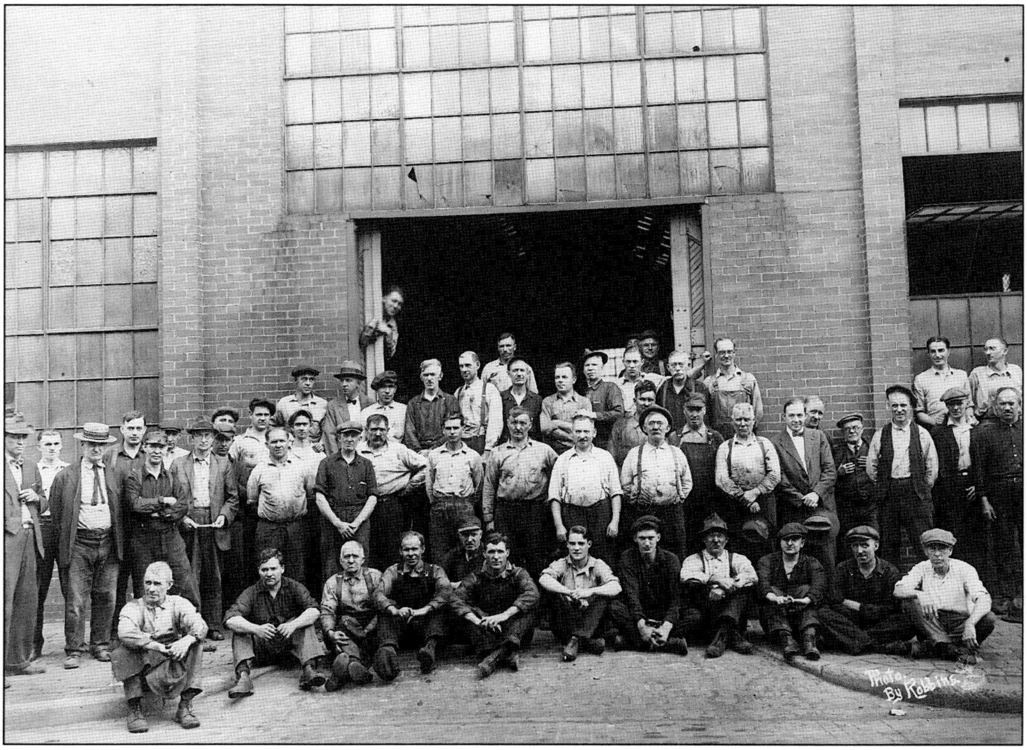

Bovaird & Seyfang Employees, 1930s. Founded in 1892, this company manufactured all sorts of oil, gas, and artesian well supplies and every class of tools.

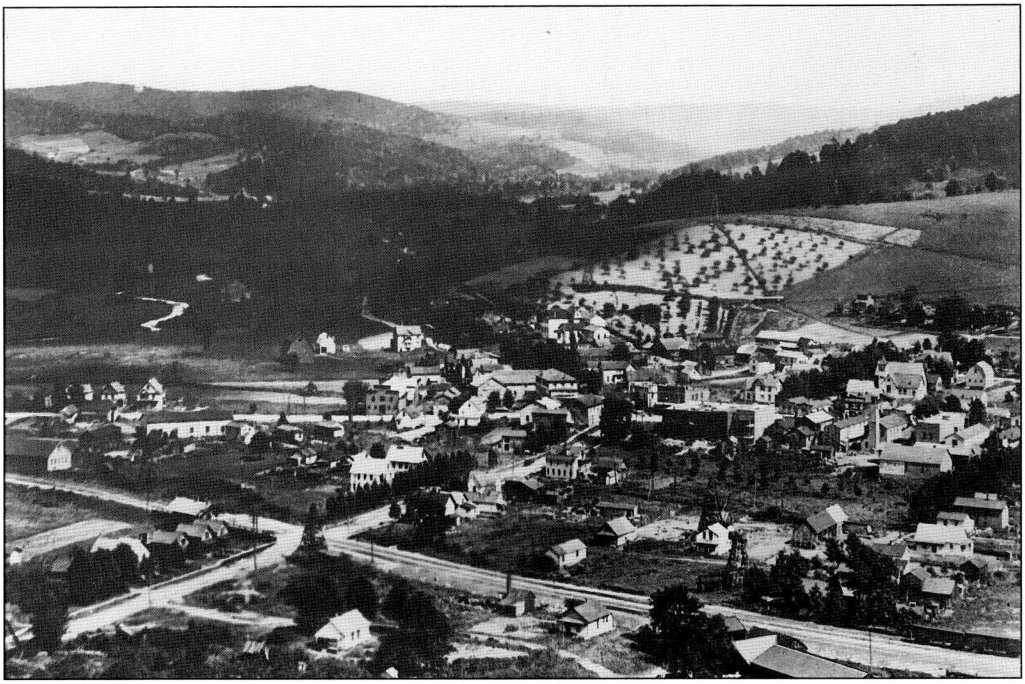

The Kendall Oil Refining Company, 1880. This is one of the earliest known photographs of the refinery. Kendall is the small group of buildings in the lower right-hand corner. The road traveling left to right is Kendall Avenue.

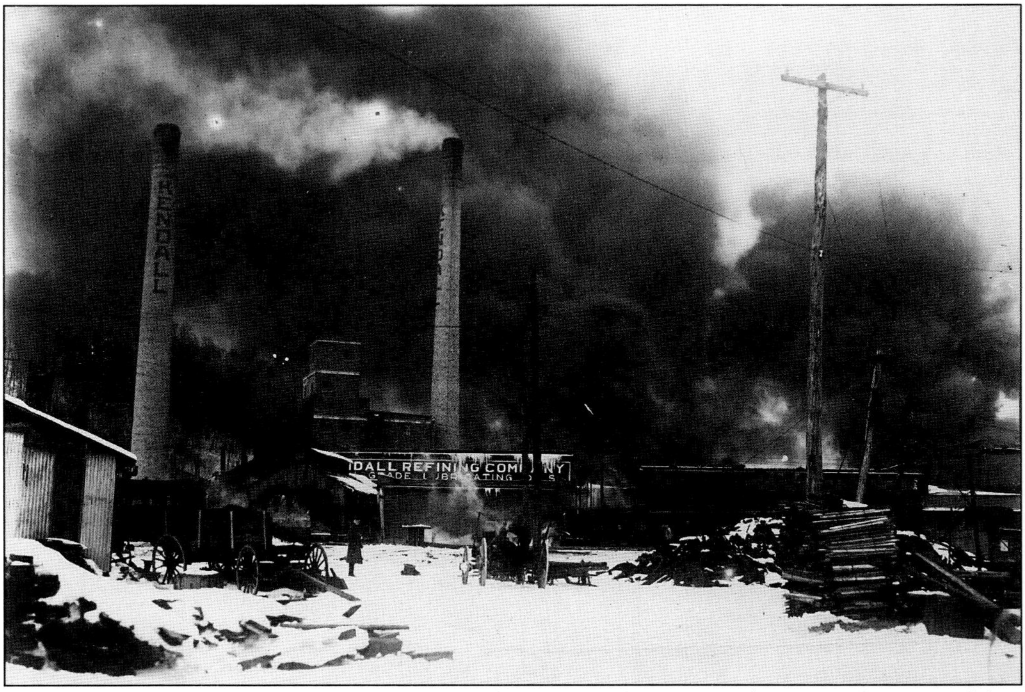

The Kendall Oil Refinery Fire, 1906. A devastating fire occurred in 1906, burning all but the wax plant. Under the direction of Otto Koch, it was rebuilt, and over the next 90 years it would become Bradford's biggest and only refinery.

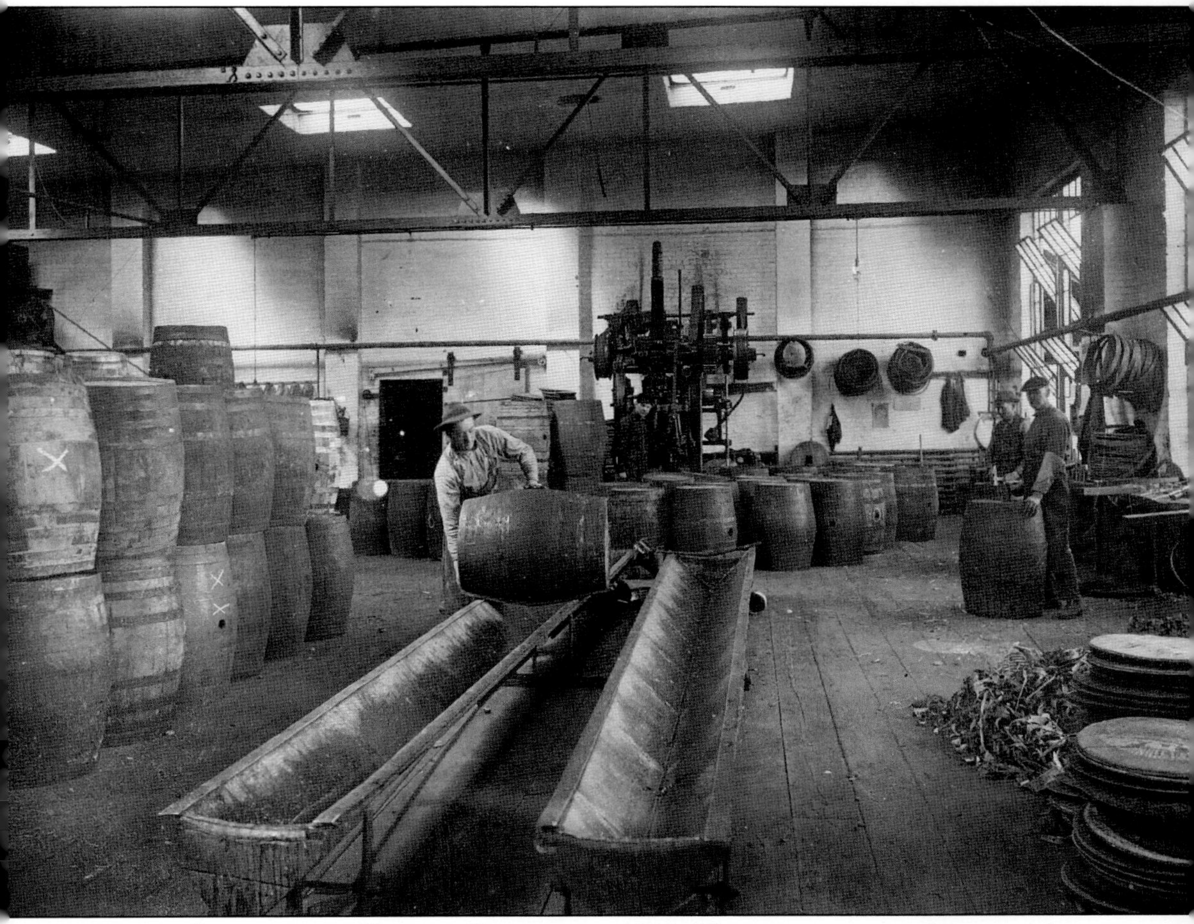

INSIDE THE BARRELHOUSE, KENDALL REFINERY, C. 1920. These men are examining wooden barrels for defects (note the "X" on the side of the barrels at the left of the photograph). A standard barrel contains 42 gallons of oil.

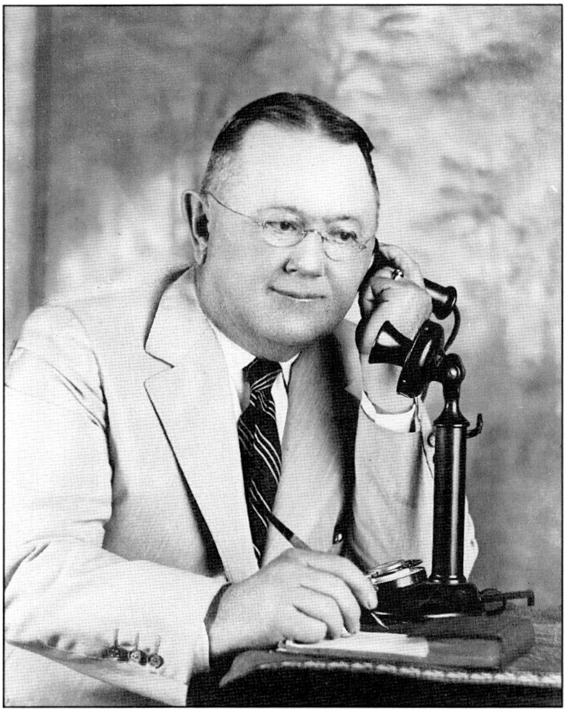

Otto Koch, c. 1938. Chairman of the board of Kendall Refinery, Koch began as a funeral director, building a business that still stands today on the corner of Corydon Street and South Avenue. In 1906 he accepted the position of manager of Kendall Refining Company, and under his supervision, it grew to be known nationwide for its lubricating oil and oil products. Koch died on Oct. 12, 1948, at age 83.

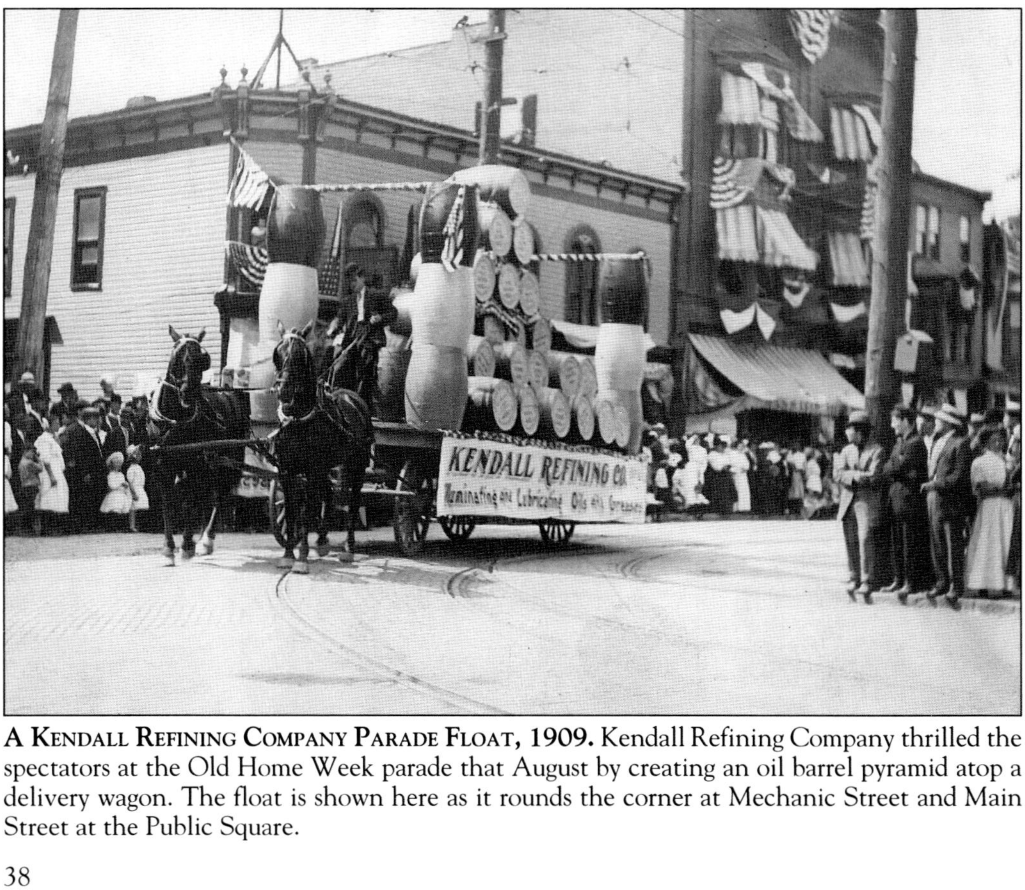

A Kendall Refining Company Parade Float, 1909. Kendall Refining Company thrilled the spectators at the Old Home Week parade that August by creating an oil barrel pyramid atop a delivery wagon. The float is shown here as it rounds the corner at Mechanic Street and Main Street at the Public Square.

MUSIC MOUNTAIN, 1937. An unexpected wildcat gusher, Niagara Oil Corporation's initial well in Lafayette Township came in on August 24, 1937, at an enormous rate, gauged at 44 barrels per hour. It was the first flowing well struck in 40 years. By the end of 1940, 292 wells had been drilled here, including some of the biggest flowing wells ever produced.

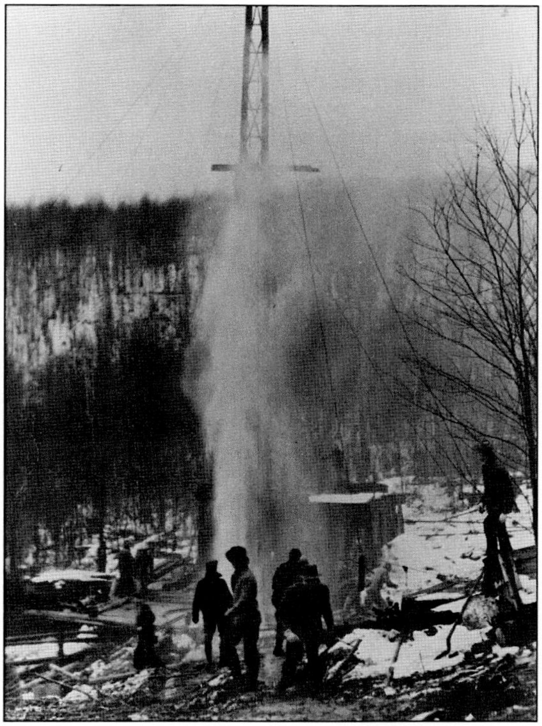

BUILDING AN OIL STORAGE TANK, c. 1948. The Lauffenberger Erection Company located at 12 N. Kendall Avenue specialized in "steel erection of all kinds, riveted and welded—any size—anywhere." Oil tanks such as this one are a common sight in Bradford.

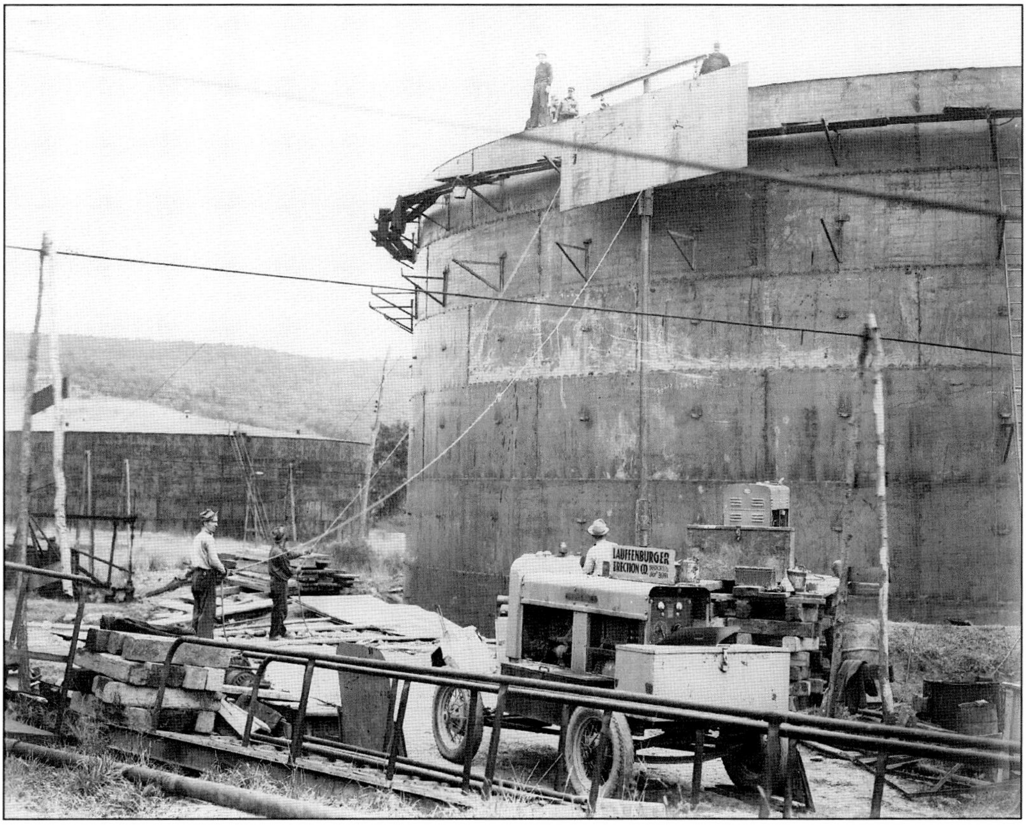

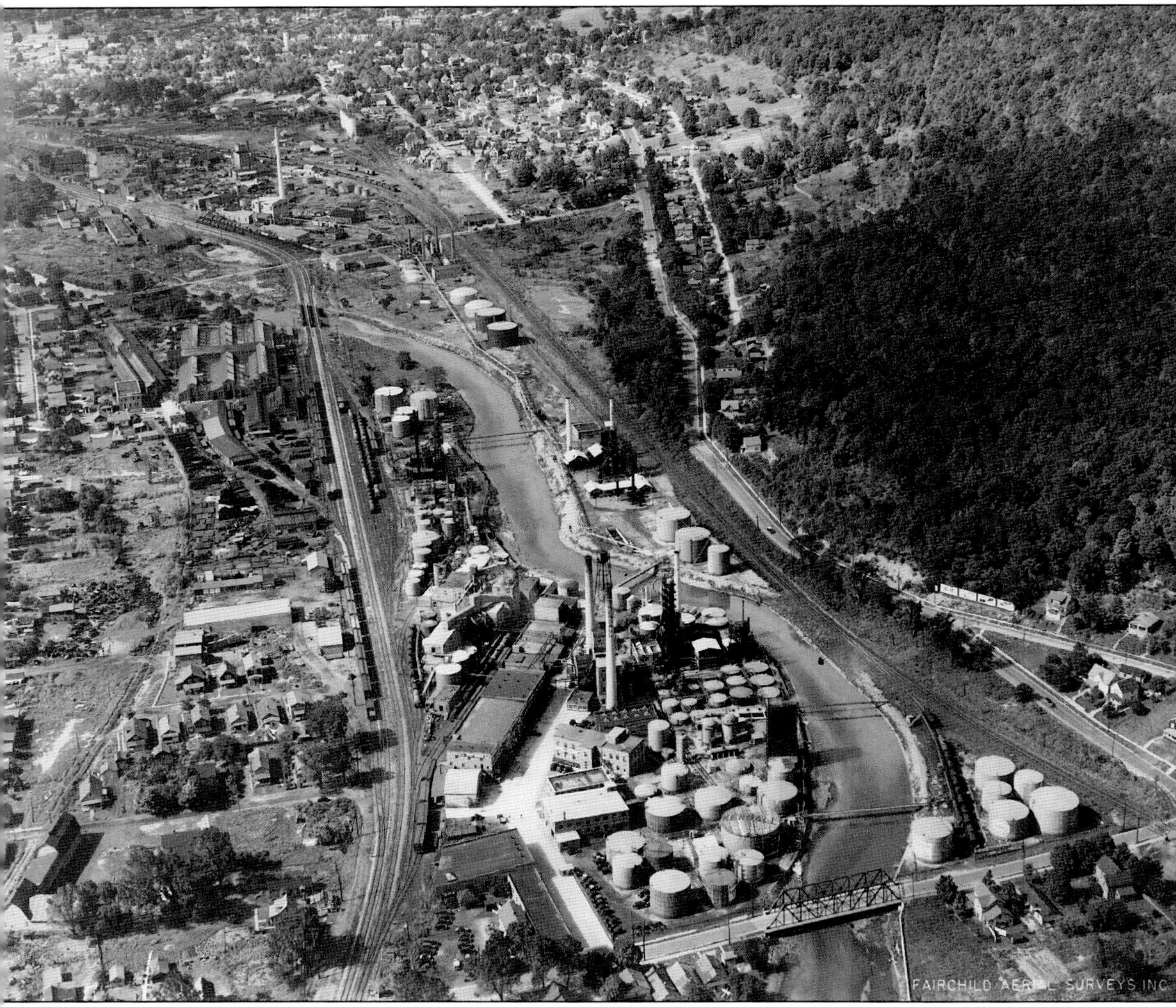

The Kendall Oil Refining Company, September 1933. The company began in 1881 as a "complete refinery capable of making lamp oil and steam cylinder oil" along Kendall Creek, and by 1928 a new distribution system would market Kendall lubricants nationwide. This aerial view of the refinery shows the extent of the refinery along the Tuna Creek. The bridge in the lower right is the North Kendall Avenue Bridge. Synonymous with Bradford, the city was heartbroken when the name "Kendall" was sold to the Sun Oil Corp. in 1996. The American Refinery Group bought the physical refinery in 1997.

Three

The Century Begins

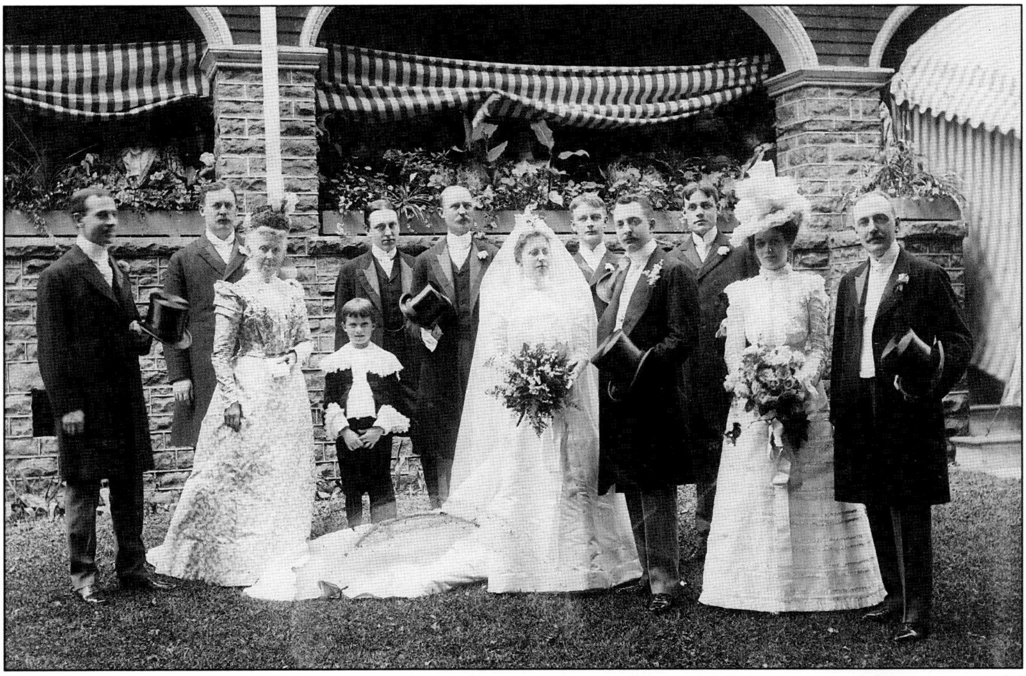

Grace Emery's Wedding, June 28, 1905. It was the wedding of the century. Thirty-year-old Grace Elizabeth Emery, daughter of Bradford oil millionaire entrepreneur Lewis Emery, married Mahlon Chapman Martin of Bogata, Columbia. Married in the Church of the Ascension, over one thousand people lined the street, hoping to catch a glimpse of the wedding party. This photograph was taken that afternoon, at the reception at the Emery estate. The marriage was short-lived, however, and following her father's death in 1924, Grace became the acting head of the Emery manufacturing empire. She died in 1948, at the age of 67. Upon her death, the flag on the Bradford Post Office flew at half-mast; the first time that it had ever been flown for a private citizen.

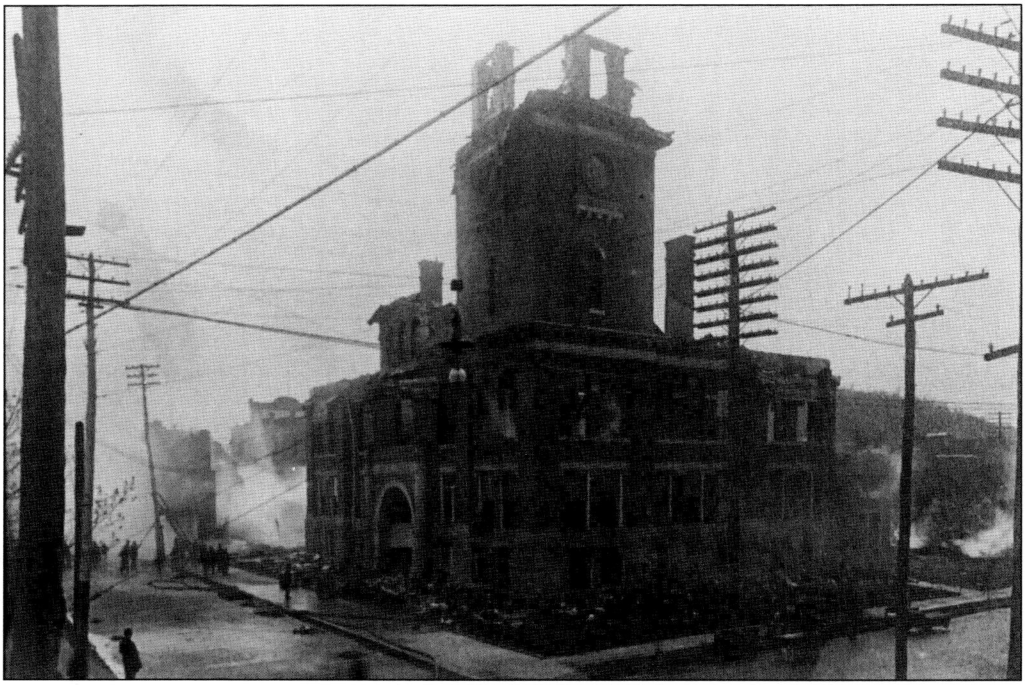

City Hall Burns, November 9, 1901. The fire began in Beamer's livery stable next door, but when it was over the roof and tower of city hall (which had just been completed in 1899) was destroyed. This photograph, taken the next day, shows the extent of the damage. Fortunately, the city records were stored in a fireproof vault and were saved but all the maps belonging to the city engineer were lost.

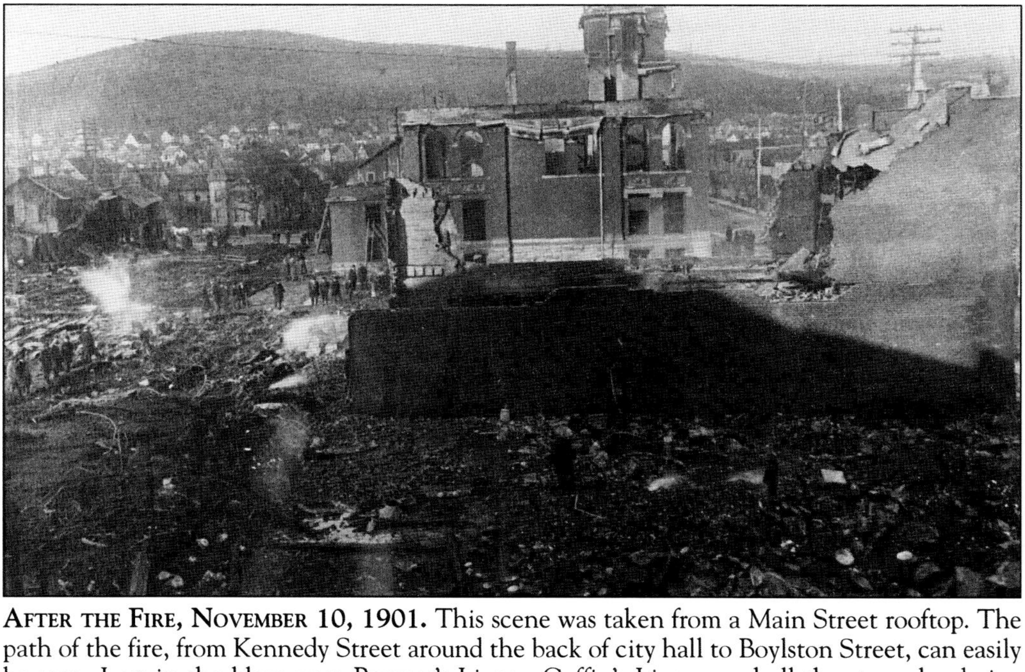

After the Fire, November 10, 1901. This scene was taken from a Main Street rooftop. The path of the fire, from Kennedy Street around the back of city hall to Boylston Street, can easily be seen. Lost in the blaze were Beamer's Livery, Coffin's Livery, and all the stores bordering them. Thirty-eight horses burned to death.

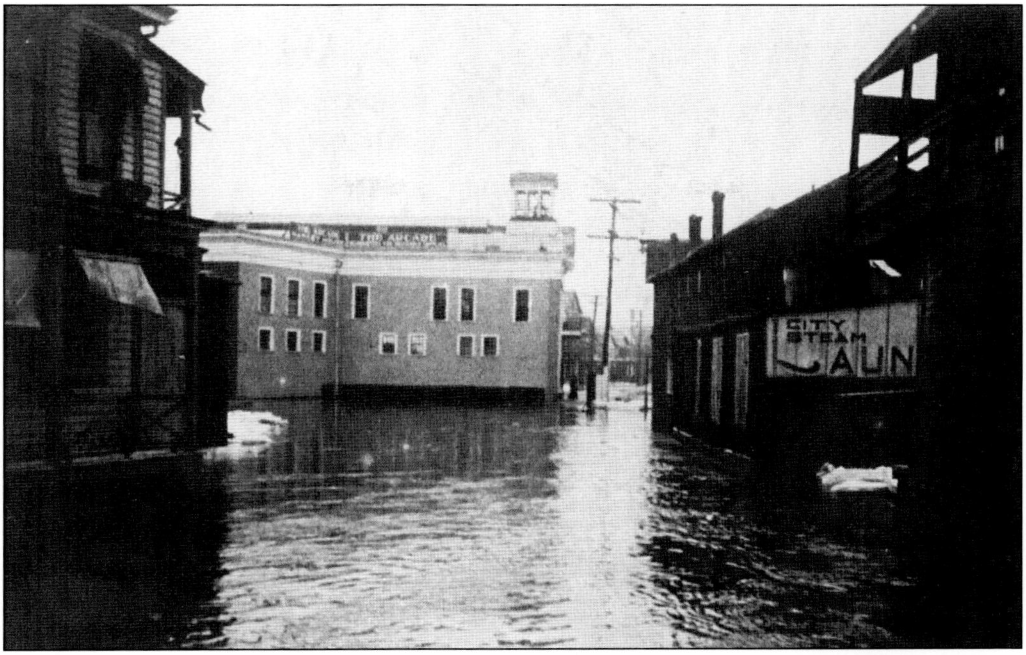

The Arcade Building, 1903. This was an architectural wonder. The building itself straddled Tuna Creek, with entrances on both Pine Street and East Washington Street. It is seen here shortly after it was constructed, in flood season. It was built on a system of trusses and girders, which would theoretically support the entire building and its contents. Regretfully though, in 1918, added weight due to an exceptionally large storage of food supplies and textile machinery stored there for World War I caused the collapse of the Arcade Building into the creek. It was repaired but never rebuilt, and stands today on East Washington Street; its back wall bricked over, facing the creek it once spanned.

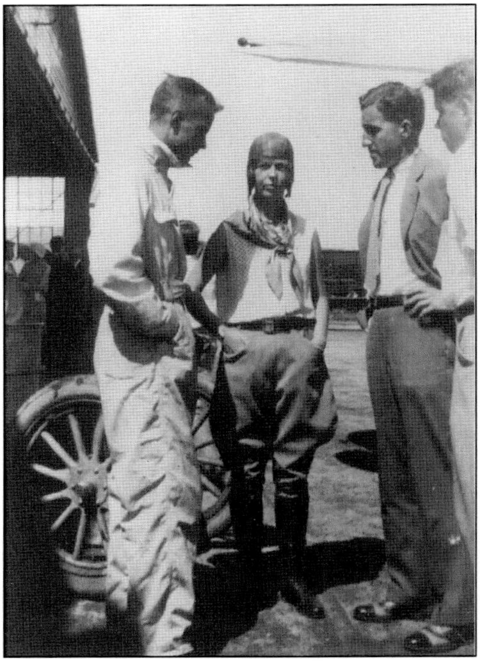

The Dedication of the Harri Emery Airport, July 7, 1929. Following the death of Harri Emery, Bradford's most famous aviator, the Bradford Airport was renamed in his memory. Visitors from all over the country flew into Bradford in his memory. Here, Elinor Smith, center, holder of the woman's endurance record in an aircraft, visits with Pete Brooks, left, and Harvey Phillips and Jim Schonblom, right.

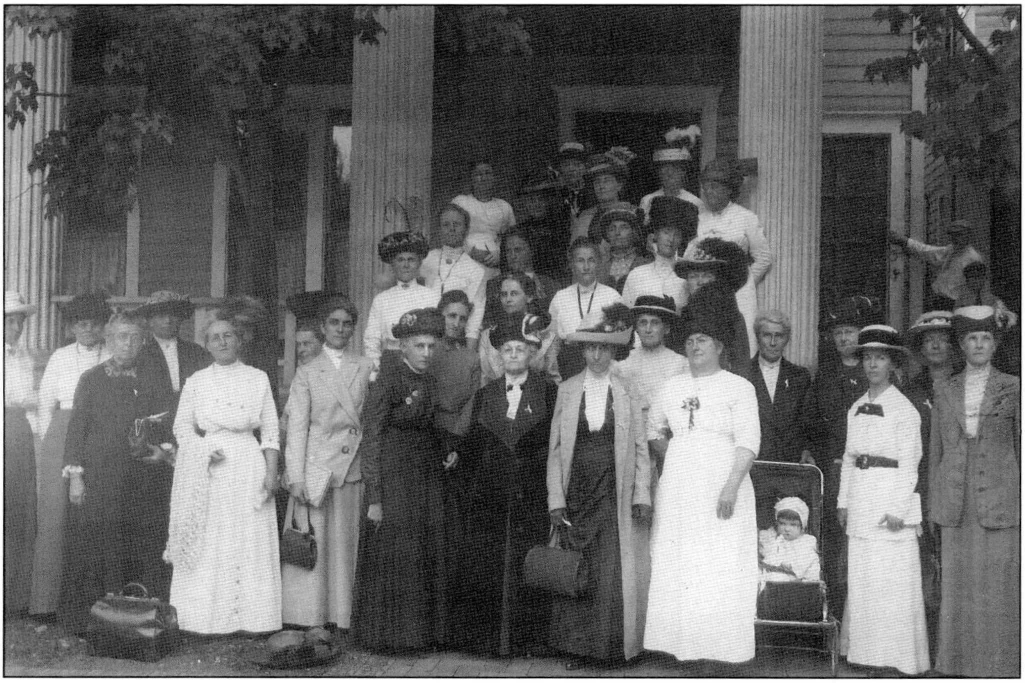

THE WOMEN'S CHRISTIAN TEMPERANCE UNION, C. 1905. The WCTU was founded on October 13, 1880 and was devoted to the abstinence of drink. The organization vigorously campaigned against alcohol, and for women's suffrage. In 1892 Susan B. Anthony came to Bradford and spoke on their behalf. By 1900, there were 150 members. Their clubhouse still stands on the corner of Congress and Corydon, where this photograph was taken. The WCTU disbanded in Bradford in the summer of 1996, citing a lack of women willing to "take the pledge against liquor."

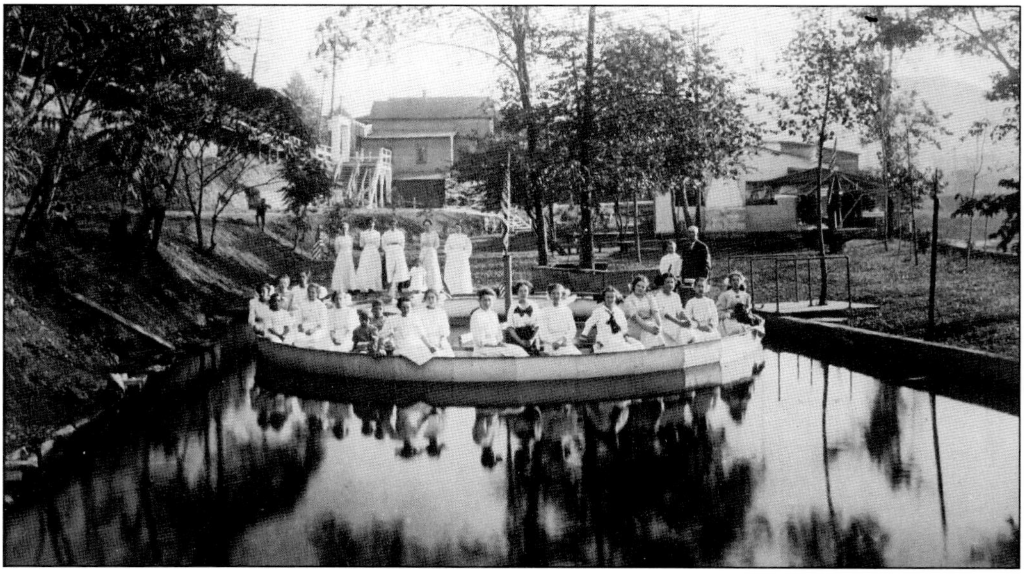

LUNA PARK, C. 1909. Located just below East Main Street (near the present-day Orak Grotto), this pleasant picnic grove was on the banks of the Tuna Creek. These young girls appear to be sitting in a circular merry-go-round that floats.

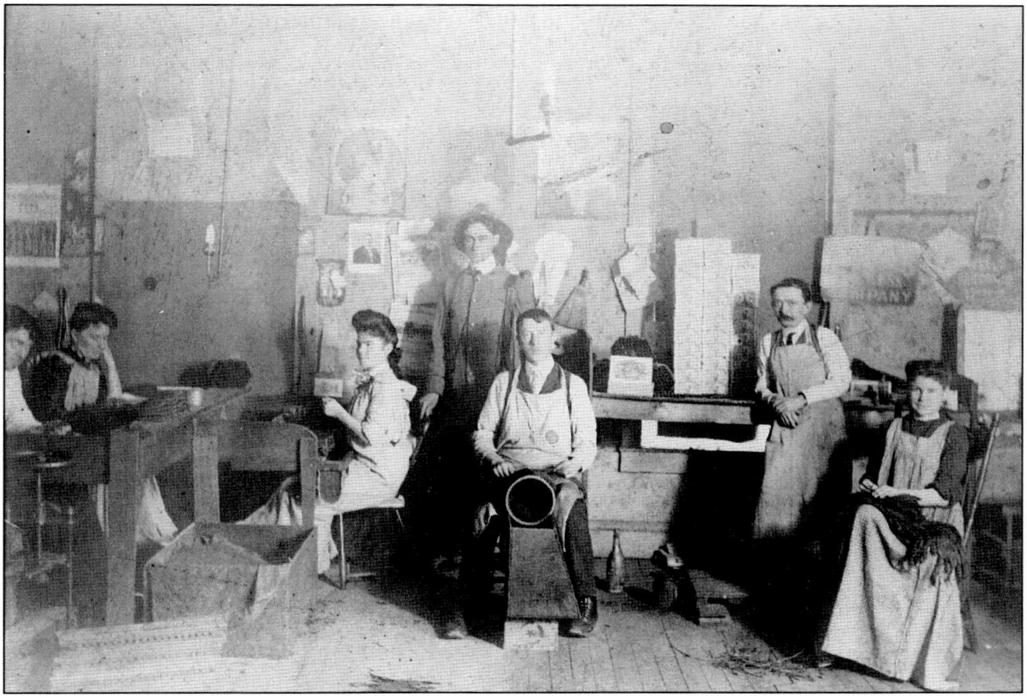

CIGAR MAKING, 1905. This small, cigar-making company was located on West Washington Street at the turn of the century. George "Commodore" Cornelius, the owner, is standing second from right, leaning on the table.

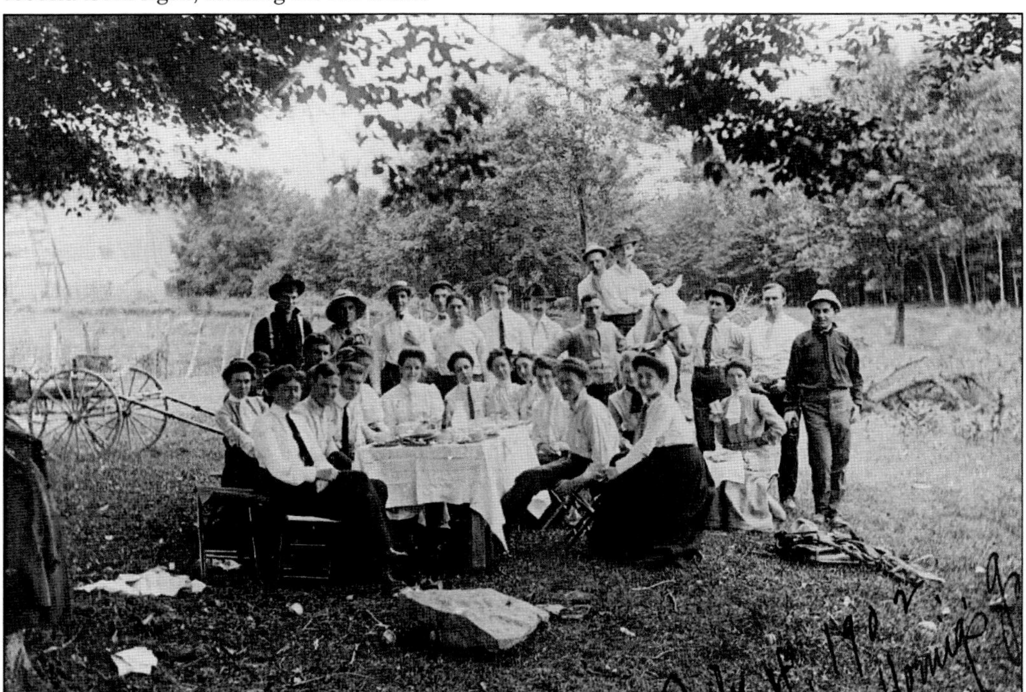

A PLEASANT DAY, JULY 4, 1902. This group has gathered for an Independence Day picnic at Hoenig's Grove near Custer City.

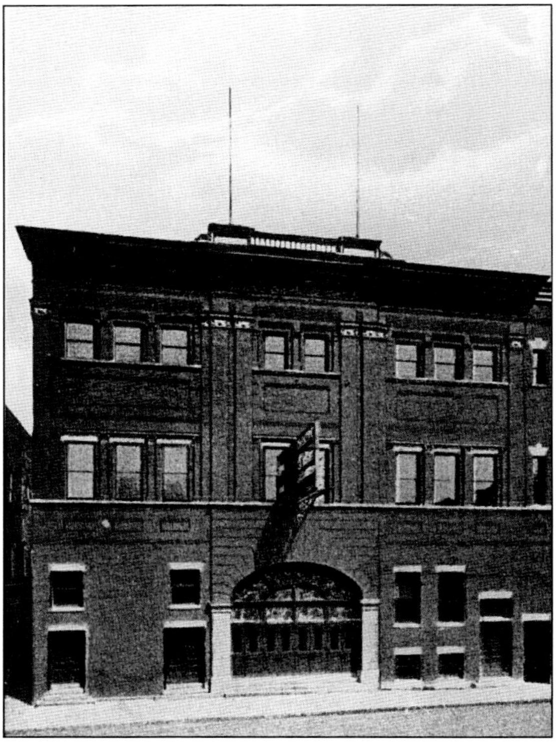

The Bradford Theater (Shea's), 1901. Located at the site of the present-day parking lot of the Seneca Building, the theater is fondly remembered by many Bradfordians as "Shea's." It was designed by Leon H. Lempert and Son, Theatrical Architects of Rochester, New York. This nationally known firm designed over 90 opera houses, including the Palace Theatre in Olean, New York, which is still standing.

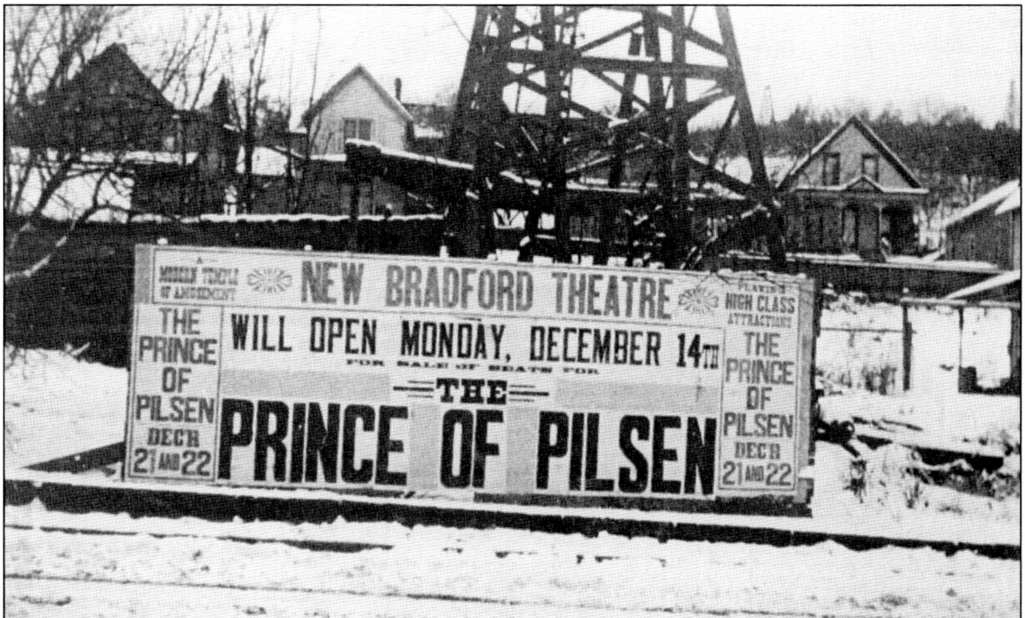

Opening Night Billboard, 1903. Billboards such as these advertised the opening of the New Bradford Theatre on South Avenue. Ticket sales for *The Prince of Pilsen* began December 14; opening night was December 21. The sign advertises the new theater as "A Modern Temple of Amusement" that played "High Class Attractions." The theater (later known as Shea's) remained in business until 1959.

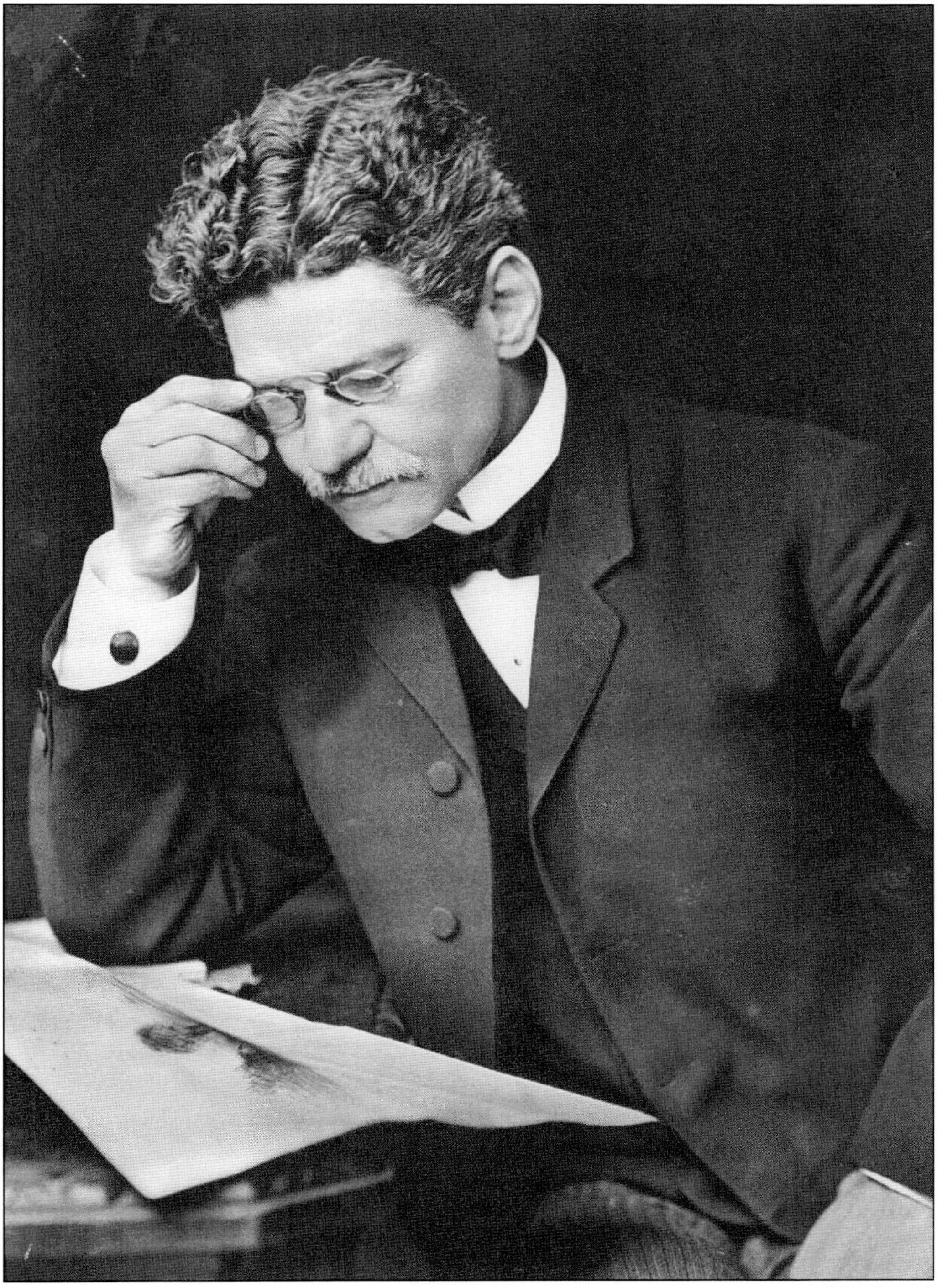

Jame Leasure, c. 1905. An entrepreneur and inventor, Leasure was responsible for 43 inventions, including the Leasure Vacuum cleaner, an automobile non-skid tire, sanitary windshield, and a durable railroad tie. He helped found McCourt Label, was employed for 19 years with Standard Oil, operated the printing department of the *Bradford Era* for nine years, and owned the St. James Hotel at the head of Main Street.

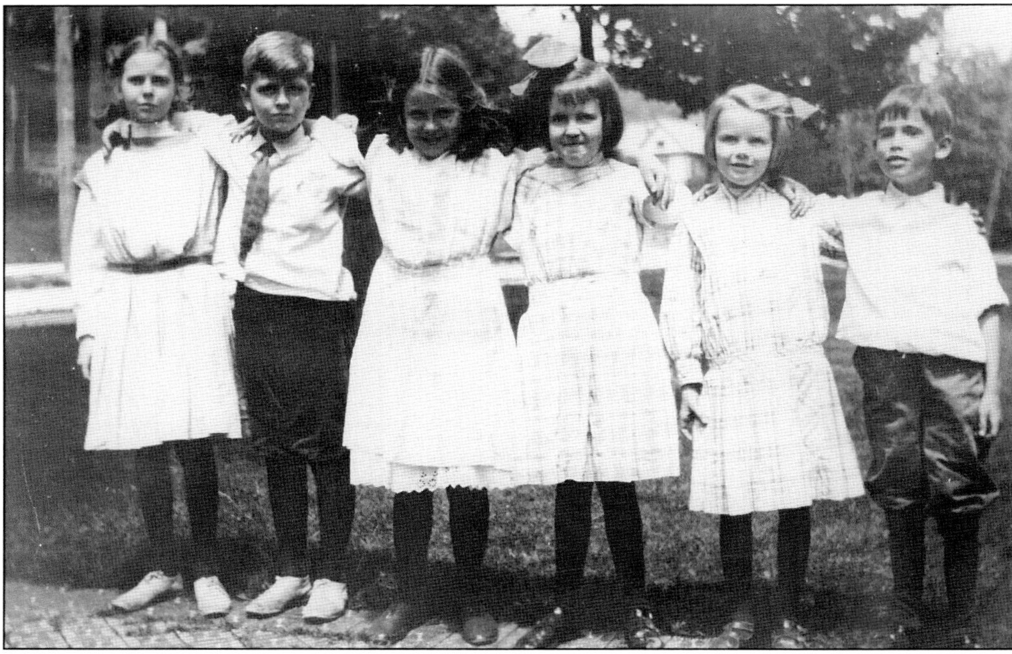

Good Friends on Jackson Avenue, 1910. The period from 1900 to the 1920s, before two world wars and a global economic depression, has been called the Age of Innocence. These children, all of whom lived on Jackson Avenue, are the hope of the new century. They are, from left to right, Cecily Bovaird, Craig (?) Bovaird, Mabel Adams (Hamilton), Julia Smith (Jones), Christine Schonblom (Fisher), and Paul Burdick.

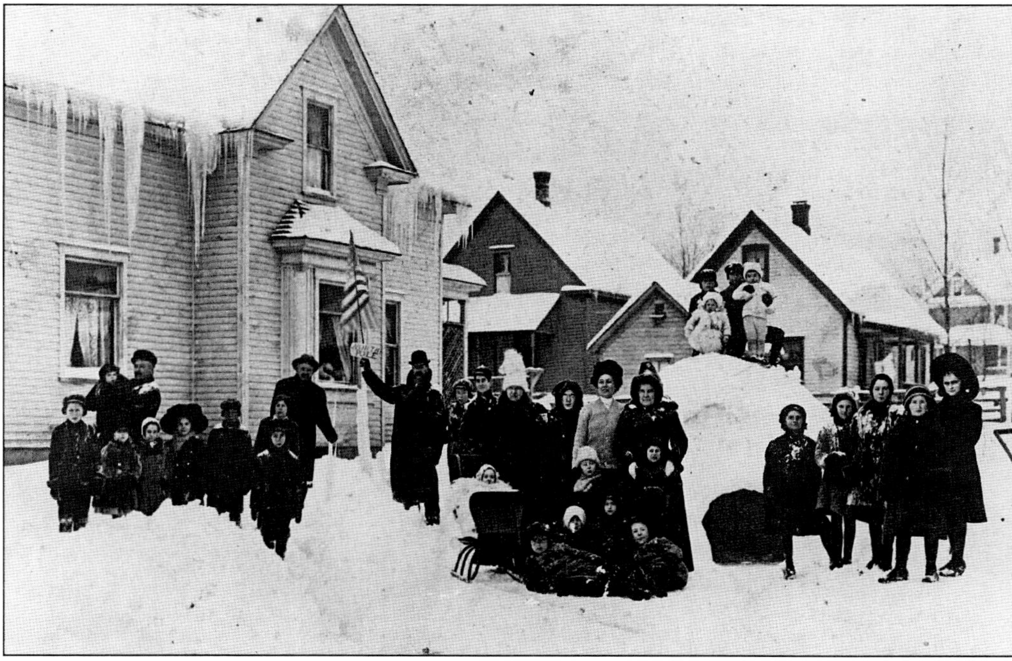

Playing in the Snow, 1910. These Cole Avenue neighbors have all come outside to enjoy the cold and snow. The man holding the flag and the sign that reads "north pole" is Rev. Charles Peterson, pastor of the Swedish Mission Church.

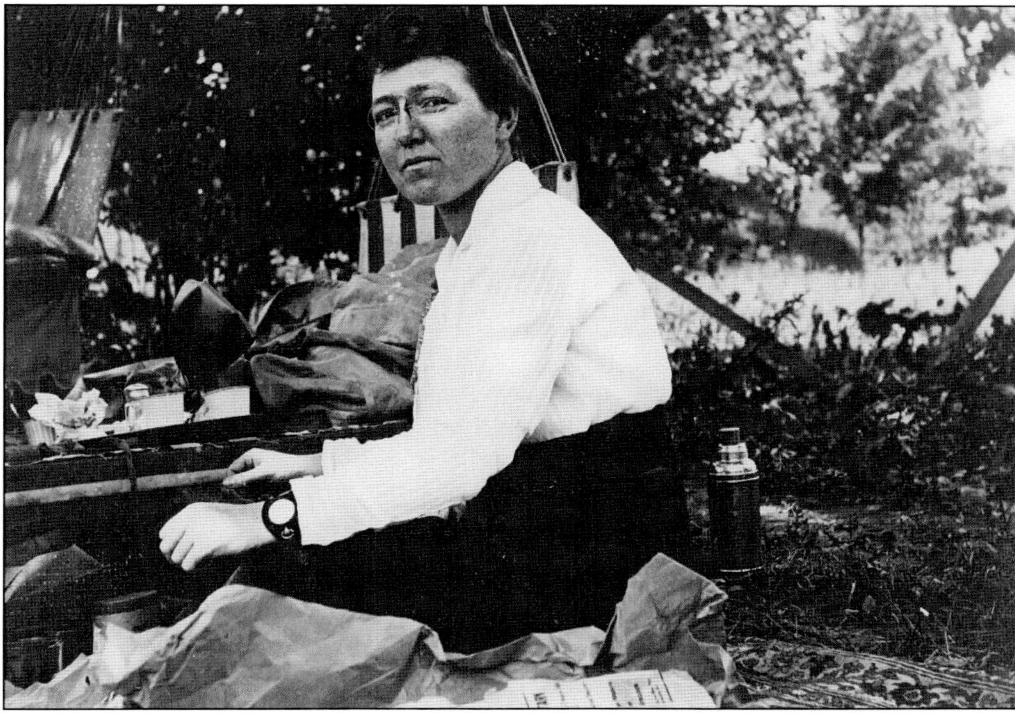

PERSIS ROSAMUNDE STRAIGHT ROBBINS, MD, 1910. Born in Bradford in 1879, she became one of Bradford's first woman physicians. She graduated from Pennsylvania State University; practicing medicine with her father, Dr. A. Straight, until his death in 1917. She began her own practice in 1927 on Pleasant Street, and continued until her death in 1963, at the age of 84.

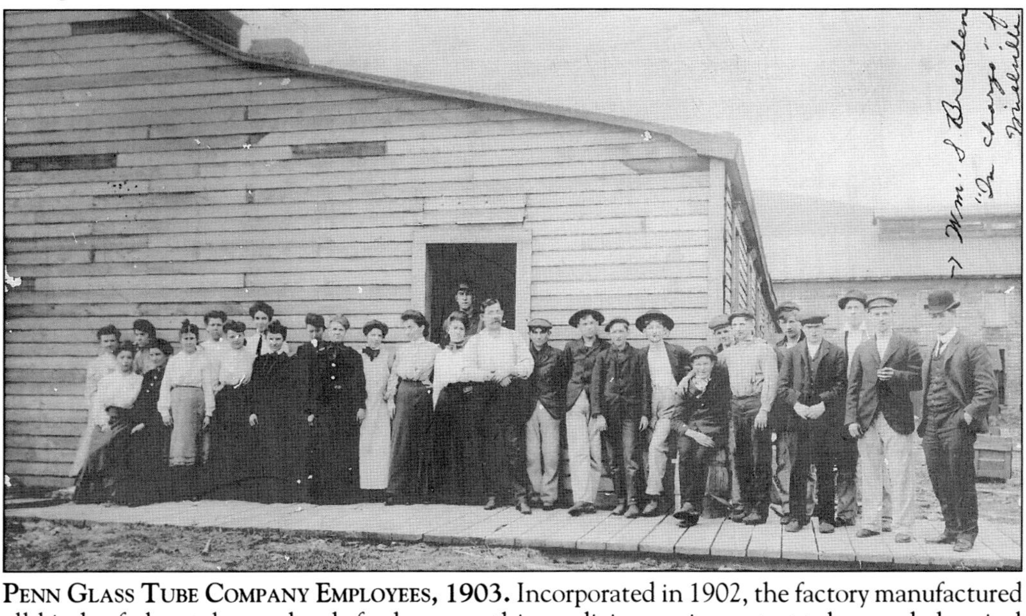

PENN GLASS TUBE COMPANY EMPLOYEES, 1903. Incorporated in 1902, the factory manufactured all kinds of glass tubes and rods for homeopathic medicine, syringes, test tubes, and chemical and scientific appliances. Located at 37 Holley Avenue, the company employed 30 workers and had an annual output of $25,000 worth of manufactured goods.

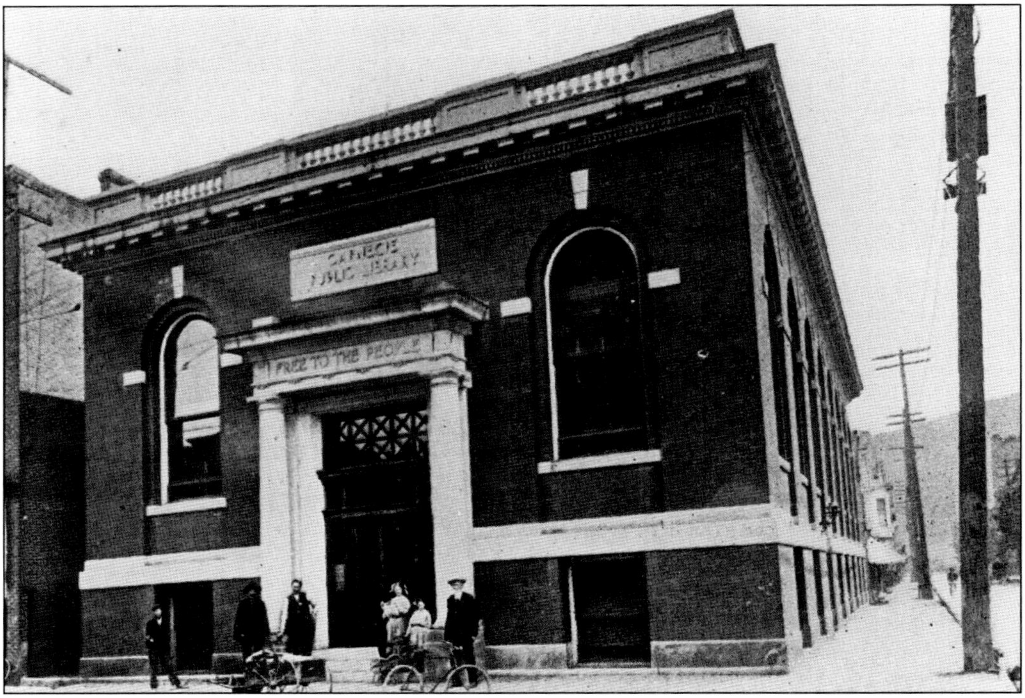

The Carnegie Public Library, 1903. It was built on land donated by the city, with a $25,000 gift from Pittsburgh philanthropist Andrew Carnegie. Located on the corner of Congress and Corydon Streets, it initially contained just 2,750 books, but by 1938 had over 152,000 volumes.

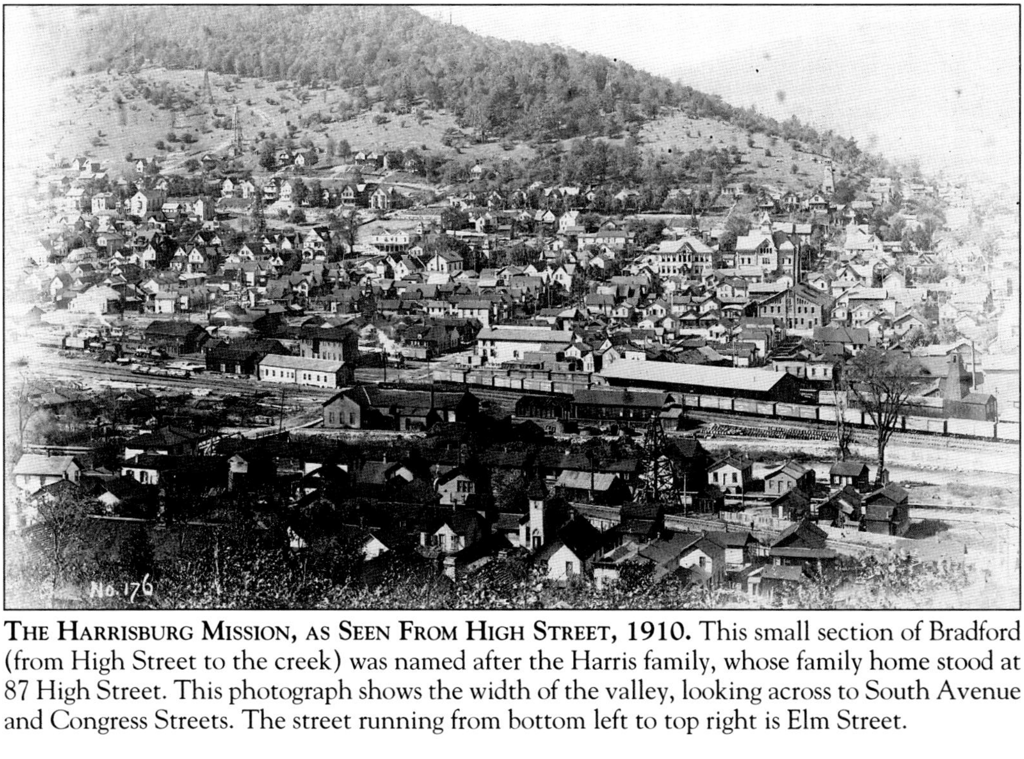

The Harrisburg Mission, as Seen From High Street, 1910. This small section of Bradford (from High Street to the creek) was named after the Harris family, whose family home stood at 87 High Street. This photograph shows the width of the valley, looking across to South Avenue and Congress Streets. The street running from bottom left to top right is Elm Street.

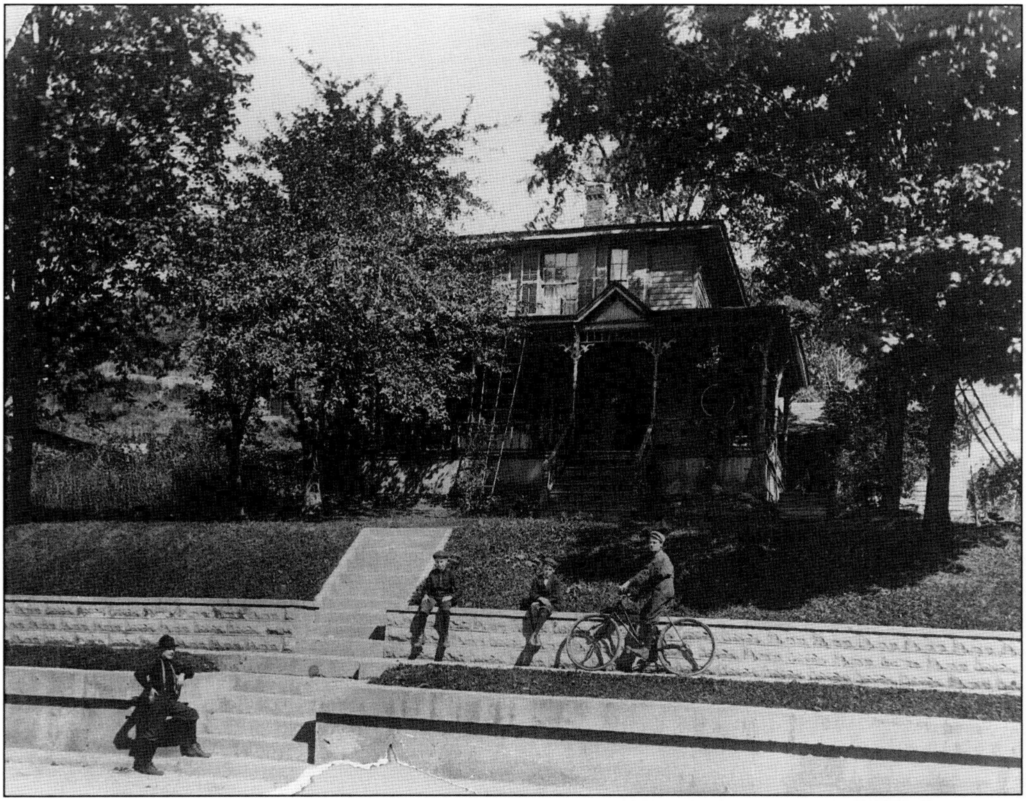

THE HARRIS HOME, 87 HIGH STREET. Located at the head of Elm Street, the Harris home was built before 1886. Marshall Harris worked as a druggist at the Thompson and Wood Drug Store on Main Street.

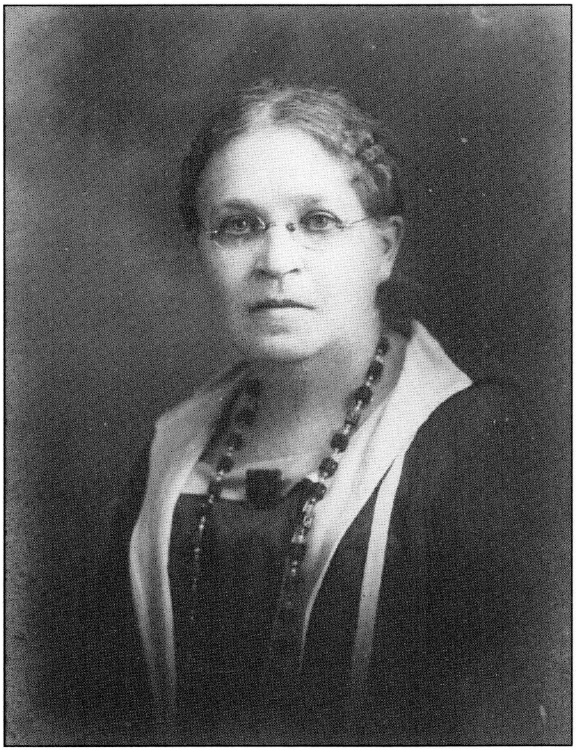

LUELLA HARRIS (1862–1946). A teacher and lifelong resident of Bradford, she was passionate about the history of the early Bradford pioneers and wrote several books on the subject. In 1925 Luella helped to found the "First Families of the Tuna," an organization dedicated to the preservation of those histories.

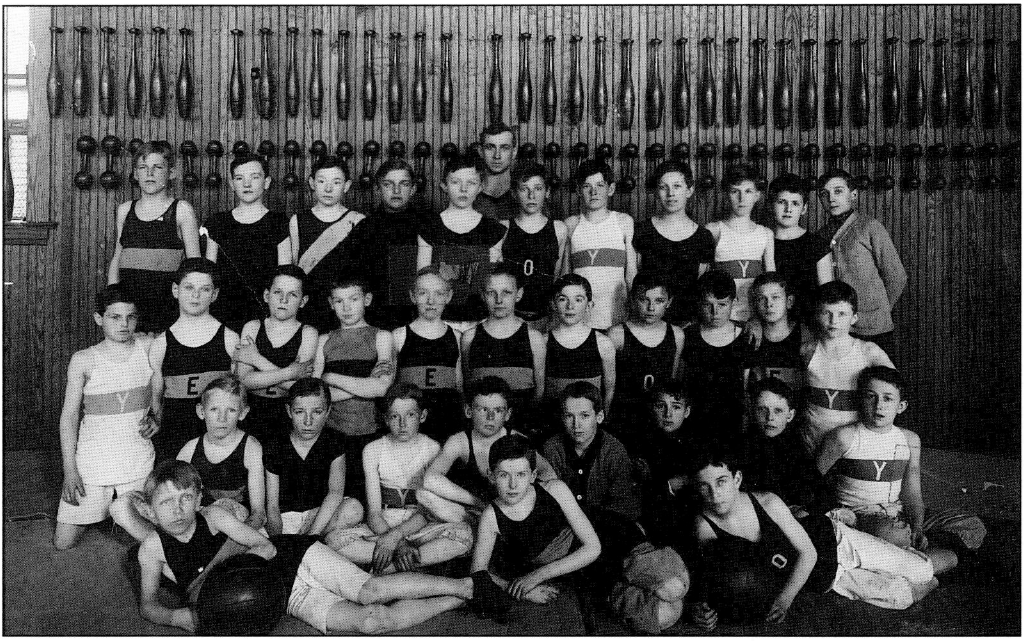

AT THE YMCA, 1909. The Indian clubs and hand weights on the wall behind these young boys were typical exercise equipment of the era.

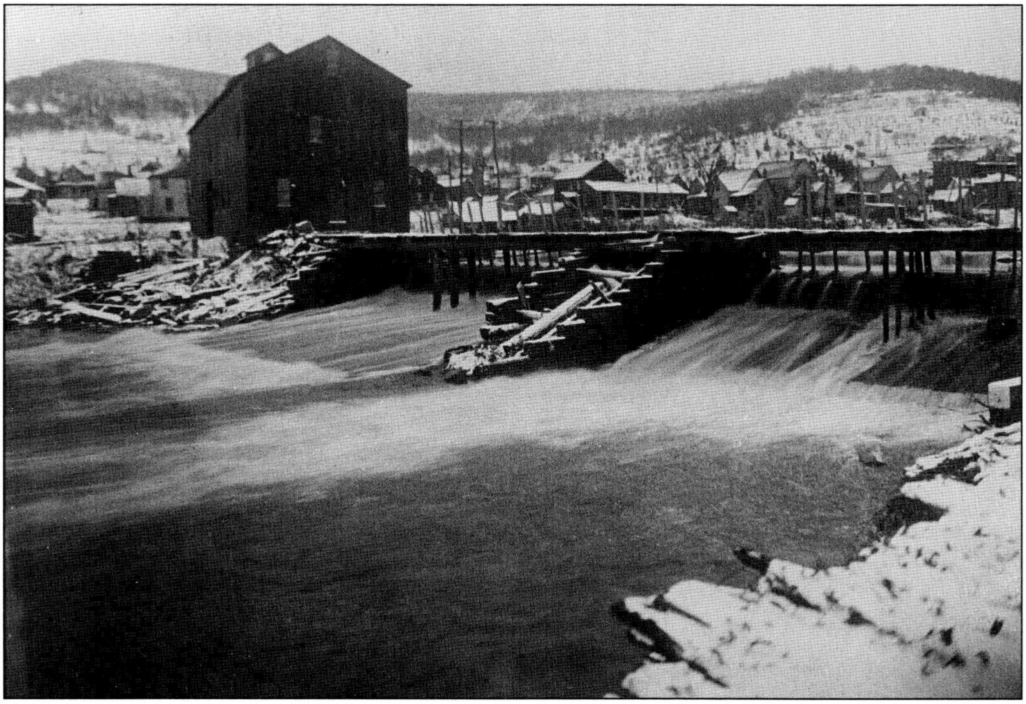

THE DOUGLASS DAM AND SPILLWAY, 1903. Operated by C.L. Douglass as a gristmill on the Tuna Creek, the dam was located at the site of the present-day Mill Street bridge. It was bought by the city for $15,000 in 1906. The bridge was constructed shortly afterward. The mill is to the left of the dam.

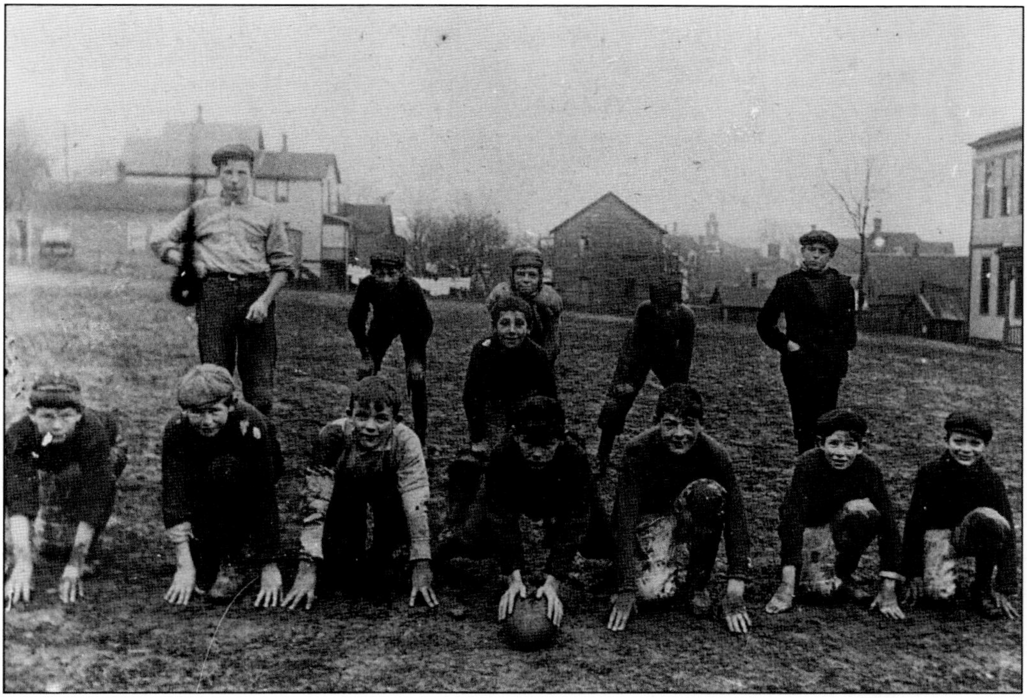

BACK LOT FOOTBALL AT THE OLD THIRD WARD SCHOOL, 1908. This playground was located behind the old Third Ward Grade School on the corner of School and Center Streets. These boys may have been among those burned when a gas well exploded on School Street on April 3, 1909. Russell Johnston—second boy from left, kneeling—was severely injured in the blast, and died a few days later.

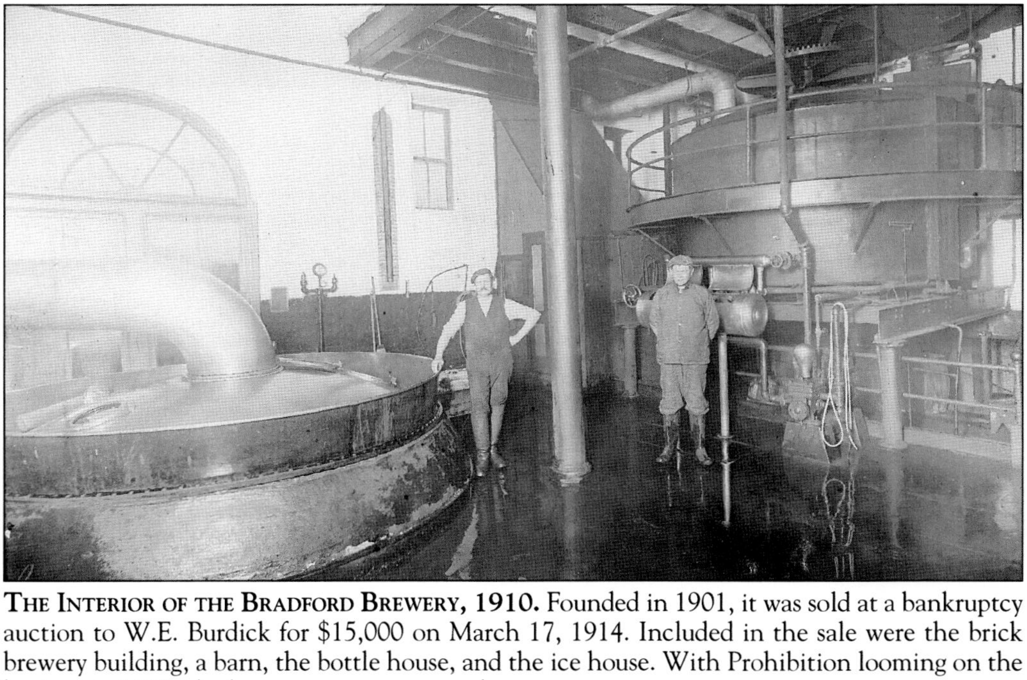

THE INTERIOR OF THE BRADFORD BREWERY, 1910. Founded in 1901, it was sold at a bankruptcy auction to W.E. Burdick for $15,000 on March 17, 1914. Included in the sale were the brick brewery building, a barn, the bottle house, and the ice house. With Prohibition looming on the horizon in 1920, the brewery never reopened.

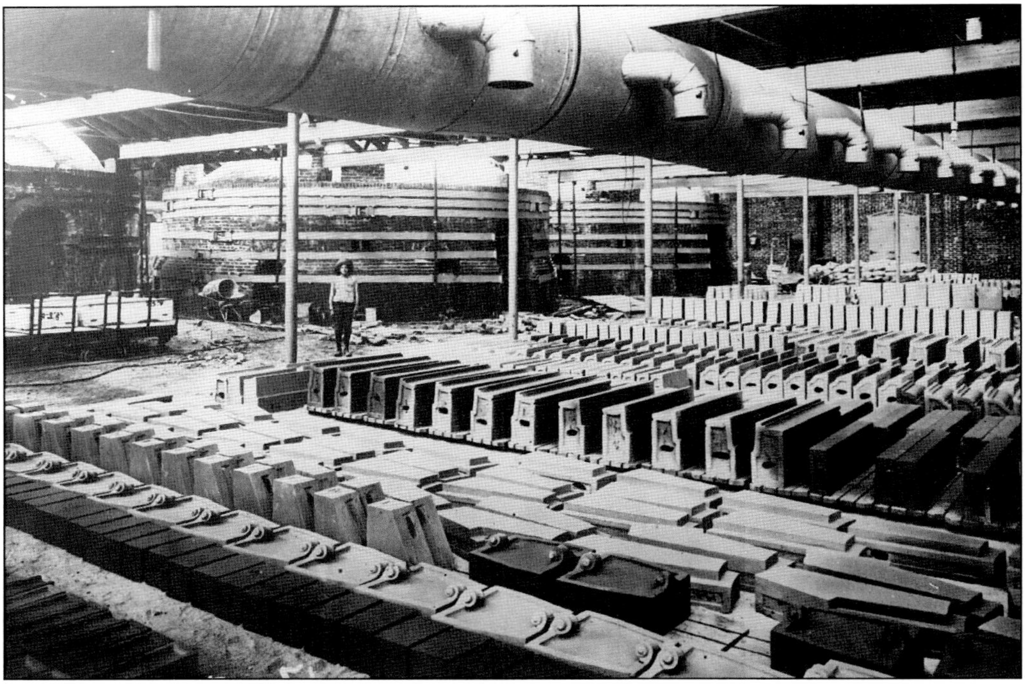

The Northeastern Terra Cotta Company, 1909. Located at the end of Grove Street, it remained in existence for only a few years, manufacturing architectural terra-cotta moldings. This photograph shows the drying floor.

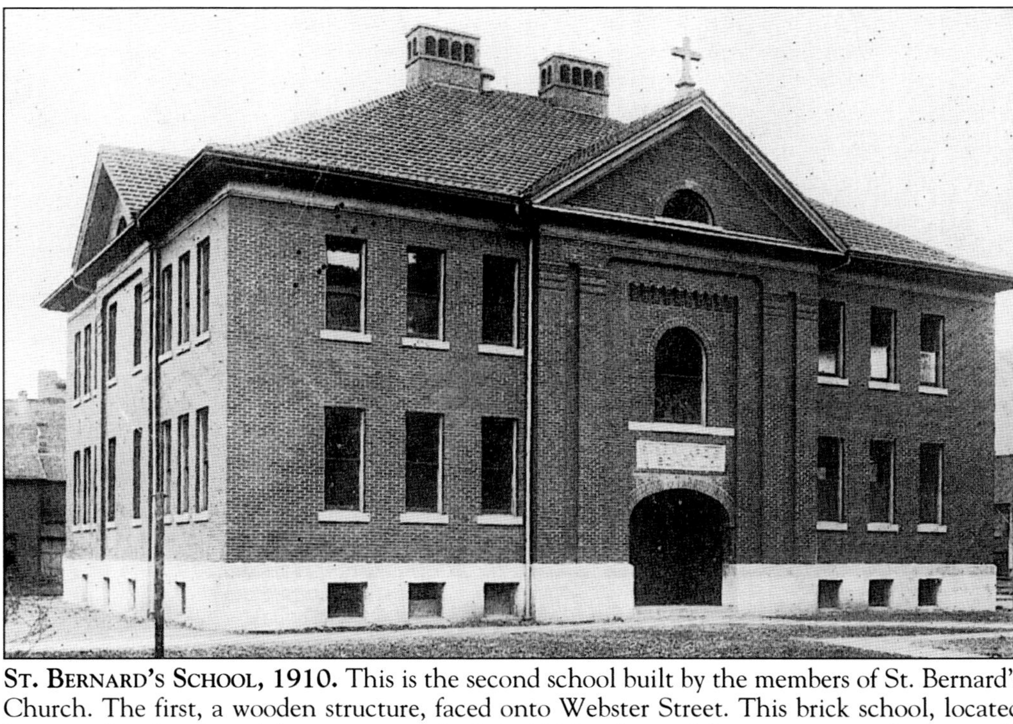

St. Bernard's School, 1910. This is the second school built by the members of St. Bernard's Church. The first, a wooden structure, faced onto Webster Street. This brick school, located between the church and the rectory, was built in 1904 and served for many years as both a grade school and a high school.

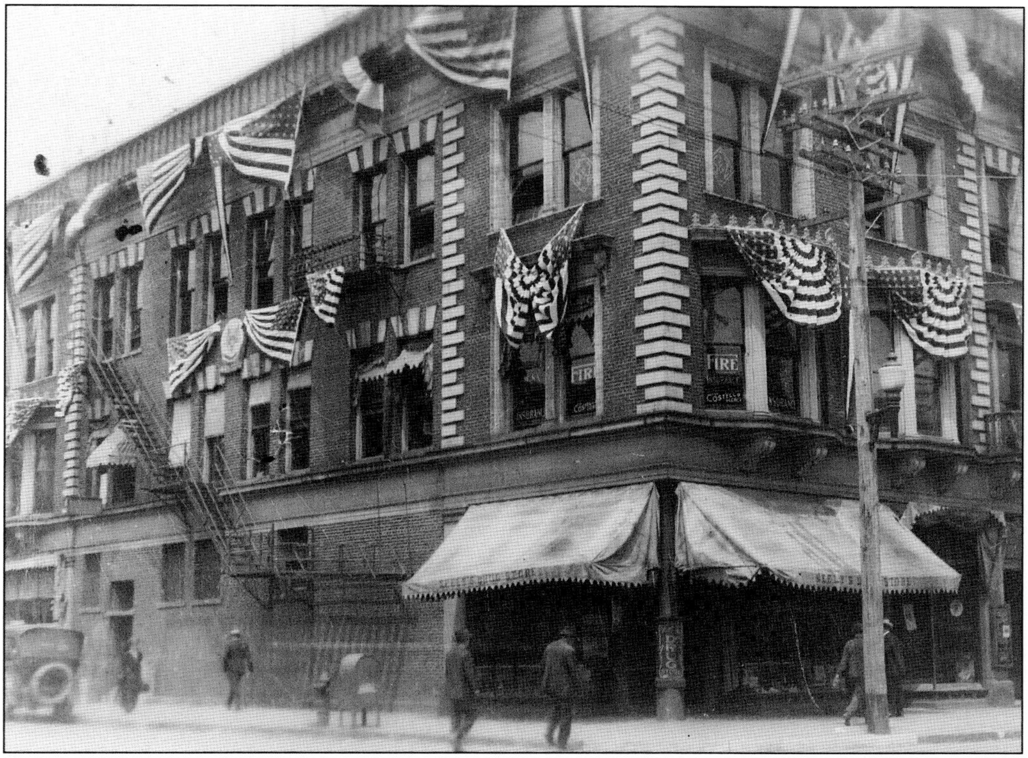

THE SCHONBLOM BUILDING, 1909. Located on the corner of Main and Kennedy Streets, this impressive structure was designed by Frederick C. French, a noted Bradford architect, who also designed the James R. Evans building across the street. Built in 1902, early tenants included a physician, a dentist, two insurance companies, a tailor, and Neely's Drug Store. Otto Schonblom, for whom this building is named, was president of the Bradford National Bank, which helped to finance the construction.

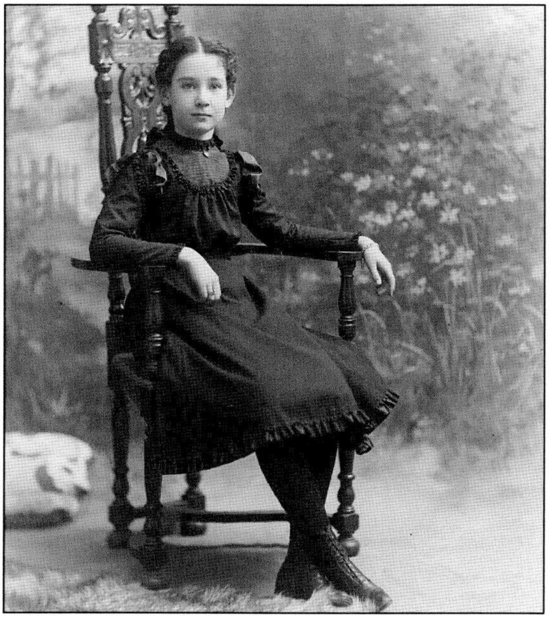

MERRY CHRISTMAS FROM GRETCHEN, 1906. From her black high-button shoes to her neatly braided hair, 11-year-old Gretchen is the picture of a turn-of-the-century girl. The only inscription on this photograph is the Christmas greeting, her name, and age—one can only wonder how Gretchen faired in the coming century.

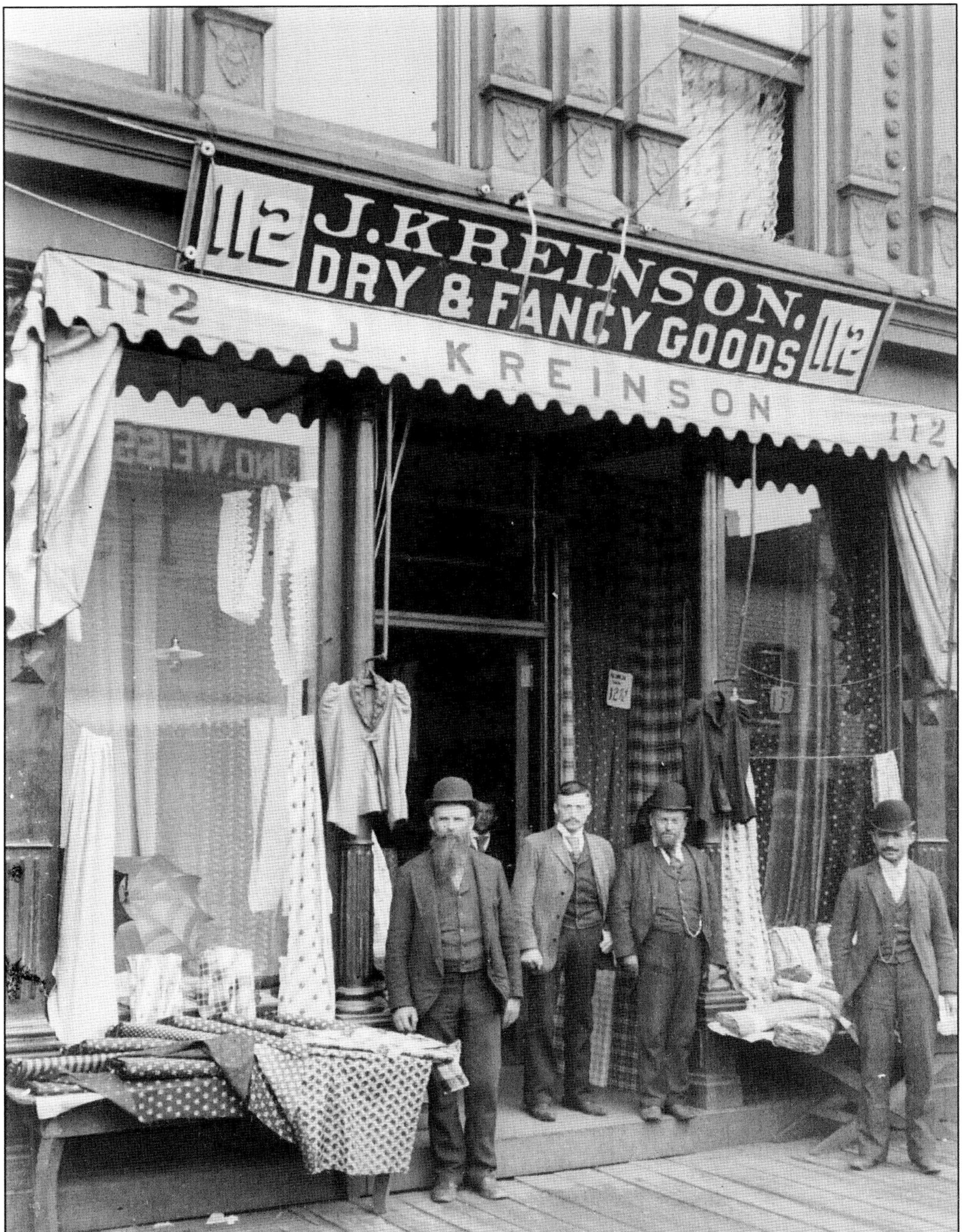

J. Kreinson's Dry & Fancy Goods, Main Street, c. 1910. The Kreinson family operated a thriving dry goods business for over 50 years. First the shop was on Mechanic Street then the business expanded onto 112 Main Street. Lazier Kreinson, at left, came to Bradford from Titusville in 1878. His 17-year-old son, Jacob Kreinson, joined him here in 1883, and helped run the business. Jacob, second from left, died in 1916 at the age of 50; he was survived by a son, David, and a daughter, Miriam.

Four

The Town Grows as War Approaches

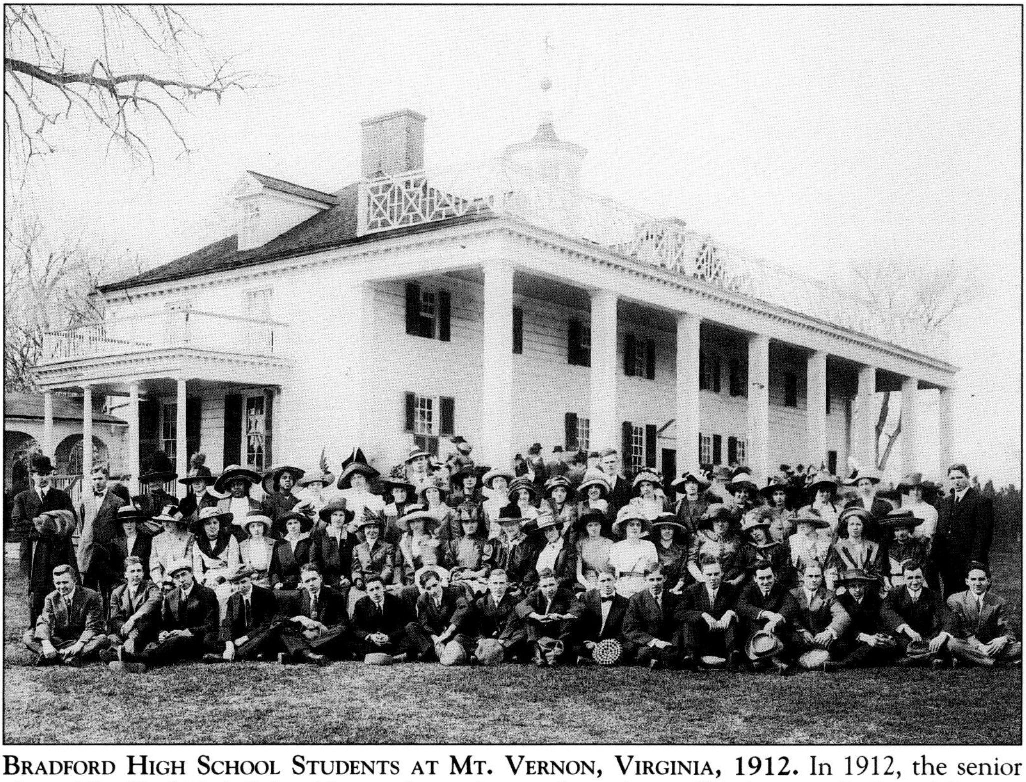

BRADFORD HIGH SCHOOL STUDENTS AT MT. VERNON, VIRGINIA, 1912. In 1912, the senior class of Bradford High School began the tradition of traveling to Washington D.C. and George Washington's home at Mt. Vernon during Easter vacation. A class photograph was taken there each year. These trips were continued each spring by the graduating class until 1941.

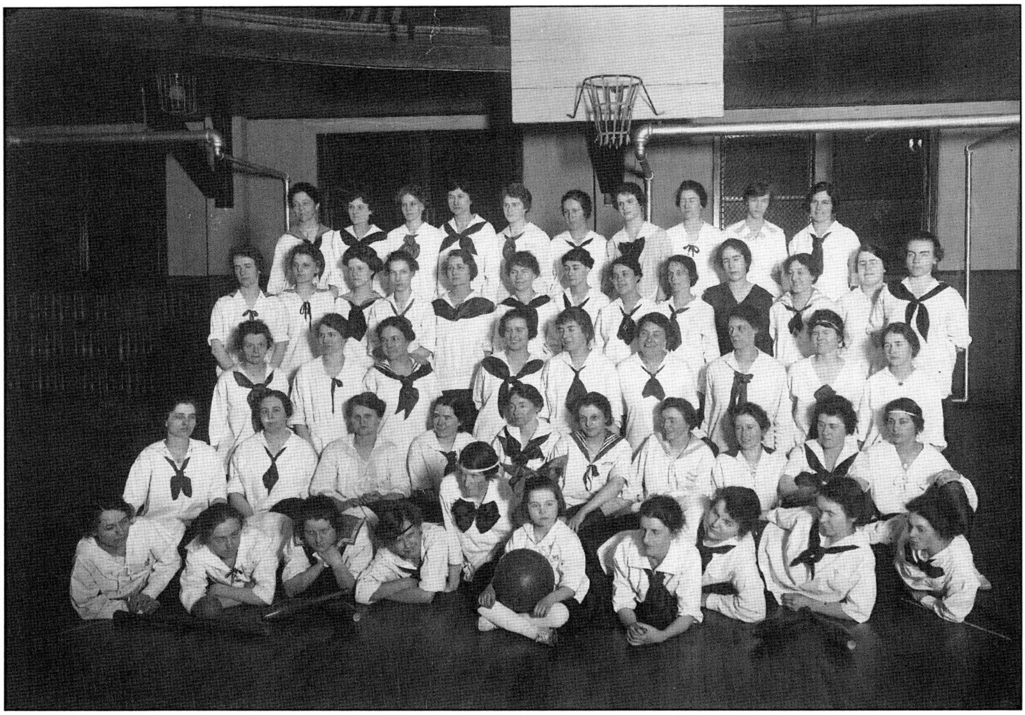

A Girls Physical Education Class, c. 1915. These girls have just finished a lesson in basketball. Seen here in the gymnasium of the high school at the head of Mechanic Street, they look quite comfortable in the official "gym" clothes of the era. Notice the upper running track around the perimeter of the gym.

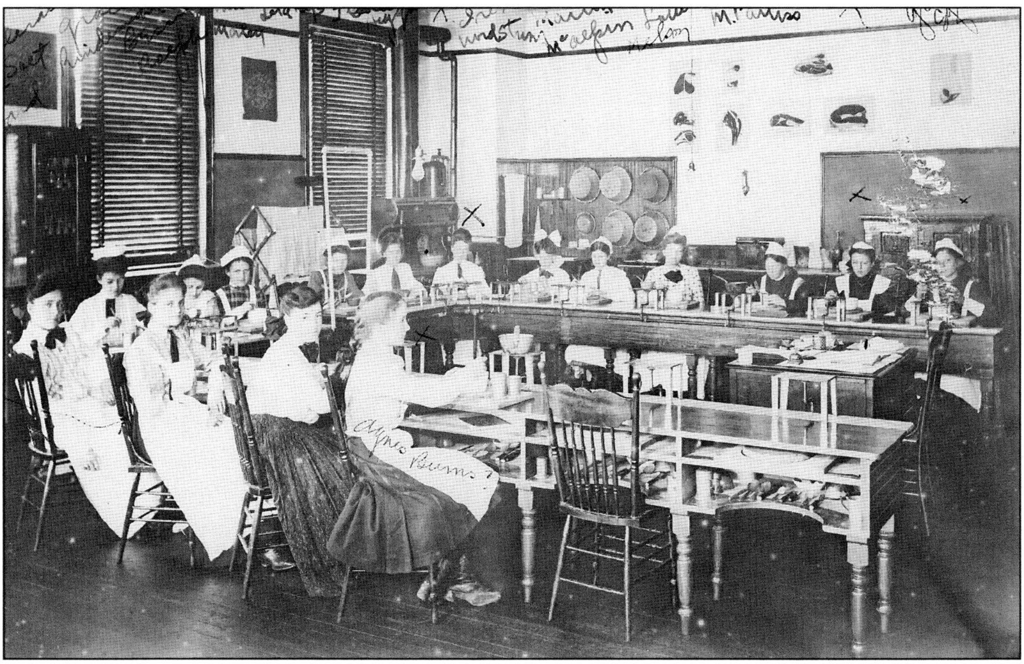

A Domestic Science Class, 1915. These high school girls are learning how to run a home efficiently, and how to cook.

HER FAVORITE DOLL, 1912. With McKinley assassinated in 1901, Theodore Roosevelt assumed the presidency and, supposedly, while on a hunting trip, spared the life of a new born bear cub. Stuffed bears soon became known as "teddy bears." Here, Evelyn Bassage, age four, is pictured with her favorite teddy.

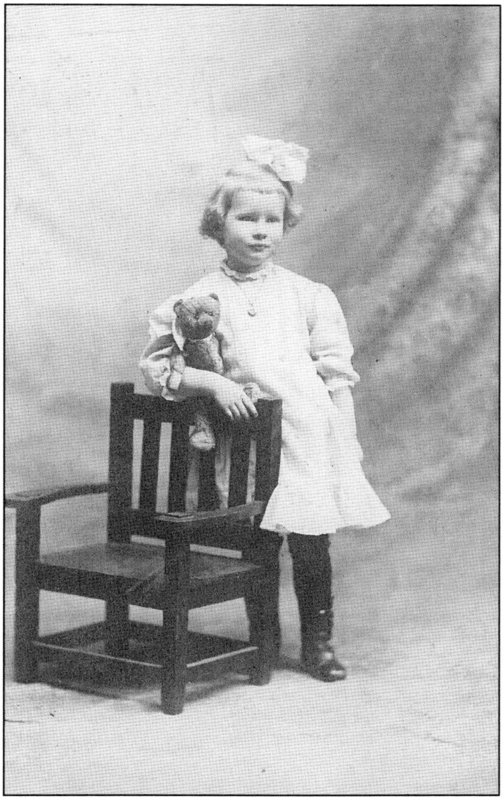

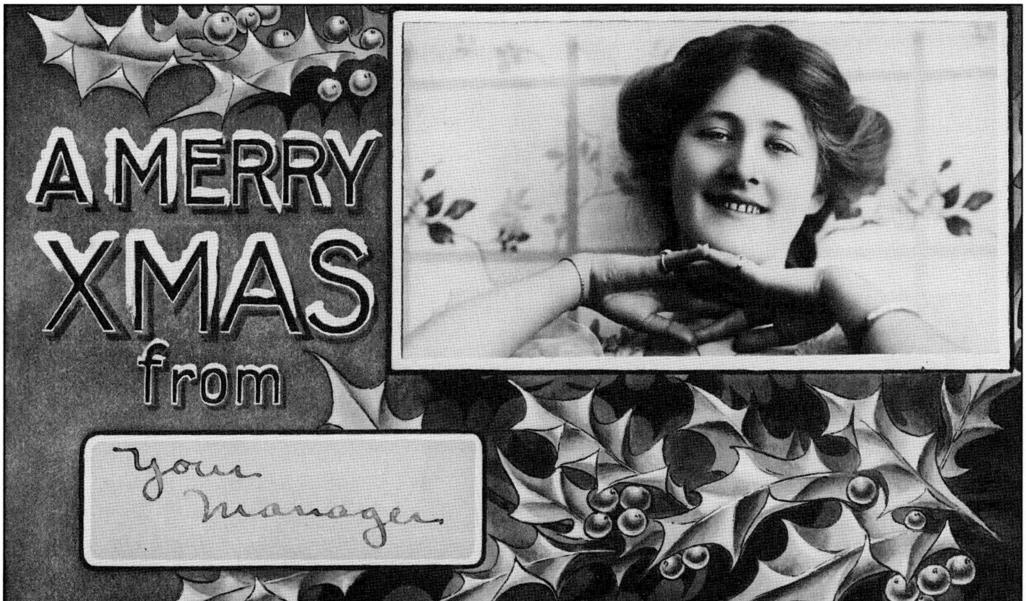

ESTELLA NORRIS, "THE NIGHTINGALE SINGER," 1912. Although crippled at an early age and confined to a wheelchair for the rest of her life, her voice became her fortune as she traveled with vaudeville shows throughout the area. She is shown here at age 22. Later she married, had a son, and lived at 62 Pleasant Street, dying at age 72 in 1962.

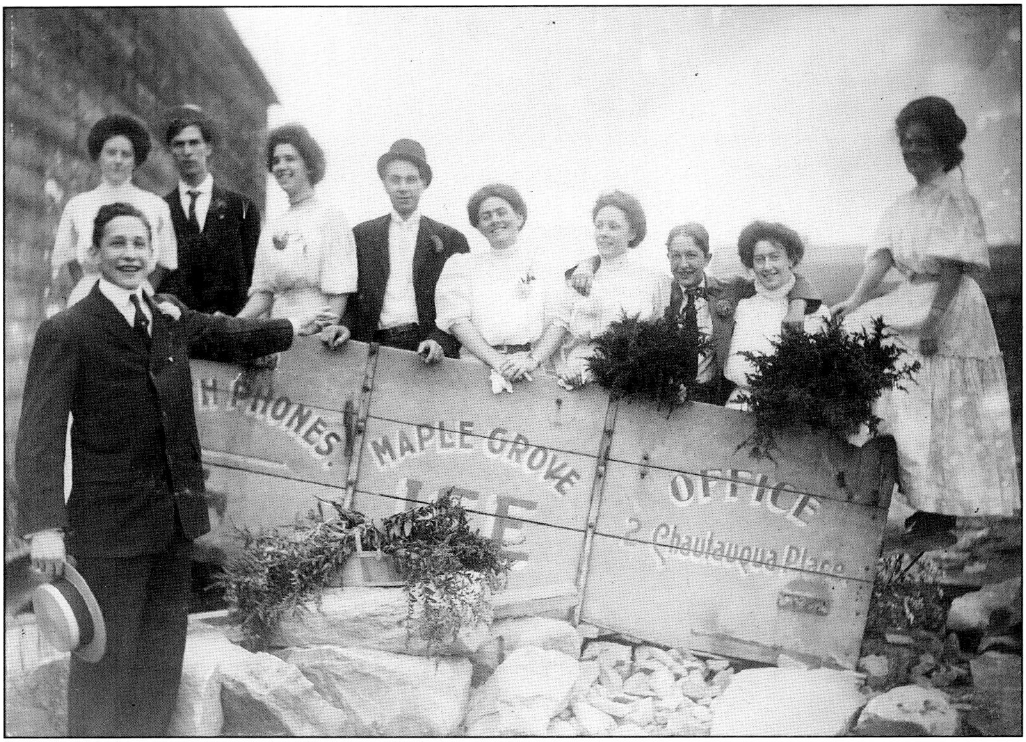

The Maple Grove Ice Company, c. 1912. Founded in 1903, the company owned four ponds for cutting ice in winter, and operated six wagons for ice delivery to the hotels, businesses, and homes throughout the area.

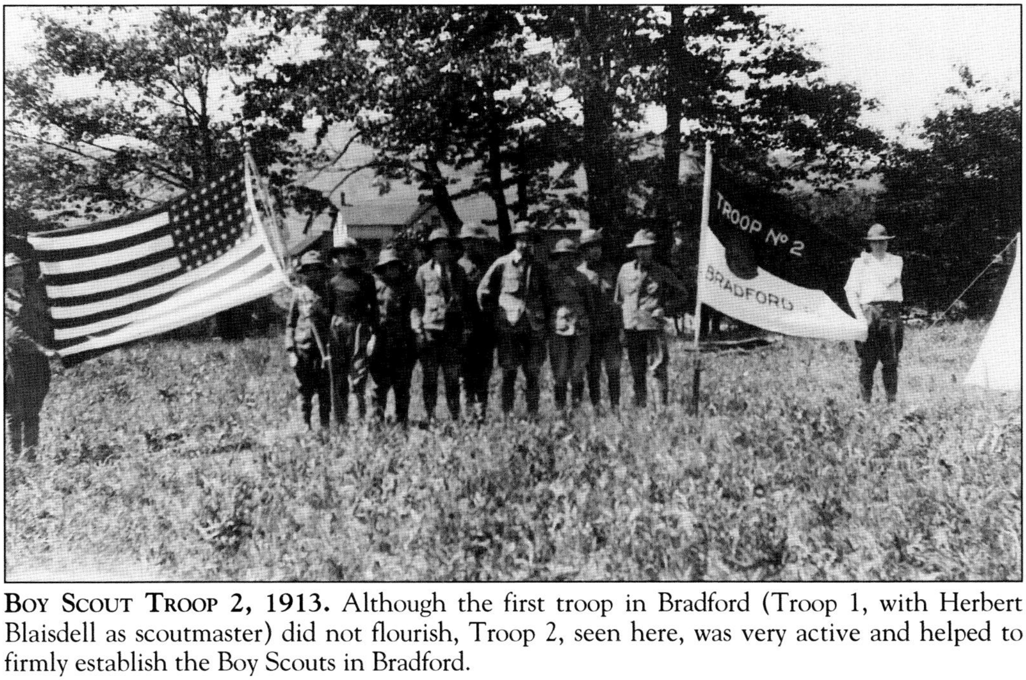

Boy Scout Troop 2, 1913. Although the first troop in Bradford (Troop 1, with Herbert Blaisdell as scoutmaster) did not flourish, Troop 2, seen here, was very active and helped to firmly establish the Boy Scouts in Bradford.

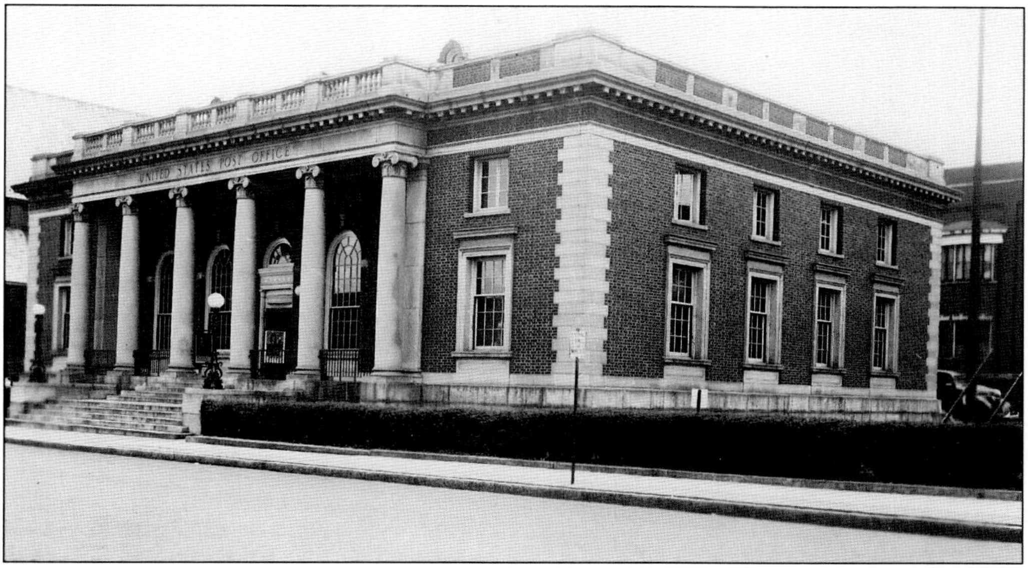

THE NEW POST OFFICE, 1913. Bradford's first federal building was dedicated on Feb. 22, 1913. The architect was E.N. Unruh of Bradford. William Hanley was the contractor. Designed to be fireproof, the roof was made of iron and concrete with copper fittings. The interior was lit with both gas and electric lights. The building has stood empty since postal facilities were moved to Boylston Street in 1982.

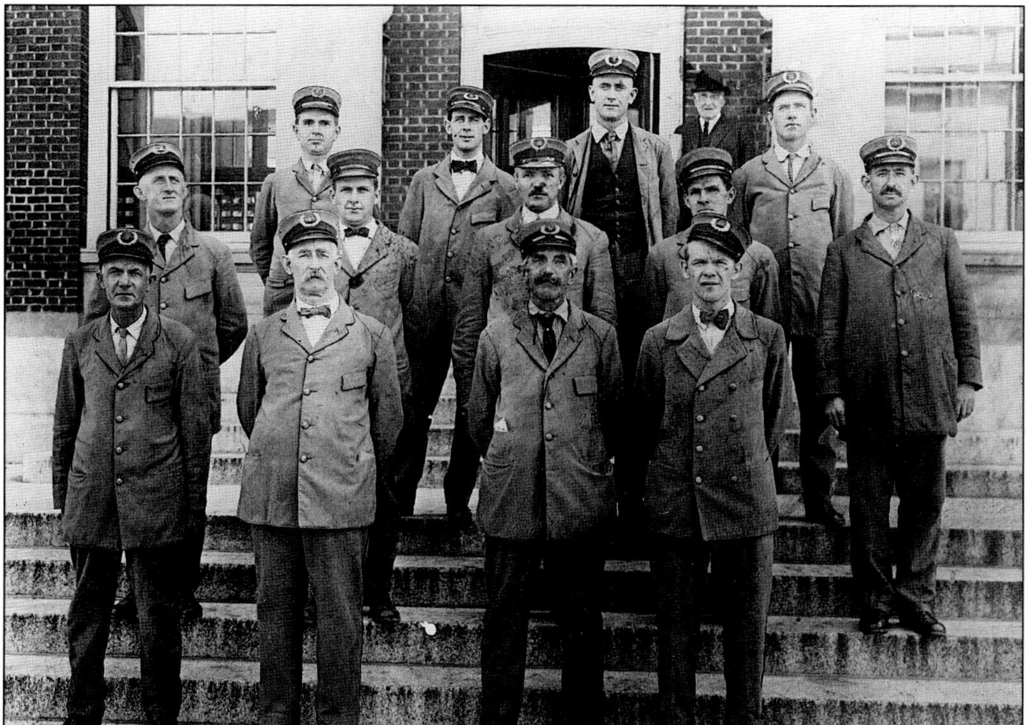

POSTAL EMPLOYEES, 1913. These postmen are a serious group as they stand on the steps of the new post office. In 1913, there were 11 city letter carriers, 10 clerks, and 1 rural carrier.

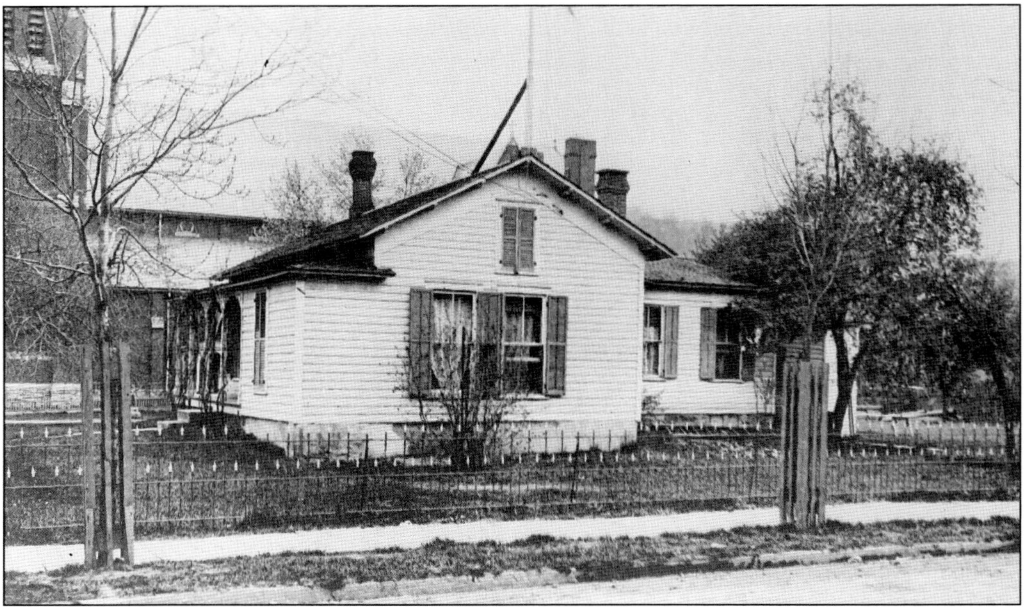

P.L. Webster's House, c. 1900. Webster arrived in Littleton as a nine-year-old boy with his stepfather, Levitt Little. He grew up with the city, saw it renamed Bradford, and became an entrepreneur, surveyor, landowner, and undertaker. He lived in this house next to St. Bernard's Church. Eventually, the federal post office would sit on this site. He died in 1915 at age 84.

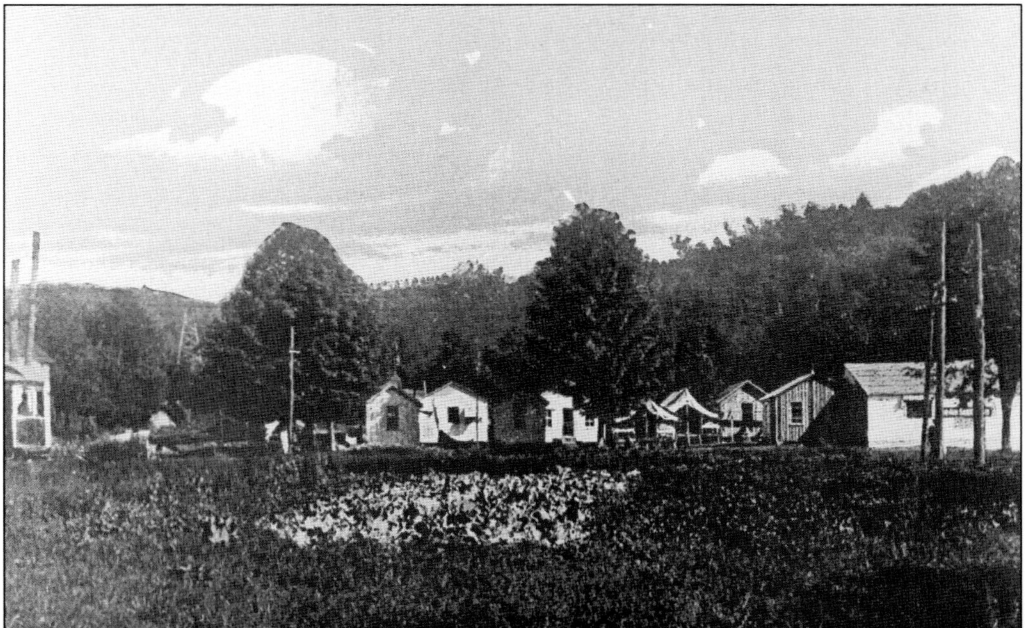

The Bon Air Tuberculosis Sanitarium, c. 1916. Founded in 1908, this tuberculosis sanitarium was located just 6 miles east of Bradford, at Bell's Camp, Pennsylvania. In 1916 there were 32 patients listed. The neighboring Cattaraugus County sanitarium, Rocky Crest, was built in the early 1920s just up the road at Rock City. With tuberculosis on the increase, such facilities were a regretful necessity.

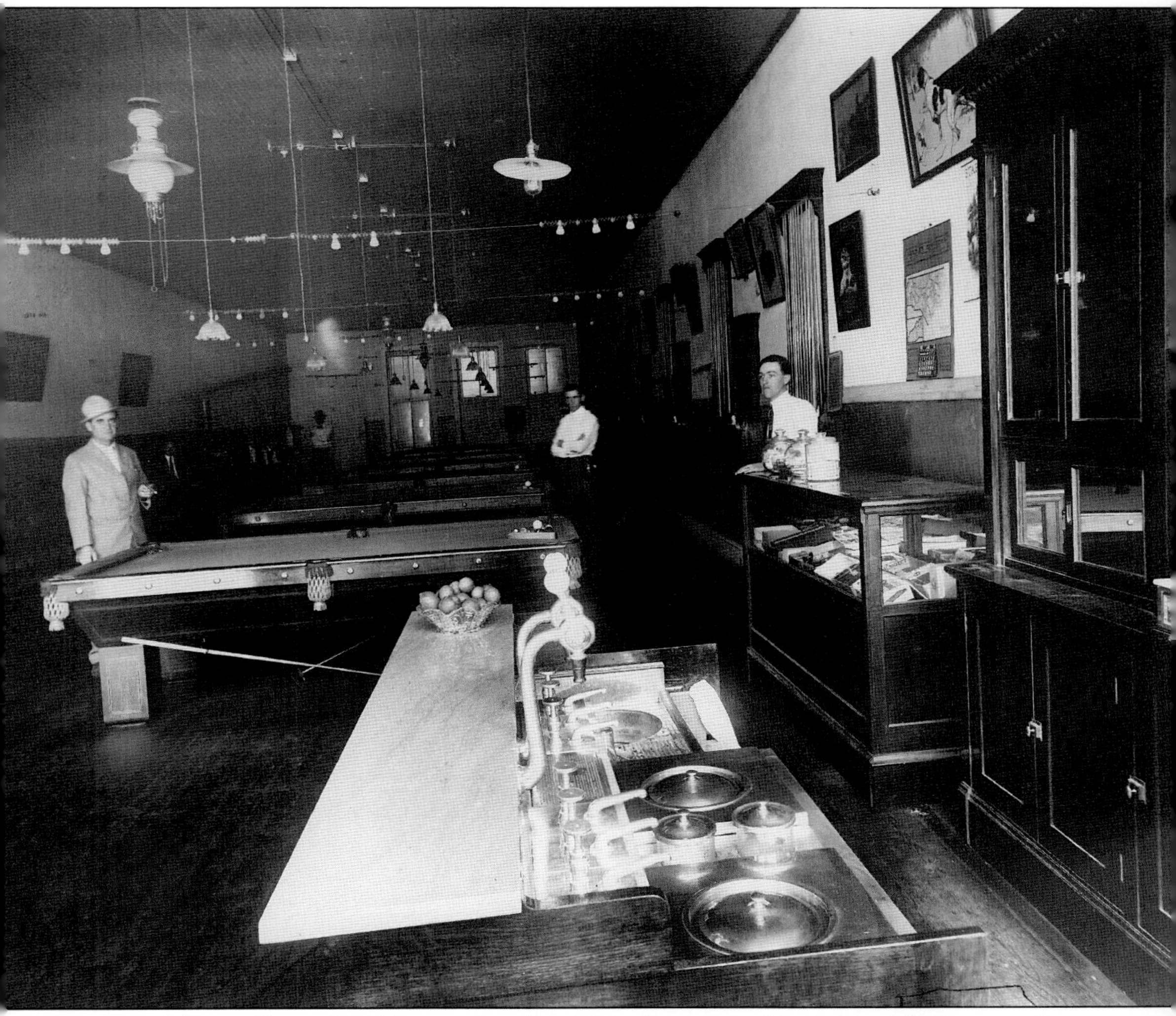

Peterson's Pool Hall, 1915. Located on East Main Street near North Kendall Avenue, the pool hall was a man's place—cigars, six pool tables, counters above the tables, and cues on the walls. No woman would come here, and kids knew better than to let their mothers see them in here, either! Trouble with a T, and that rhymes with P—and that stands for pool!

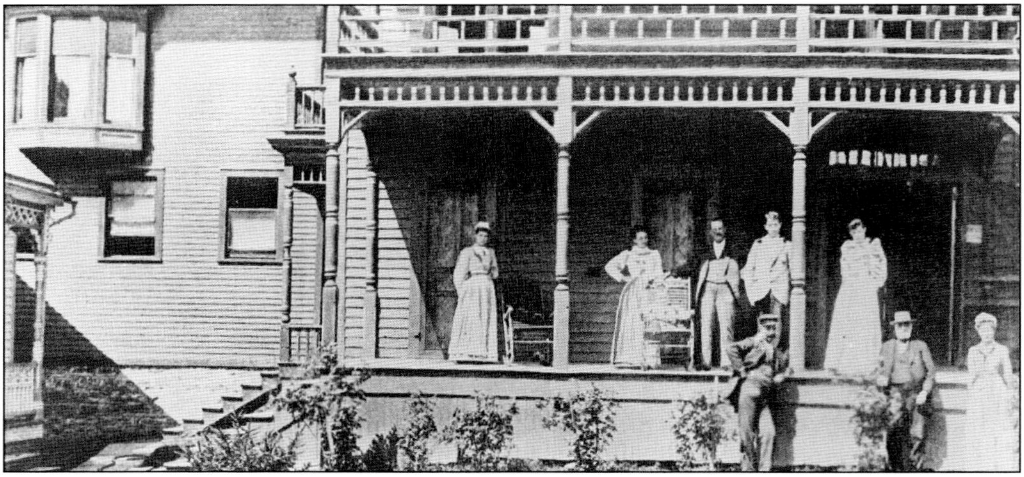

THE BRADFORD HOSPITAL, C. 1887. The original hospital, seen here, was a renovated farmhouse, containing 14 beds and a 3-member staff. Electric lights were installed in 1893. It was razed in 1917 to make way for the Hamsher House.

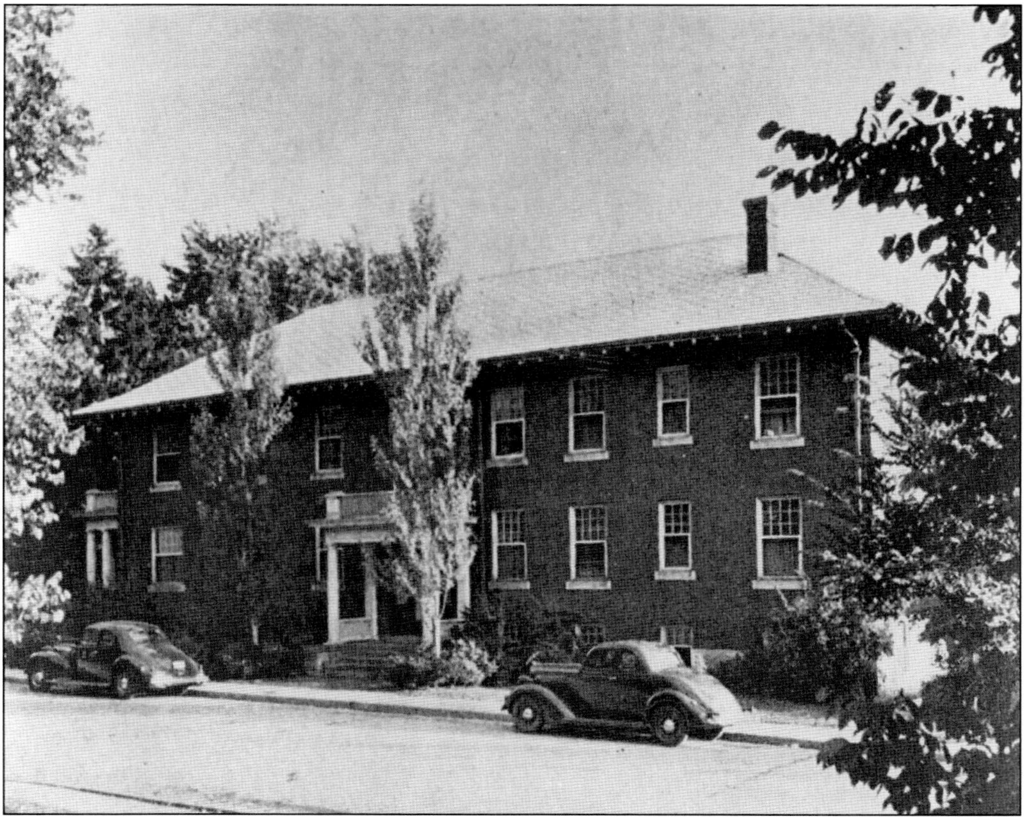

THE HAMSHER HOUSE. Donated to the Bradford Hospital School of Nursing by Sarah G. Hamsher in memory of her late husband, Lewis Hamsher, the Hamsher House on Pleasant Street was designed as a dormitory for nursing students. Built in 1917 by E.N. Unruh on the site of the original farmhouse hospital, it was expanded in 1924, eventually containing living quarters and 43 private rooms. Today it houses the Medical Arts building.

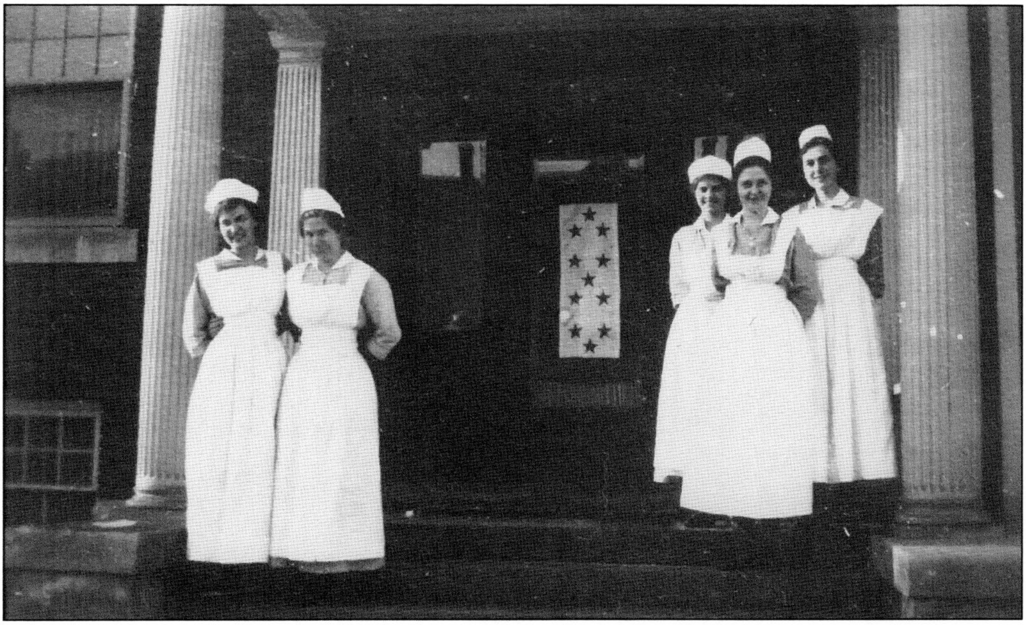

Bradford Hospital School of Nursing, 1917. Established in 1896, it strove to give each student "an understanding of the principles of the art of nursing," by providing a three-year course of study with an integrated program of experience and theory. These nurses are standing on the steps of Hamsher House.

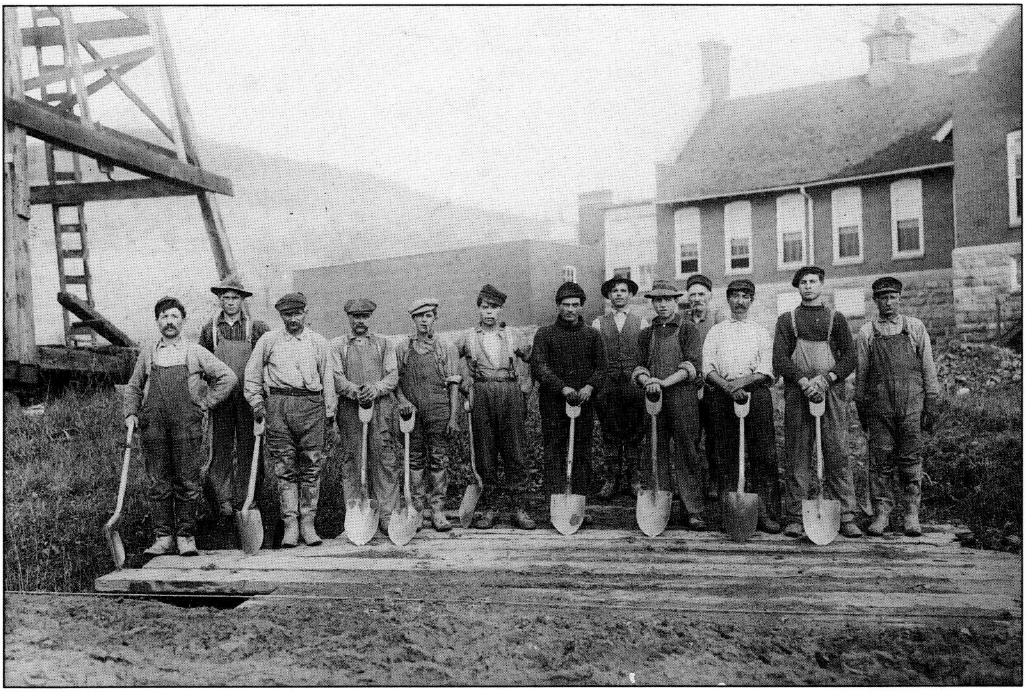

Constructing the Children's Wing, 1914. This construction crew has stopped to have their photograph taken and the pride they feel in their work is evident. The hospital was continually expanding in the 1920s as Bradford's population and medical needs grew.

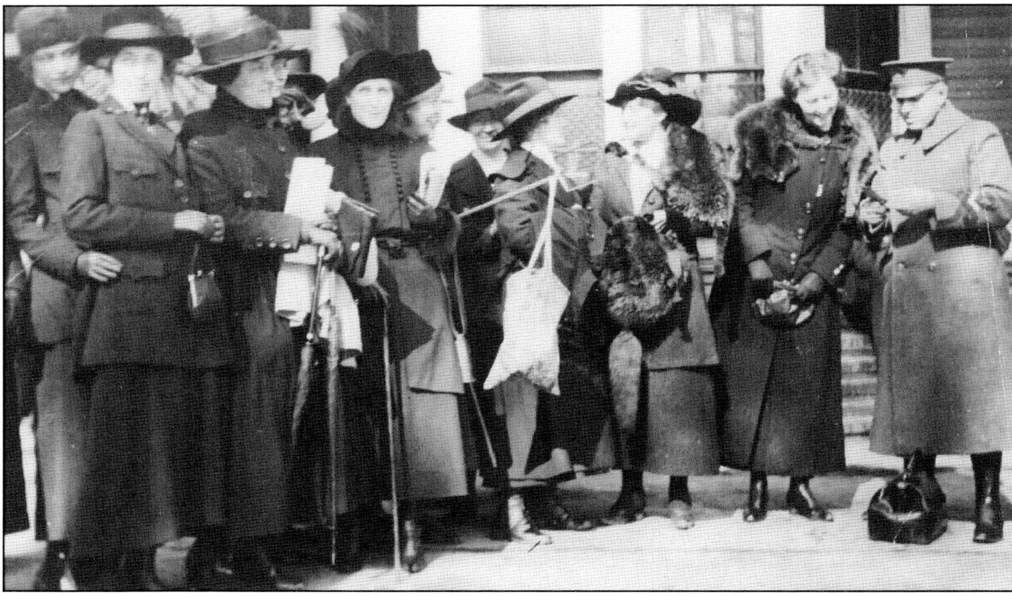

Frances Sherman, 1917. A graduate of the Bradford School of Nursing, Sherman, age 29, volunteered as a nurse in France during World War I. Ill health forced her early return from the war, and she died in 1925. The Frances Sherman Auxiliary of the VFW was named in her honor. Sherman is the second woman from the left.

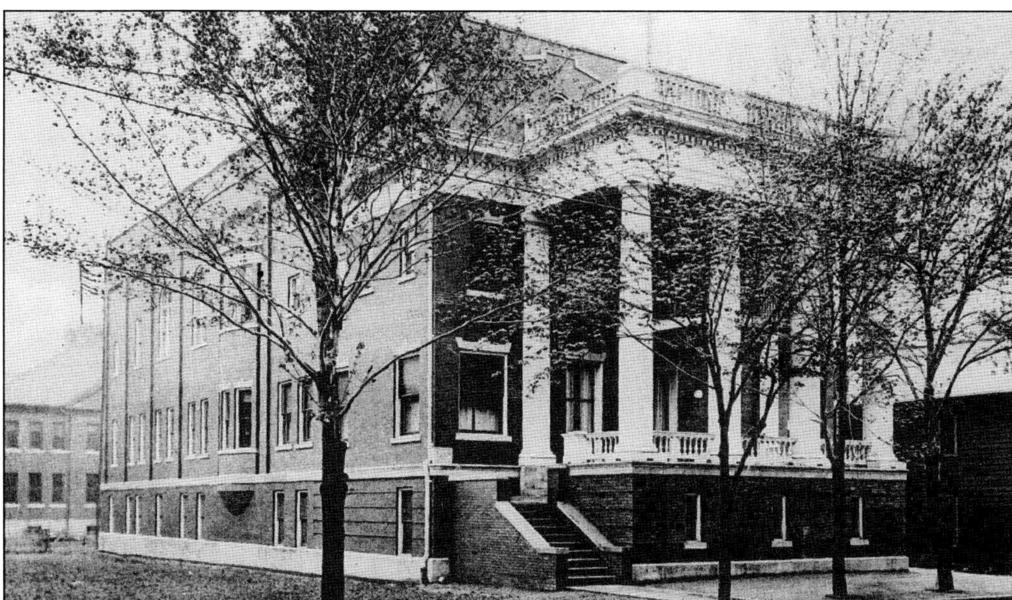

The Knights of Columbus Hall, c. 1917. Built in 1915 behind St. Bernard's Catholic Church and facing Chestnut Street, the K. of C. was a popular place for dances and events. It was razed during the 1960s as part of Bradford's redevelopment phase.

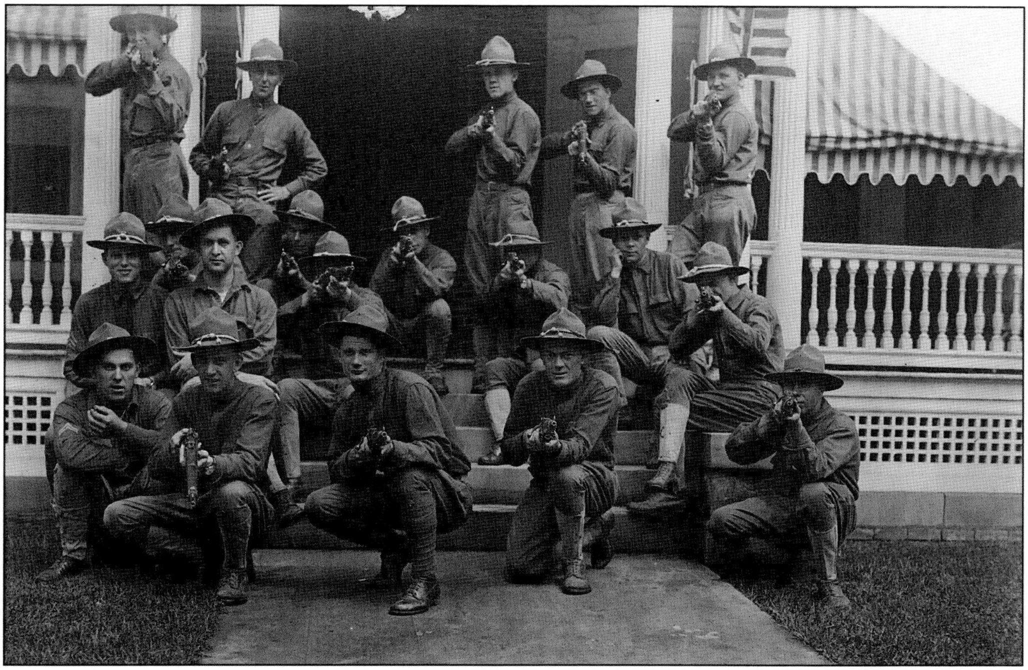

On Their Way to Mexico, June 22, 1916. In 1916, the U.S. National Guard was sent to Camp Pershing near El Paso, Texas, to guard the border and stop guerrilla raids led by Mexican revolutionist Pancho Villa. These members of Company C, seen here before their departure, jokingly point their guns at the camera. All men returned safely home to Bradford on January 10, 1917.

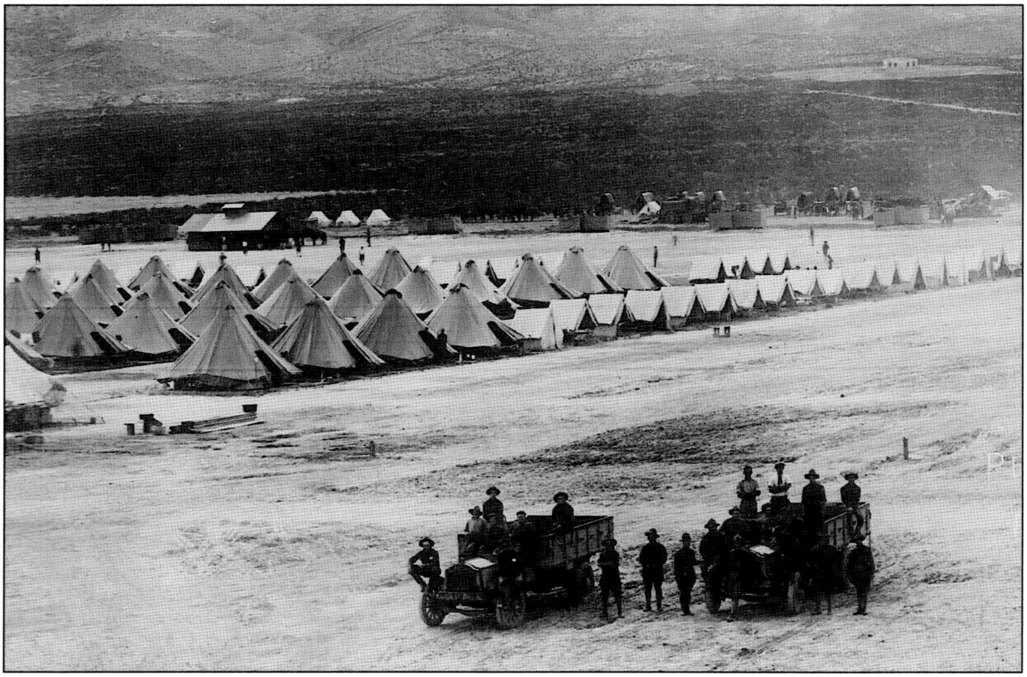

On the Texas Border, 1916. This is just a fraction of the camp of the Pennsylvania Division, 16th Regiment, stationed at El Paso during the Mexican border conflict.

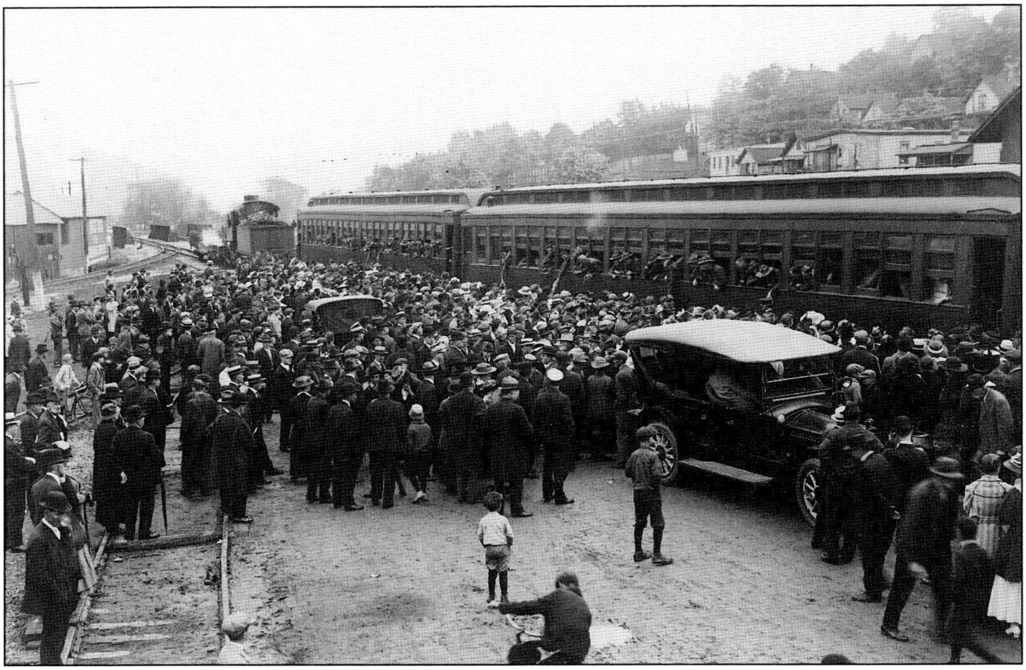

LEAVING FOR GEORGIA, SEPTEMBER 8, 1917. On April 6, 1917, the United States entered World War I and the National Guard was called upon. These men of the 16th Pennsylvania Infantry Machine Gun Company and the 16th Pennsylvania Infantry Sanitary Detachment are leaving for Camp Hancock on the 9:30 a.m. train. According to the *Bradford Era* this train "moved out from the depot through a lane of waving handkerchiefs and cheers."

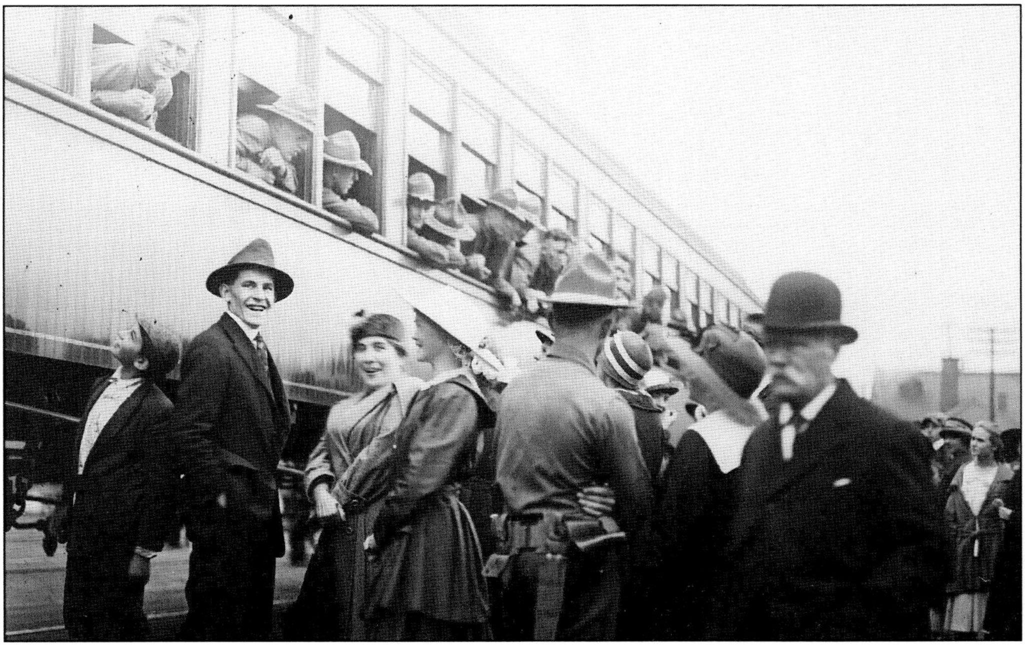

FAREWELL AT THE STATION, SEPTEMBER 8, 1917. The mood of the soldiers was very jovial as they leaned out the train windows to wave good-bye to their families. Most of these men were sent to France, where nearly one hundred of Bradford's soldiers were killed in the war.

NATE NESSELSON, 1917. Nesselson, age 24, of Pearl Street was a member of the machine gun company that left on that train. He was killed in battle at Tisme, France, on August 11, 1918. His body was returned to Bradford after the war, and is buried in the Beth Israel Cemetery on West Washington Street.

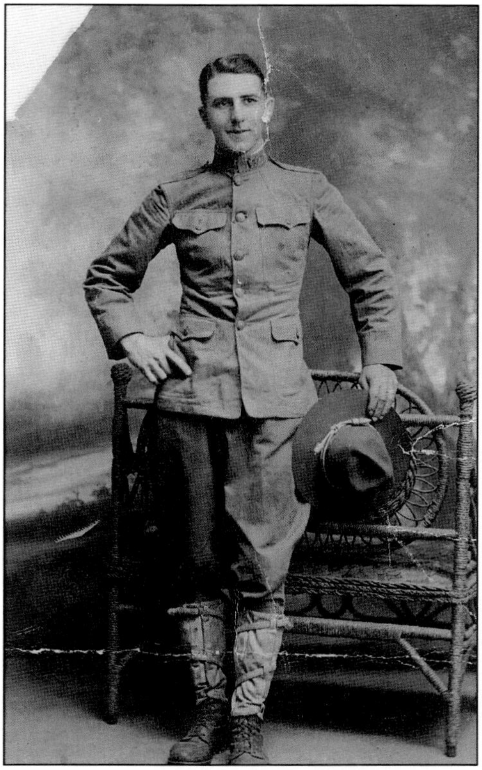

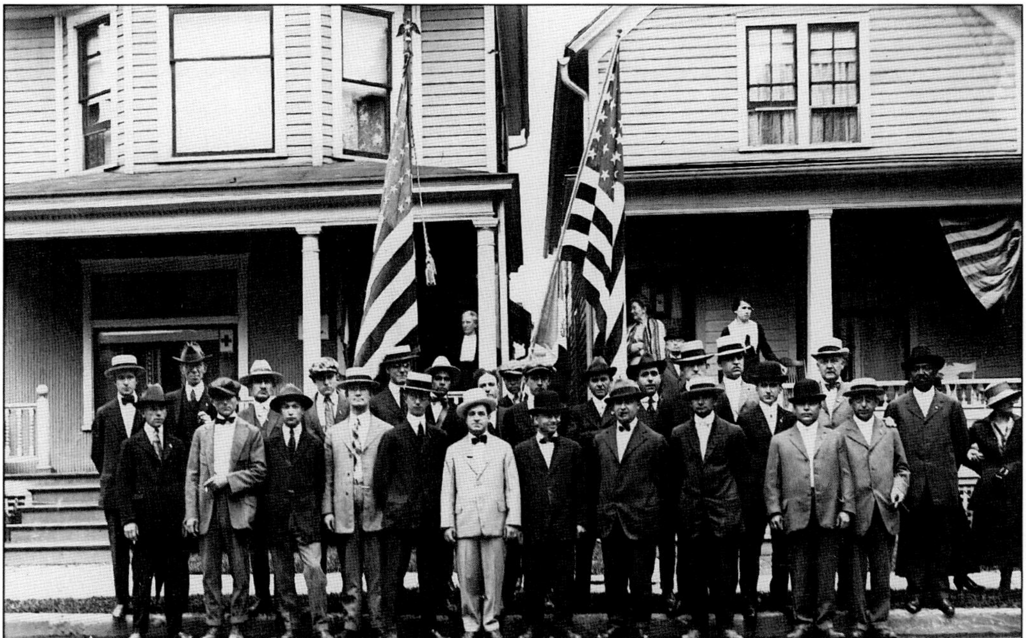

DRAFTEES LEAVING FOR CAMP LEE, MAY 29, 1918. Eventually, more men were called up as the war continued. These men will soon be leaving for Camp Lee in Virginia, and from there, overseas to fight "the Great War." This photograph was taken on Bushnell Street, near the armory. A large demonstration was held on the morning they departed.

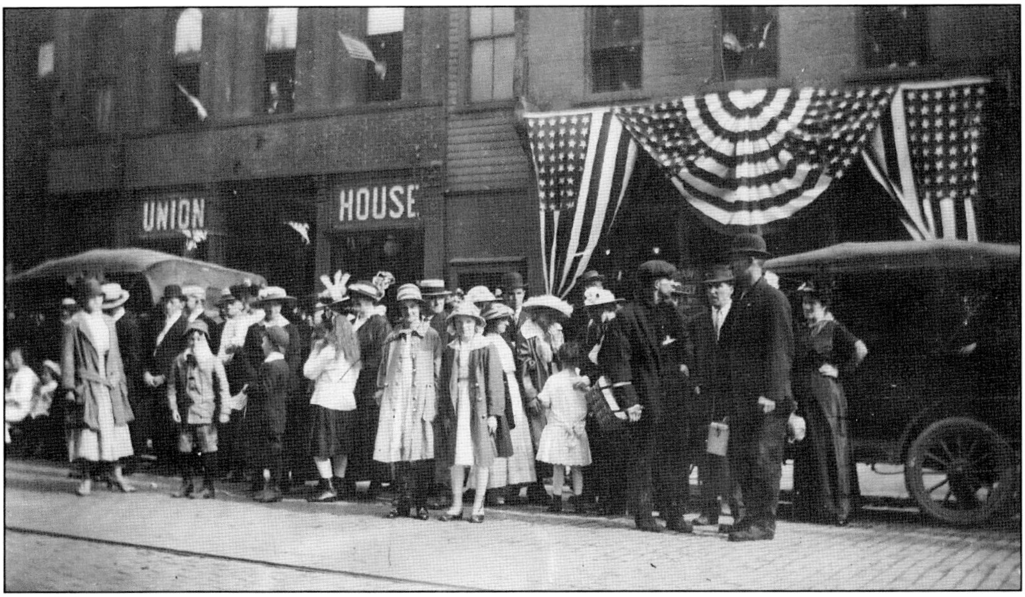

BRADFORD BIDS FAREWELL, MAY 29, 1918. It had been a year since the United States had entered the war, and Bradford was more patriotic than ever. Here, crowds line Main Street near the Union House to watch as the soldiers head towards the 9:15 a.m. train. It would be another year before most of these men returned home.

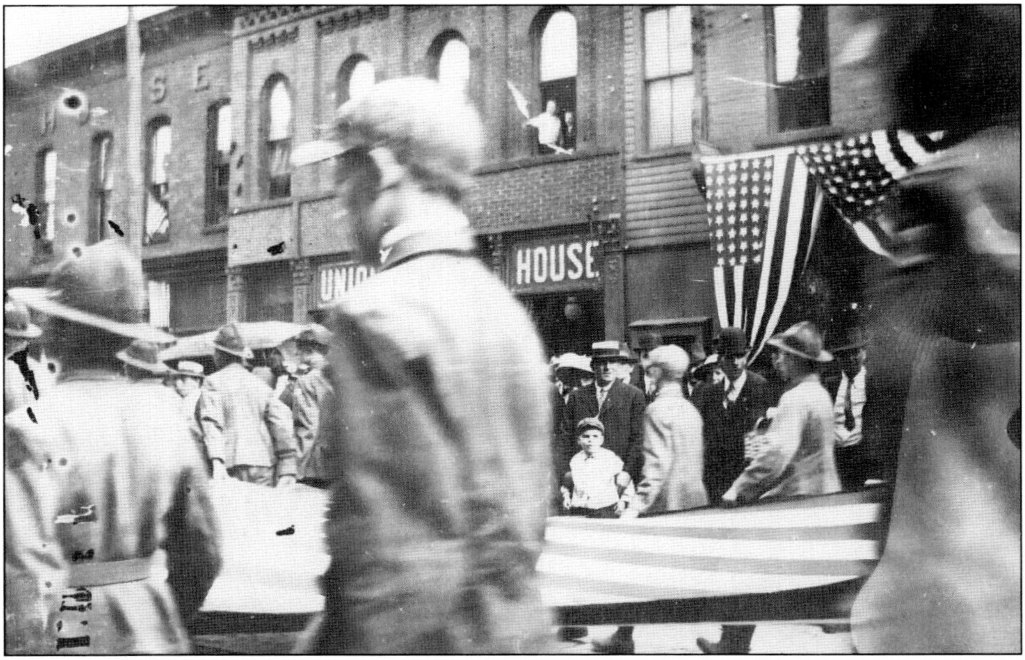

BOY SCOUTS FORM HONOR GUARD, MAY 29, 1918. The Boy Scout Troop 2 was honored to be part of the farewell parade. The boys carried a large canvas flag, which was filled with donated candy, chewing gum, cigars, tobacco, cigarettes, and over $500 in cash. "Last farewells were waved amid a din of automobile horns, locomotive and factory whistles" read an article from the *Bradford Era*.

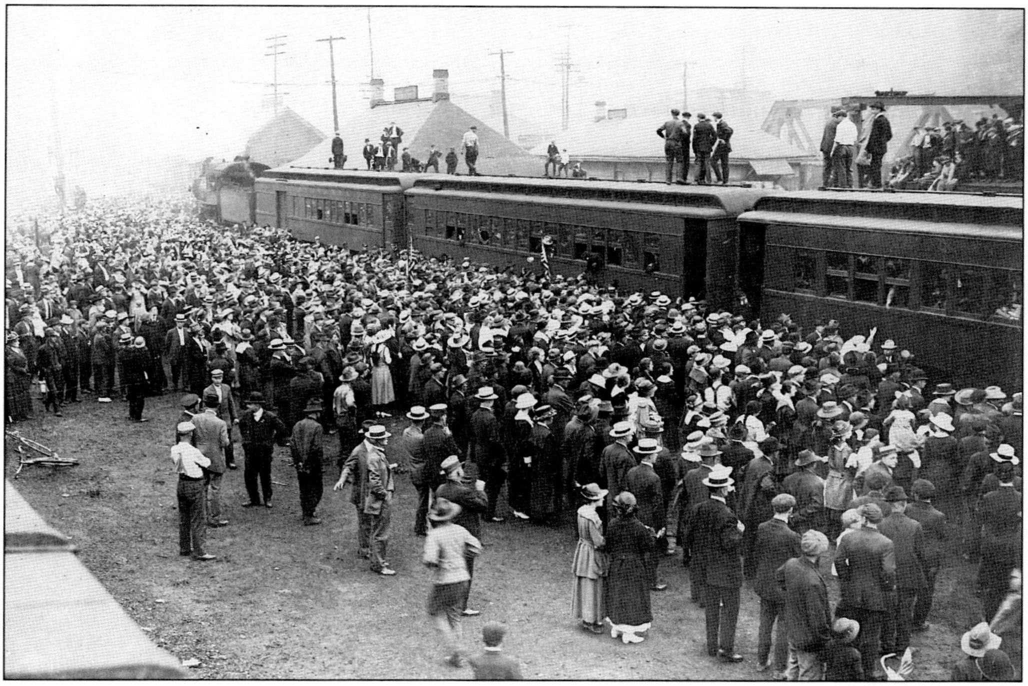

SCENE AT THE RAILROAD STATION, 1918. As before, thousands of people turned out at the foot of Main Street. This scene is nearly identical to the one on Sept. 17, 1917.

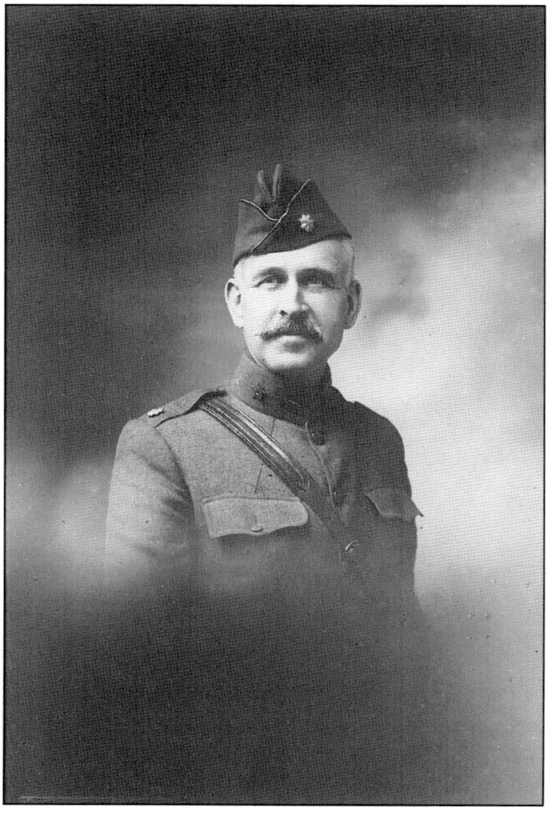

CAPTAIN FREDERICK SCHOONMAKER, 1917. Captain of the National Guard, Company C, that fought in the Mexican Insurrection of 1916, he also fought in France during World War I and achieved the rank of Lt. Colonel. A law partner of W.W. Brown, he was eventually appointed a federal judge of western Pennsylvania. He died in 1945 at the age of 72.

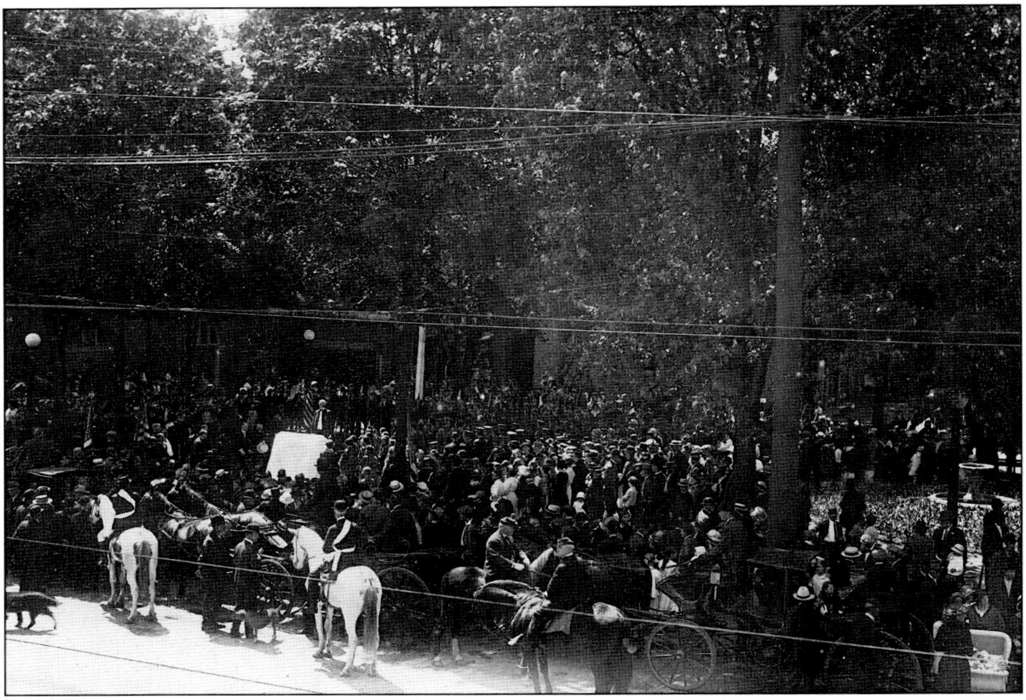

July 4, 1918. A subdued celebration took place that summer in the public square, due to the war overseas. Here, Mayor North and invited guests gave speeches that were "teeming with patriotic expressions and forecasts of allied victory" according to the *Bradford Era*.

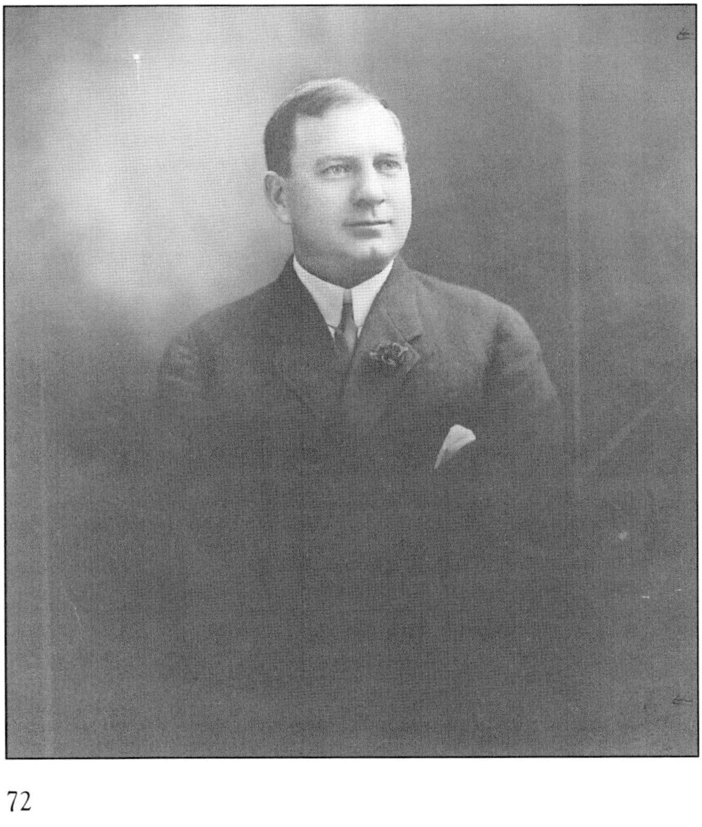

Maxwell J. Moore, 1919. A passenger conductor on the BR&P Railroad for 49 years, he also served as city controller and a member of the Pennsylvania Legislature. He died April 20, 1952, at the age of 81.

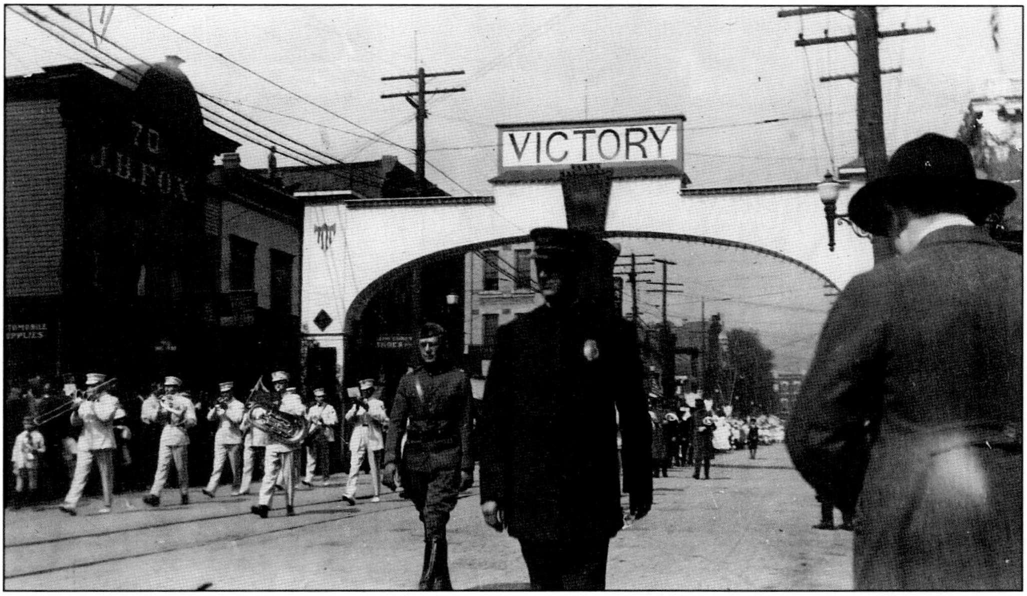

The Victory Arch, 1919. When the war ended, and Bradford's young men returned on May 7, the town rejoiced and celebrated with a huge parade down Main Street, part of which is seen here. This "Victory" arch was constructed near Webster Street and spanned Main Street.

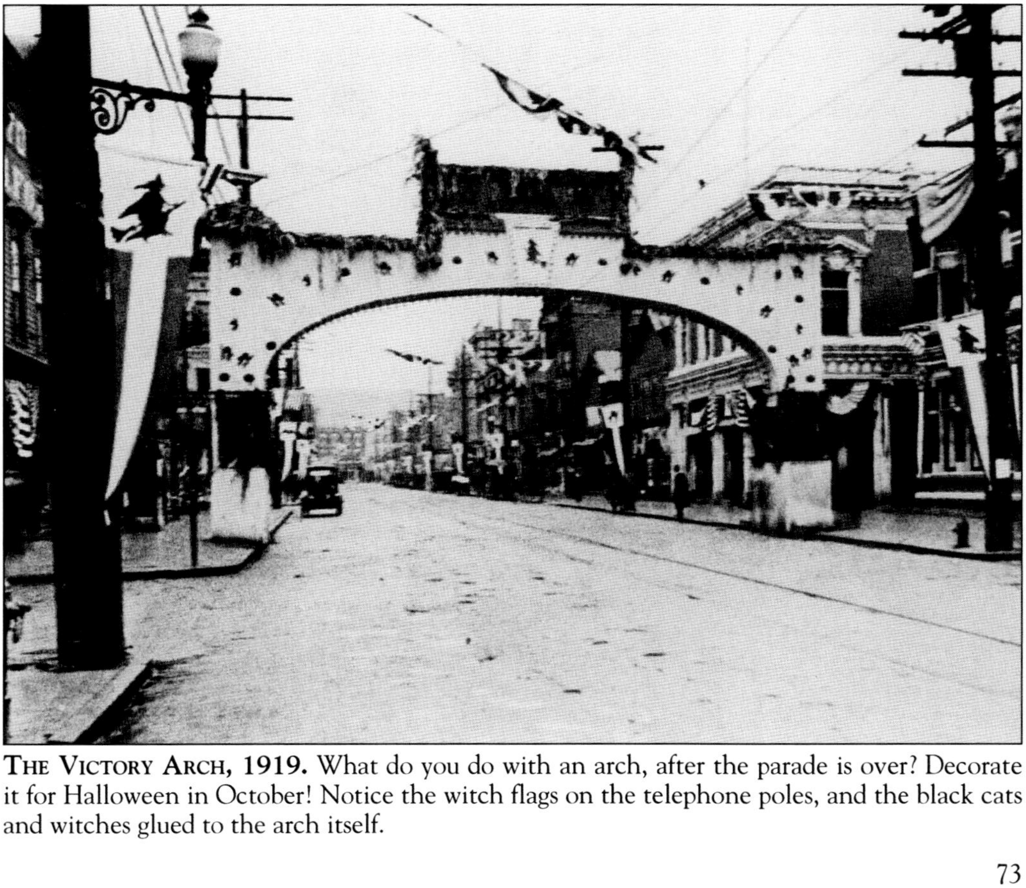

The Victory Arch, 1919. What do you do with an arch, after the parade is over? Decorate it for Halloween in October! Notice the witch flags on the telephone poles, and the black cats and witches glued to the arch itself.

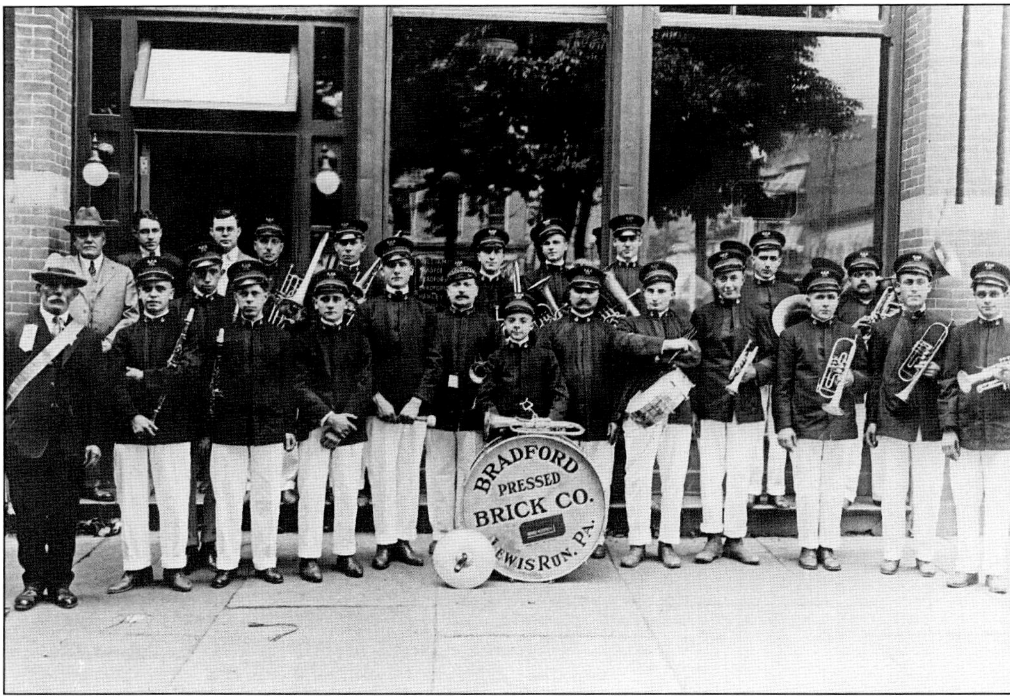

THE BRADFORD PRESSED BRICK COMPANY BAND, 1917. The band played regularly in the annual St. Rocco's Day festival in Bradford. Posed here in front of the brick company's office in Lewis Run are company owner William Hanley (at far left, second row). The band members include Barb Costanza, Santo Valenti, Tony Piscitelli, Mike Langianese, Jim Piscitelli, Lib Monago, Pete Monogo, Mike Thomas, Carl Pietranton, Carm Vigilotti, John Romano, Clem Piscitelli, Frank Piertranton, Pete Tompetti, Ray Haven, Don Monago, Mr. Zanelli, Lib Costanzo, Ben Iaderosa, and Val Veroche.

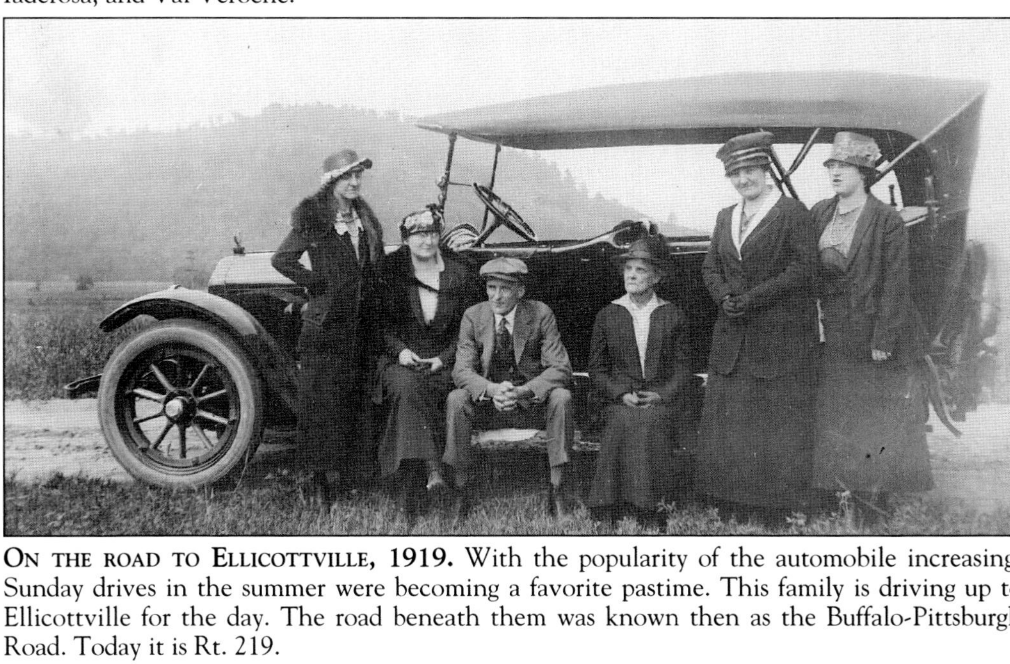

ON THE ROAD TO ELLICOTTVILLE, 1919. With the popularity of the automobile increasing, Sunday drives in the summer were becoming a favorite pastime. This family is driving up to Ellicottville for the day. The road beneath them was known then as the Buffalo-Pittsburgh Road. Today it is Rt. 219.

Five

Let it Roar! Bradford in the 1920s

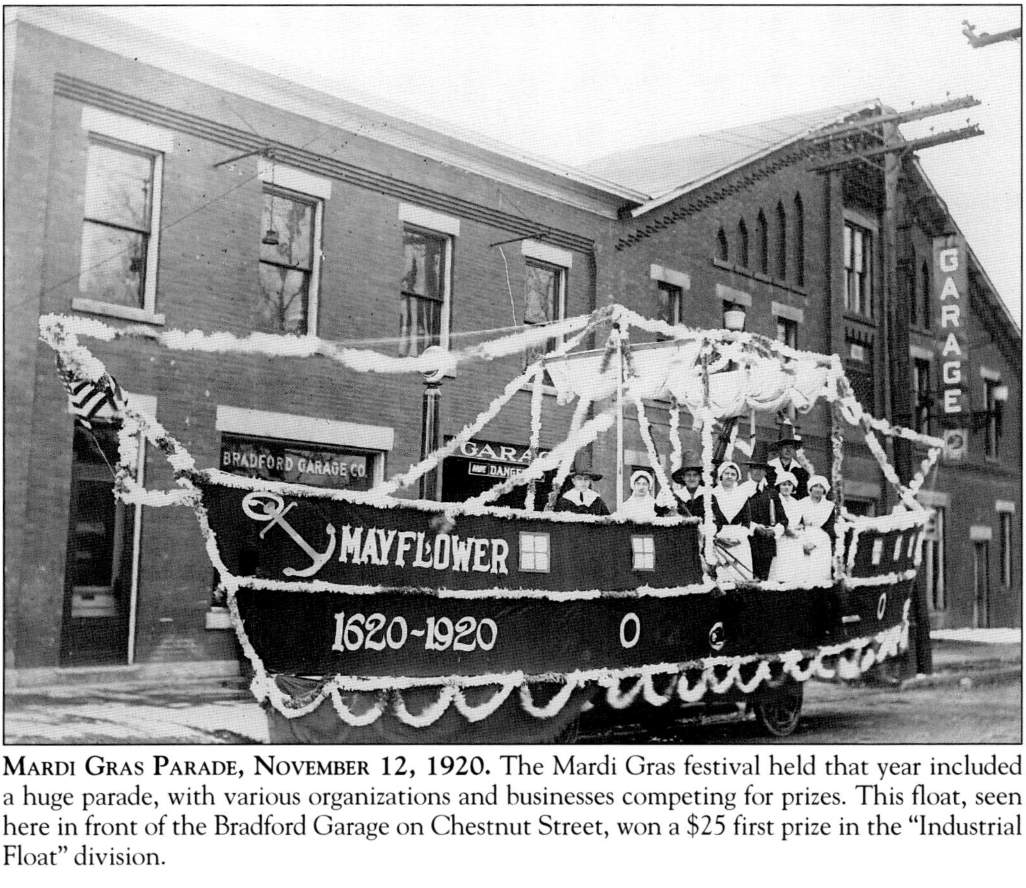

MARDI GRAS PARADE, NOVEMBER 12, 1920. The Mardi Gras festival held that year included a huge parade, with various organizations and businesses competing for prizes. This float, seen here in front of the Bradford Garage on Chestnut Street, won a $25 first prize in the "Industrial Float" division.

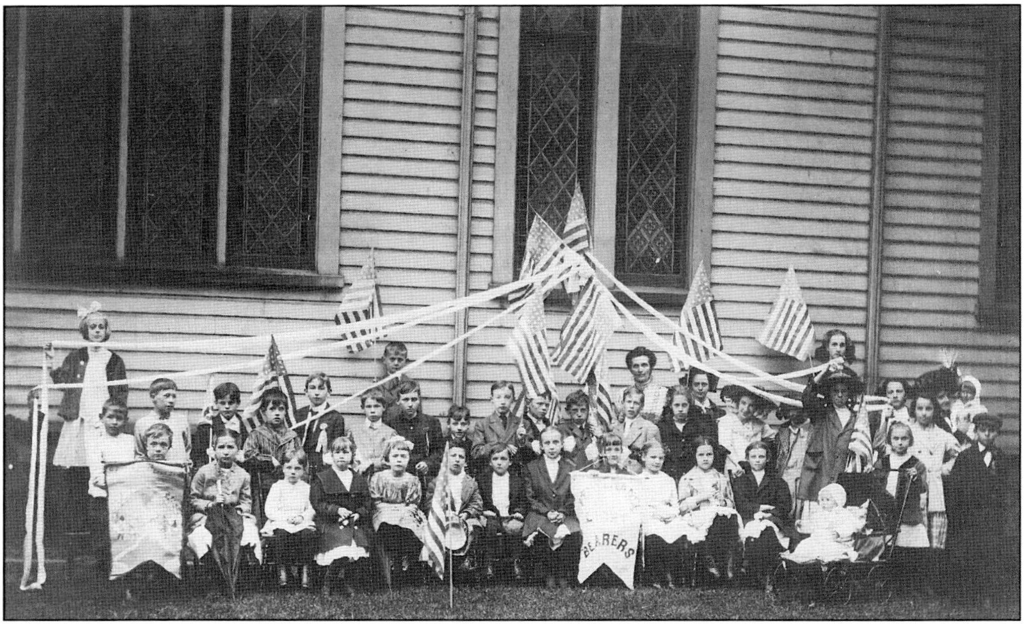

The Temperance Light Bearers, 1920. With American flags flying, and a banner reading "And a Little Child Shall Lead Them," these children of the First Methodist Church on Chambers Street are doing their part to support Prohibition. Prohibition remained in effect from 1920 until 1931. This church was replaced by the present stone building in 1927.

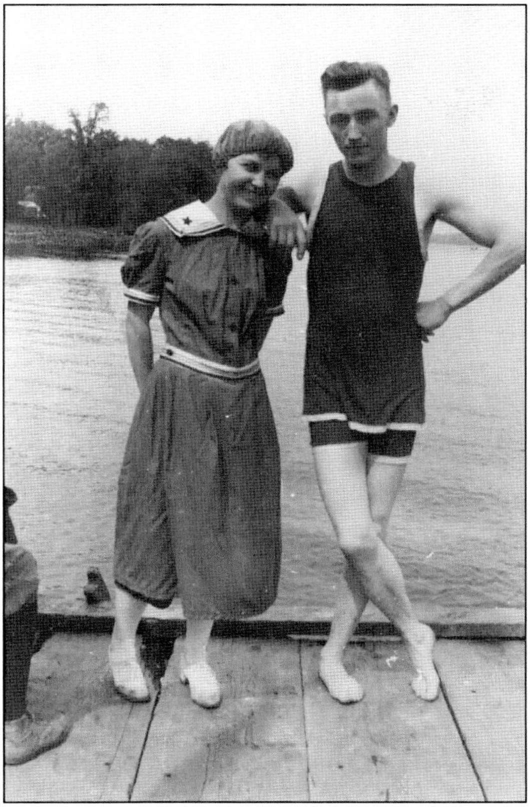

Bathing Beauties, 1920. This couple is wearing the latest in bathing suit fashions of the 1920s. Note her "bathing shoes," cap, and demur skirt. He is dressed in the typical two piece man's suit. Both swimming suits were probably made of wool.

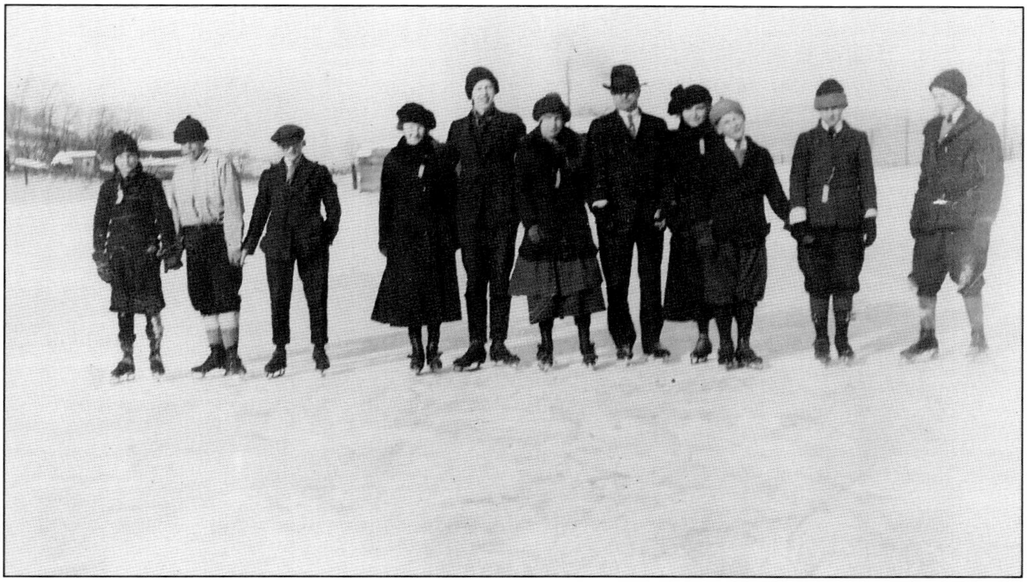

Skating at Graham's Pond, 1920s. Located behind the former Graham greenhouse on Seaward Avenue, the skating pond was a favorite spot for winter entertainment, and hundreds of people could be seen skating each weekend. Here, the Tierney family is out for a "Sunday skate."

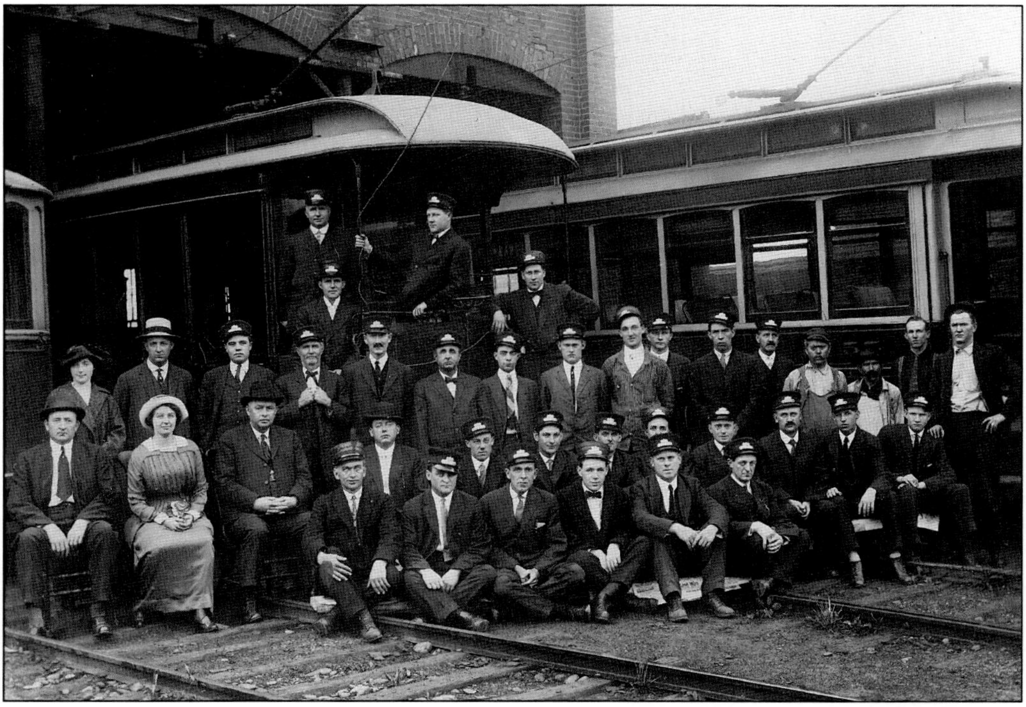

The Trolley Barn, 1920. Although a romantic ideal, electric trolley service in Bradford only existed for about 30 years (there were horse-drawn trolleys before 1896). This trolley barn was located at 361 Congress Street (now the site of the Zippo Museum). Shown in this photograph are the motormen, conductors, mechanics, and office staff. Trolleys were discontinued in October 1927, and Dodaro's bus service was instituted.

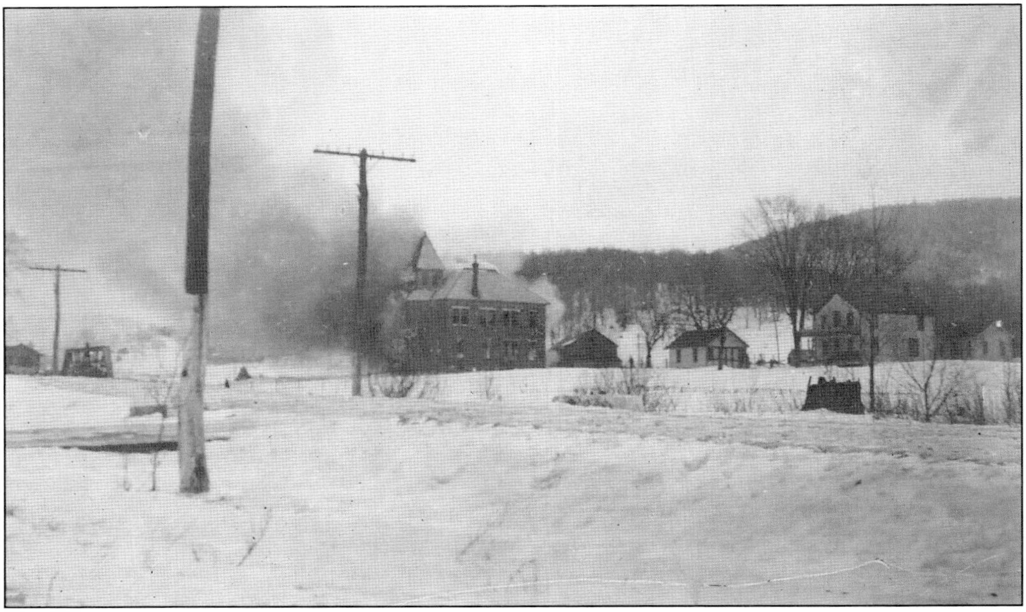

THE DERRICK CITY SCHOOL FIRE, MARCH 6, 1920. Caused by a gas leak, the fire burned quickly, owing to high winds and a lack of fire fighters. Chief Henderson of Bradford refused to send the city's fire department to the aid of the school, claiming that a lack of water supply in Derrick City and the rapid spread of the fire could not justify sending his men and fire trucks. With no effort to save it, the school burned to the ground.

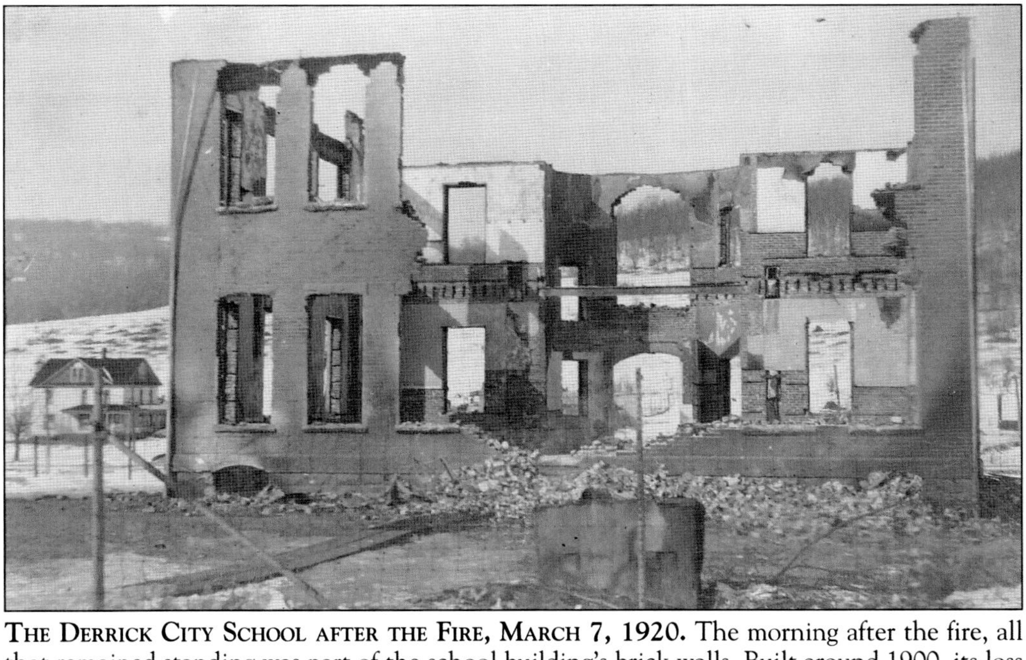

THE DERRICK CITY SCHOOL AFTER THE FIRE, MARCH 7, 1920. The morning after the fire, all that remained standing was part of the school building's brick walls. Built around 1900, its loss was devastating to the people of Derrick City. Fortunately, the fire occurred on a Saturday, or a much greater tragedy would have resulted. In 1922, the current Derrick City School was built in its place.

CHIEF CHARLES D. HENDERSON, FIRE CHIEF. The son of Scottish immigrants, he was appointed fire chief here in 1908; under his tenure the central fire station was built, the first motorized truck was bought in 1911, and all horse-drawn fire apparatus was eliminated in 1919. He died of a heart attack on January 2, 1928, at the age of 66.

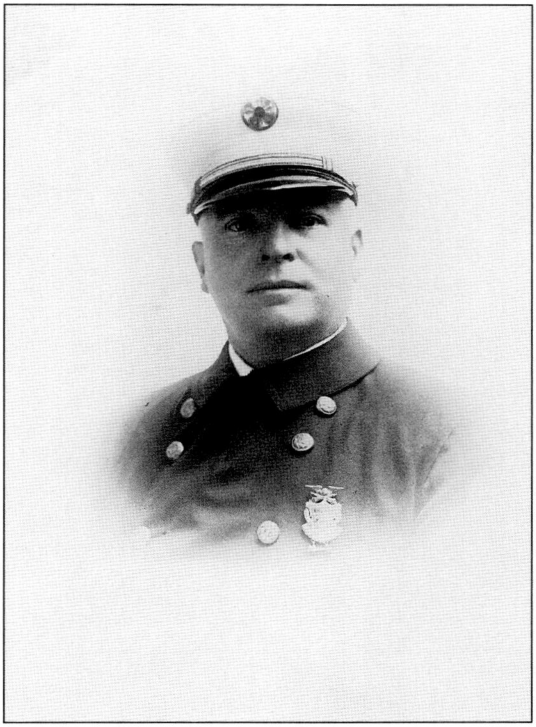

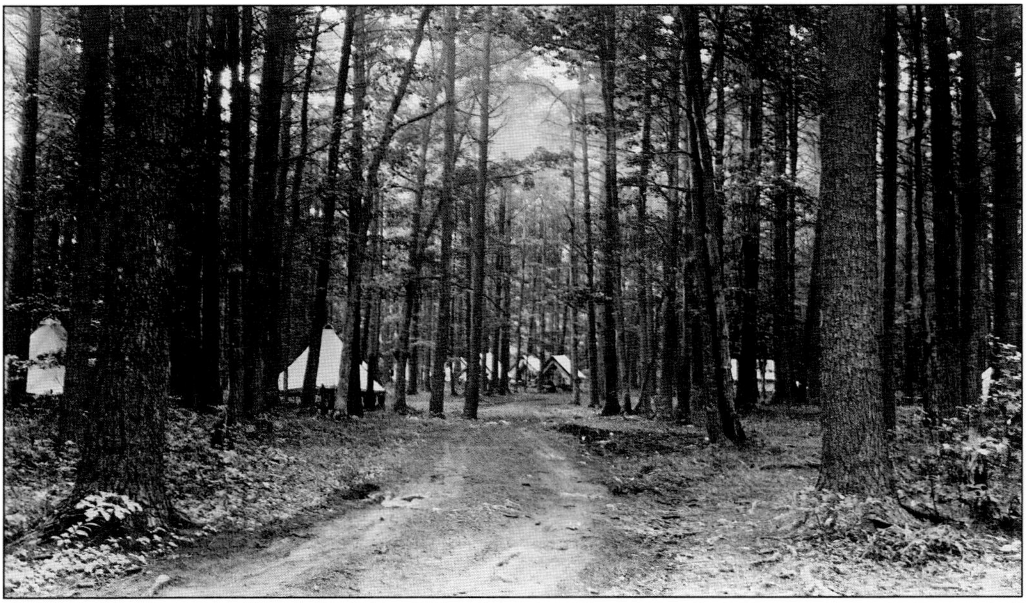

ALLEGHENY STATE PARK, 1925. The park was created in May 1921 in response to an increasing interest in nature and the outdoors. Two sizes of tents, each with cots and mattresses, could be rented quite cheaply. In 1927 cabins were built, renting at $12 per week. Blankets and extra cots were also available. ASP is currently the largest state park in New York State.

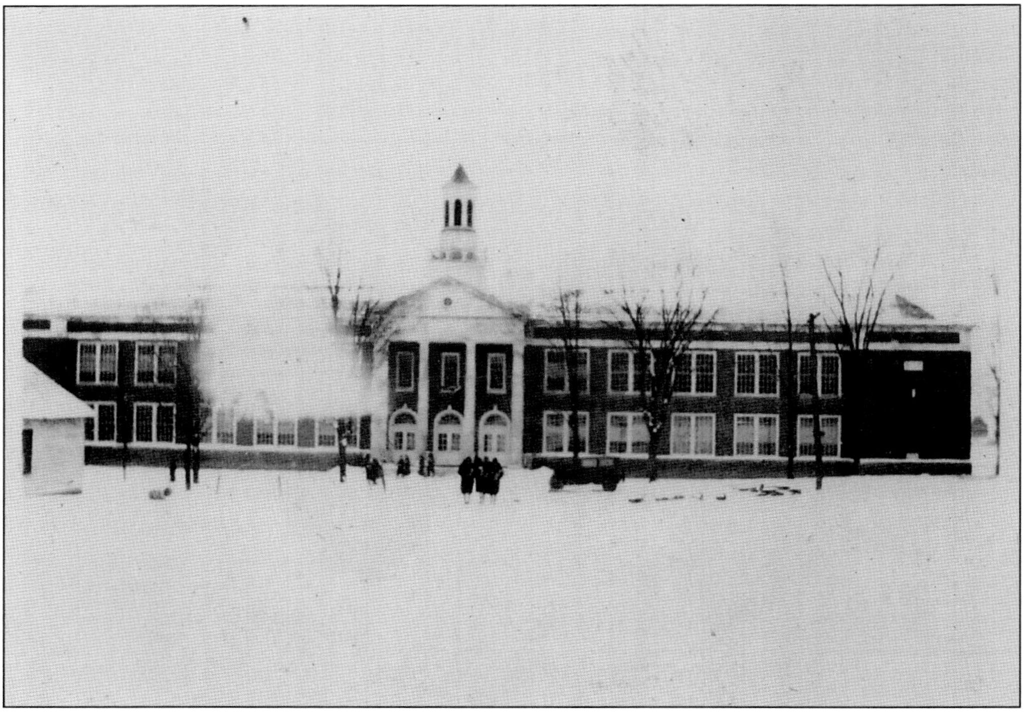

The New Bradford High School, 1926. By the early 1920s, increasing enrollment and a deteriorating high school at the head of Mechanic Street required the construction of a more modern and spacious building. After much debate, the site on Bennett Brook Road was chosen (known later as Interstate Parkway). The new $500,000 high school opened the day after Labor Day 1925 with over 570 students enrolled.

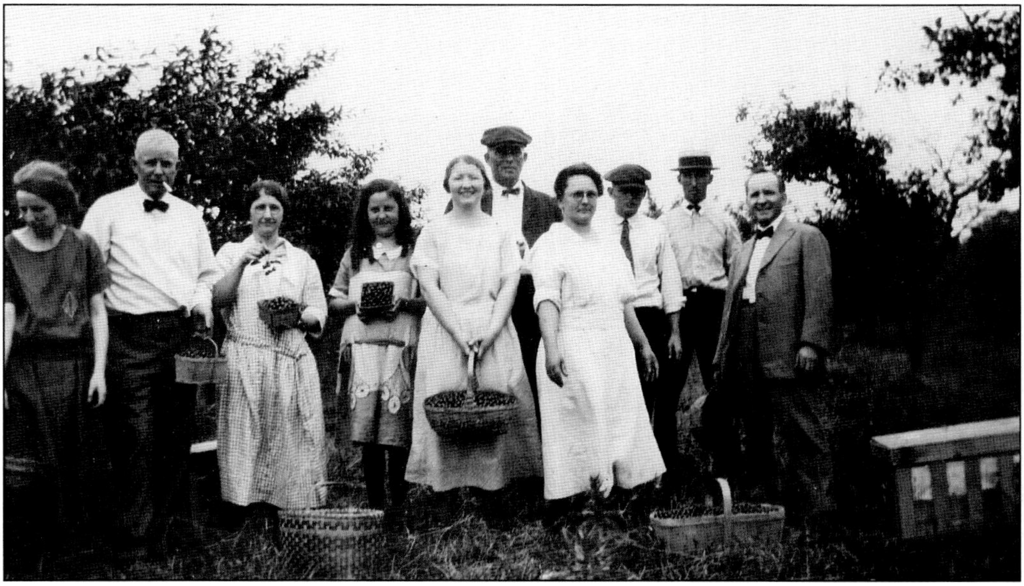

Cherry Picking, c. 1925. These family members are proudly displaying the baskets of cherries that they have picked.

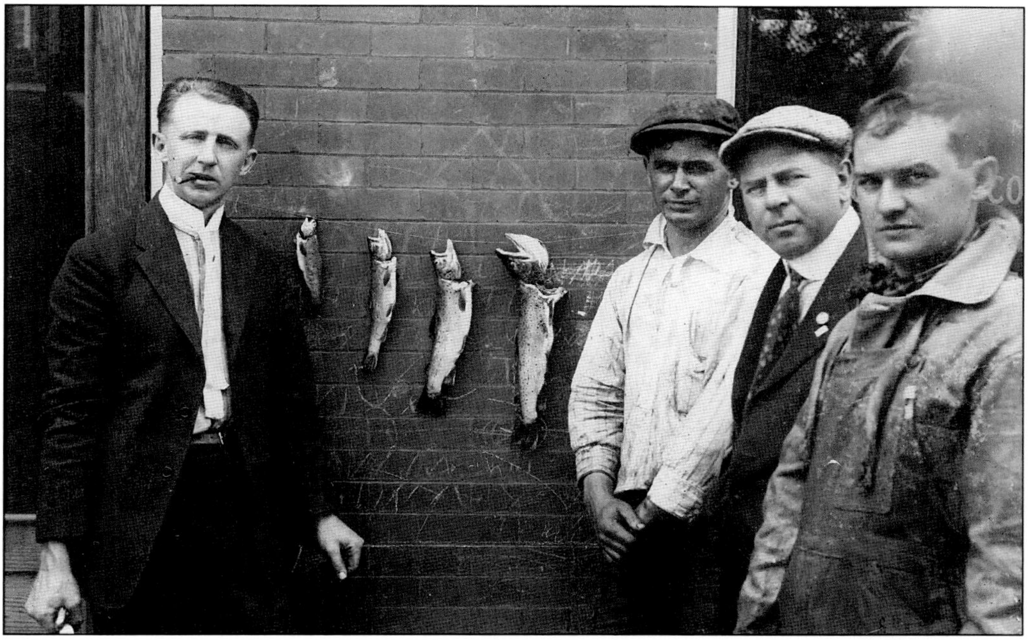

ADMIRING THEIR CATCH, 1920s. Each spring, the Emery Hardware Store had a "fishing contest" to see who caught the biggest trout on the first day of fishing season. These men seem quite proud of their catch.

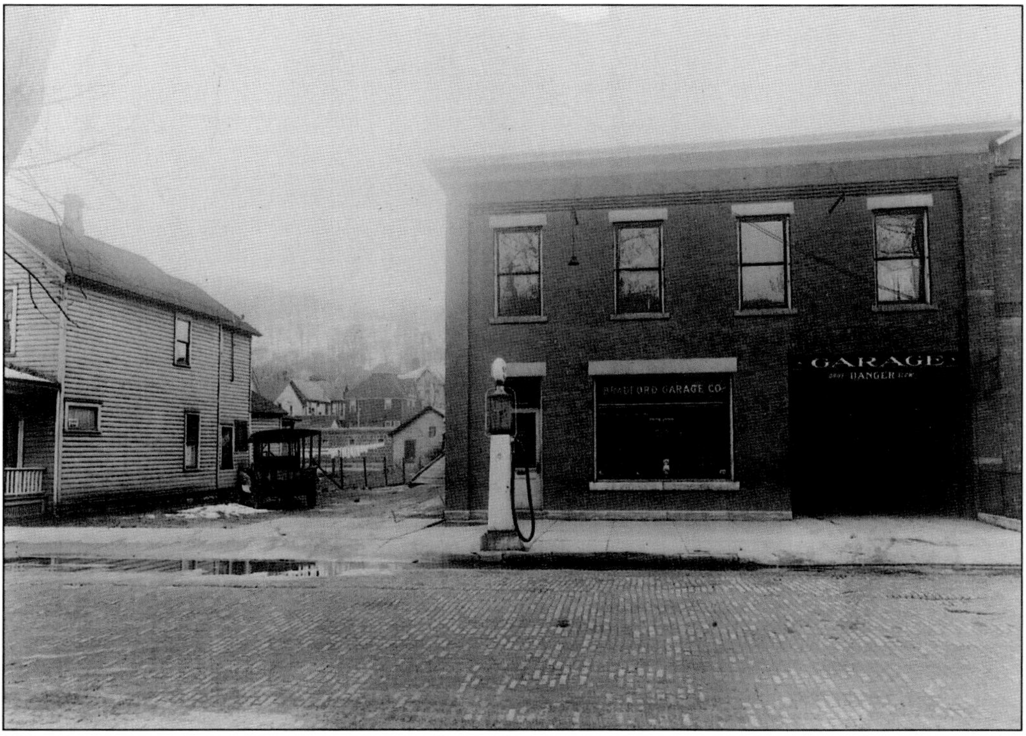

THE BRADFORD GARAGE, 1928. Located on Chestnut Street, it served as a gasoline station for automobiles in the 1920s. The building is still standing, and is known today as the Bradford Printing Co.

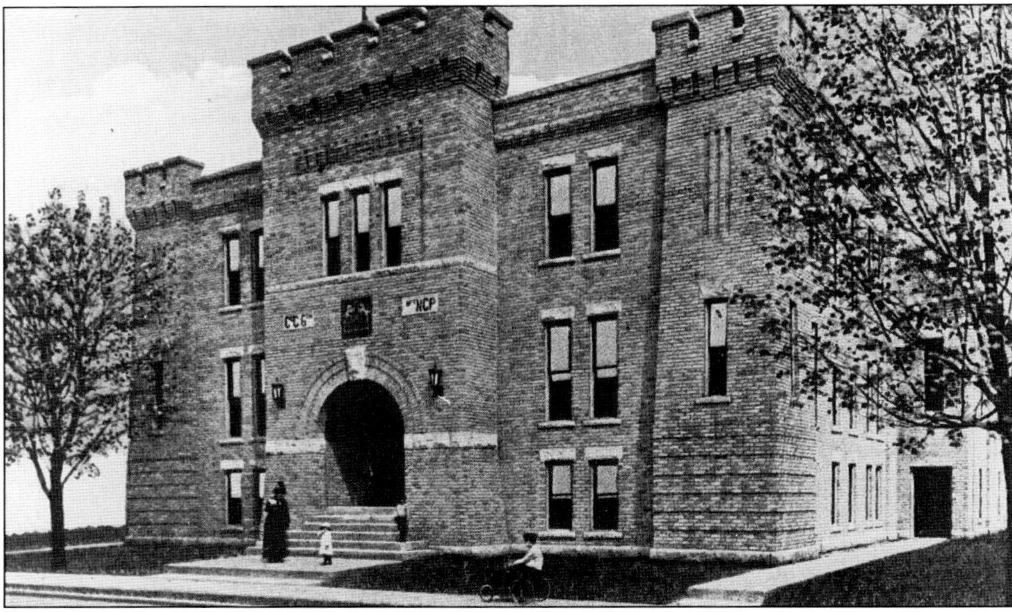

THE ARMORY, 1927. Home to Bradford's National Guard, Company C, this building was officially opened on November 26, 1912. Architecturally unique because of its "T" shape design—there are only 37 armories in the United States with this design—the armory was placed on the National Register of Historic Places in September, 1992.

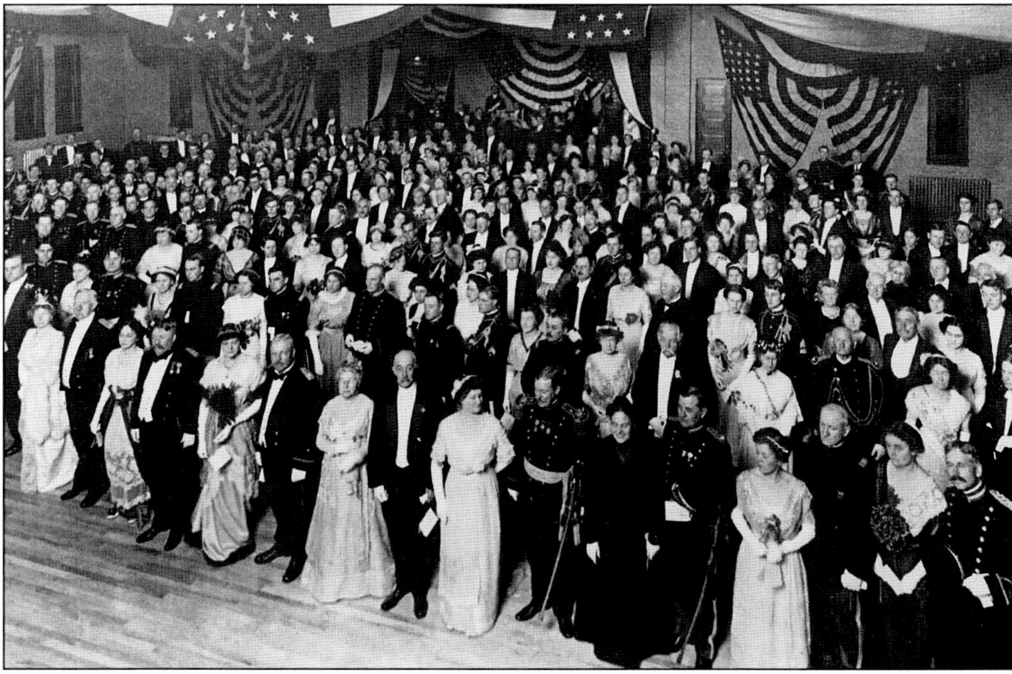

THE DEDICATION BALL AT THE ARMORY, NOVEMBER 1926. It was a gala affair. Music was played by Jamison's Orchestra, and dancing went on to midnight. John K. Tener, governor of Pennsylvania, members of the state armory board, and selected military officers led the grand march into the armory. Built by Tuna Manufacturing, it still serves as the home the Pennsylvania's National Guard.

THE FIRST BAPTIST CHURCH, c. 1923. Erected in the winter of 1880, and dedicated January 18, 1881, this church stood on the corner of Corydon and Congress Streets until its demolition in 1941, when the current Baptist church on Congress Street was built.

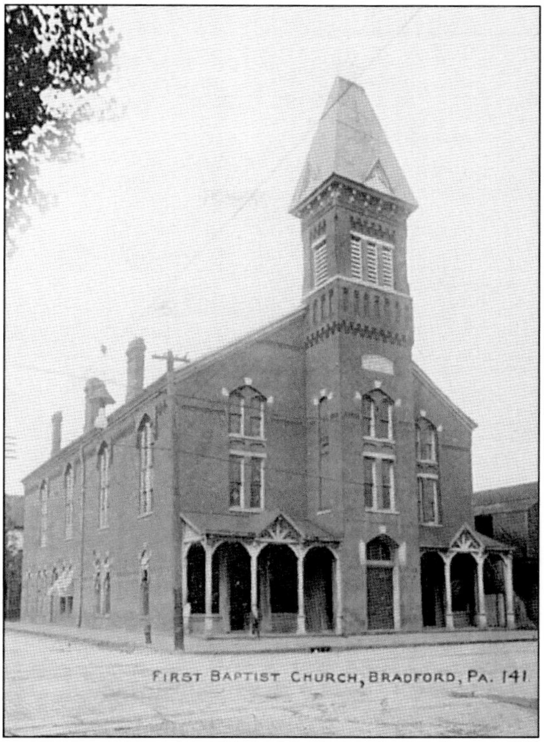

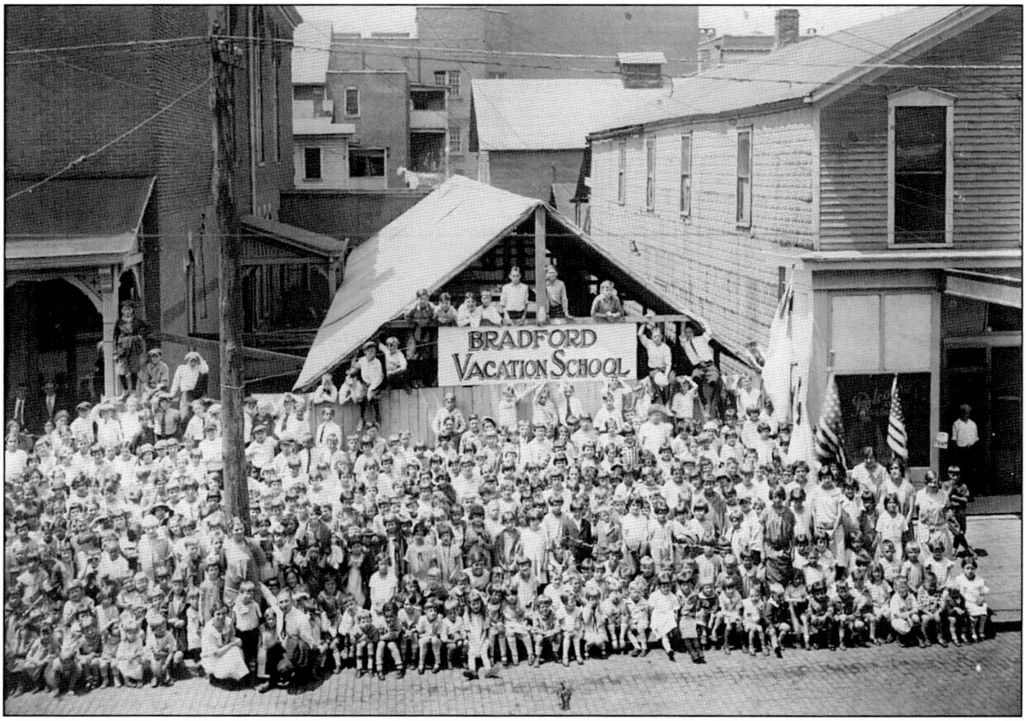

THE FIRST BAPTIST SUNDAY SCHOOL, JULY, 1923. This well-attended Sunday school was held under a large tent in a vacant lot next to the First Baptist Church. Many children in the 1920s were sent to such church-sponsored summer classes.

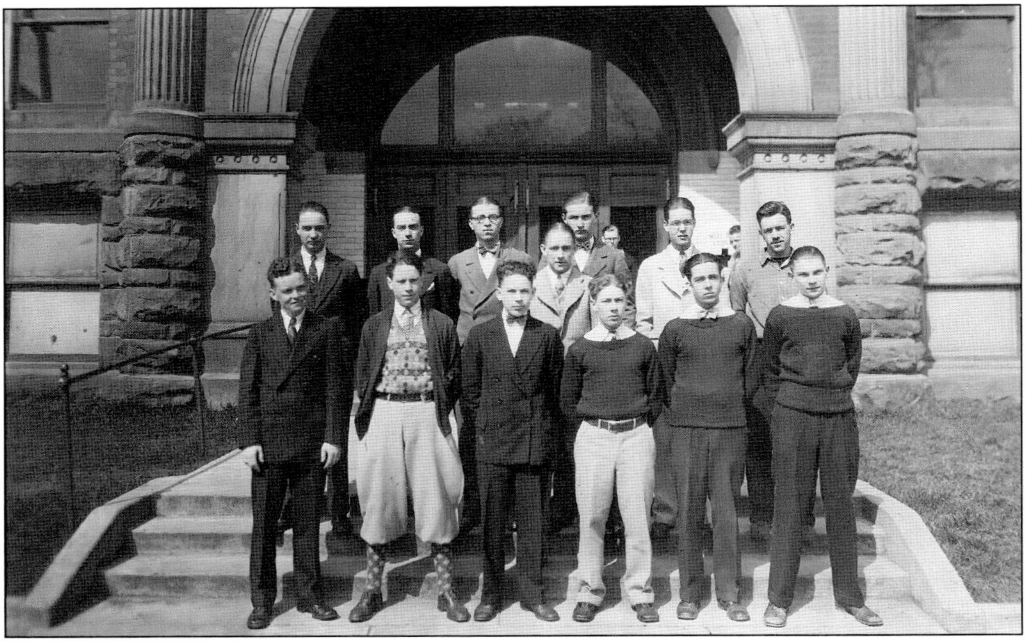

HIGH SCHOOL STUDENTS VISITING CITY HALL, 1927. These Bradford High School and St. Bernard students have been chosen to serve as honorary city officials for the day. Listed from left to right are as follows: (front row) P.J. Carroll, Jack Stewart, Ed Walker, Luther Conroe, Norman Rathfon, and an unidentified student; (back row) Frank Stack, Wylie Reed, Chester Olson, Tom McDowell, Bill Loveland, and Jake McKenzie. The boy in the middle is unknown.

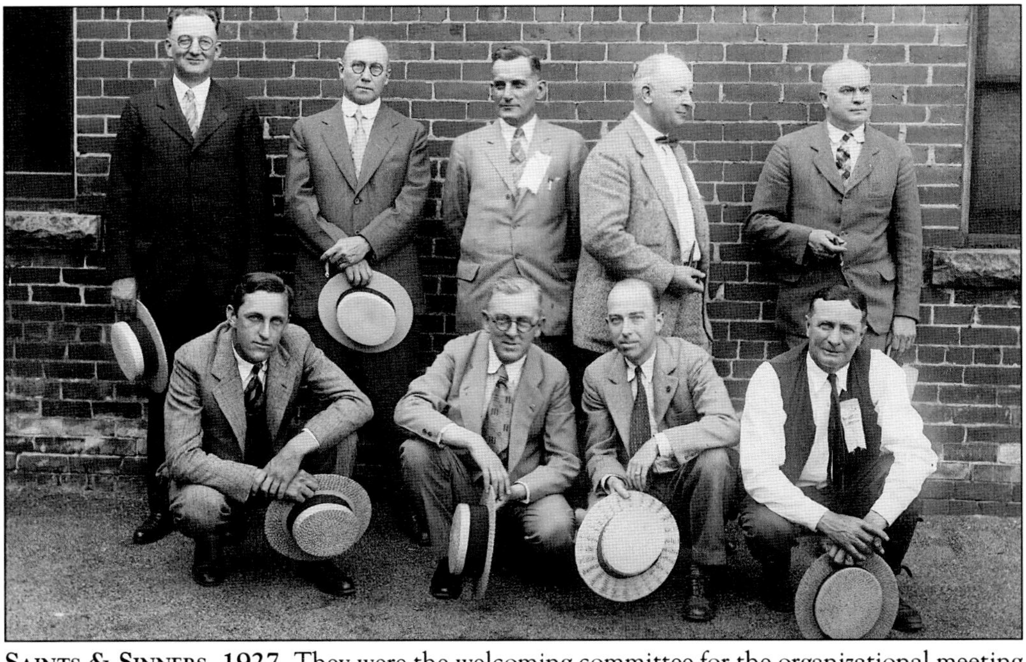

SAINTS & SINNERS, 1927. They were the welcoming committee for the organizational meeting of the Bradford Circus of the Saints & Sinners. Listed from left to right are as follows: (front row) Ed Hanley, Art Haggerty, Art Dort, and Fred Heckel; (back row) Bob George, Thede Barnsdall, Tommy Thompson, Fred Waggoner, and Jake Heckel.

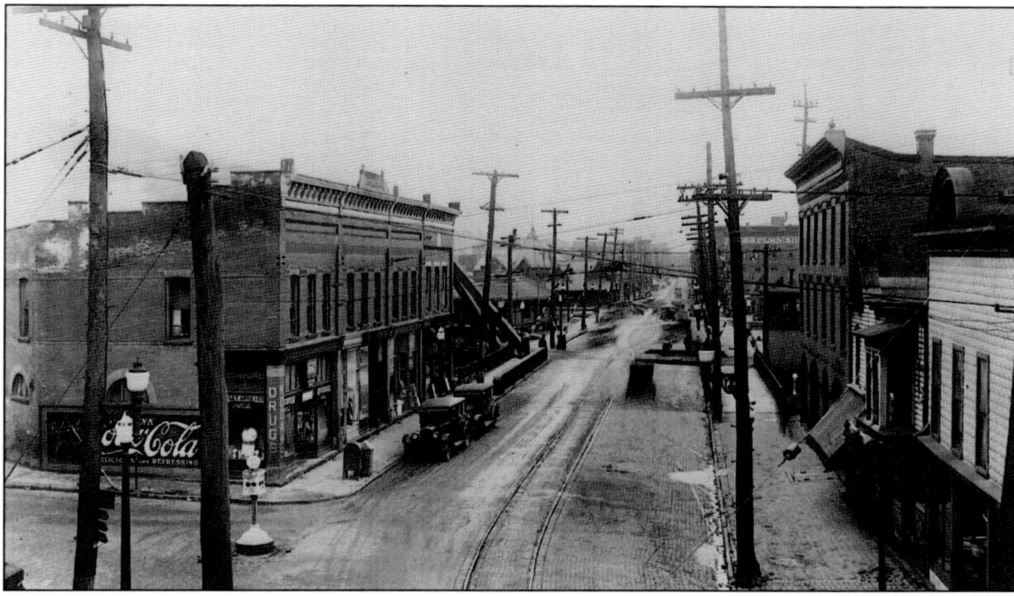

Before Main Street, 1927. Progress can certainly be seen in these two photographs, taken just one year apart. This photograph looks up Main Street—telephone and streetcar-line poles stretch along both sides of the street. Note the traffic light island at the left of the picture in the middle of High Street and the "old fashioned" streetlights—dating to 1897—along the sidewalks.

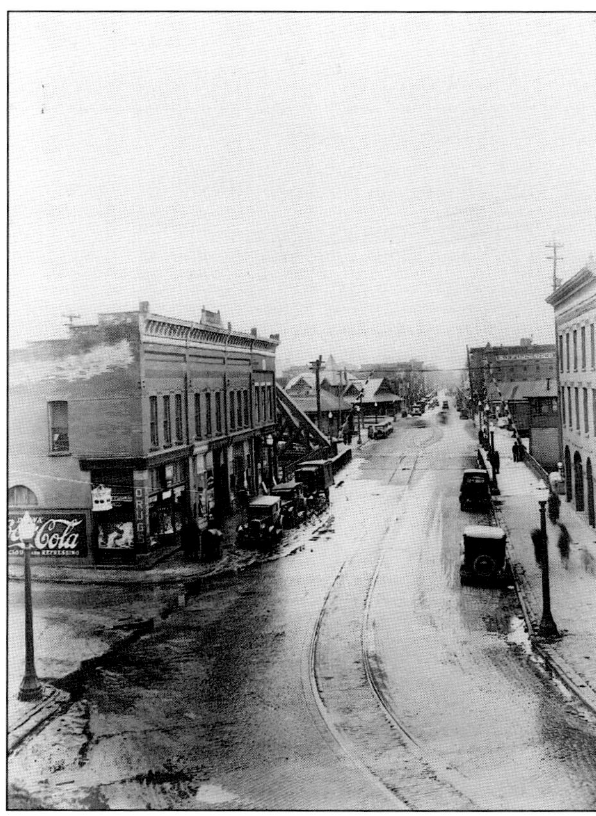

And after Main Street, 1928. Within a year, the telephone and electric streetcar poles have disappeared and modern street lights have been installed. The traffic light is now suspended from wire above High Street. The remaining poles near the railroad station are telegraph poles—they belonged to the railroad and were not removed when the other poles were taken down.

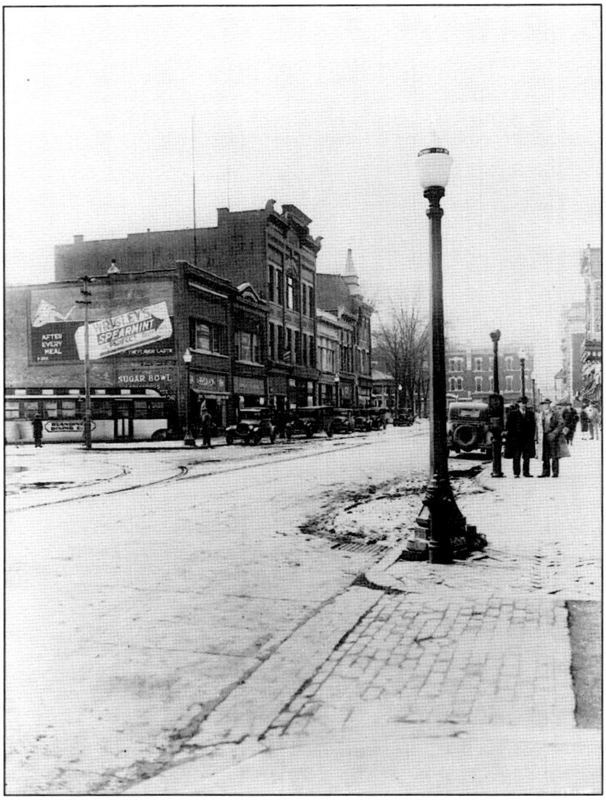

LOOKING UP MAIN STREET, SPRING, 1928. Although tracks are visible, trolley service was discontinued in the fall of 1927. The Sugar Bowl can be seen near the corner of Congress Street. Blandings Dining Car was moved in October 1928 to a site beside Graham's Florist Shop on Kennedy Street. A new business concept—a gasoline station—took its place.

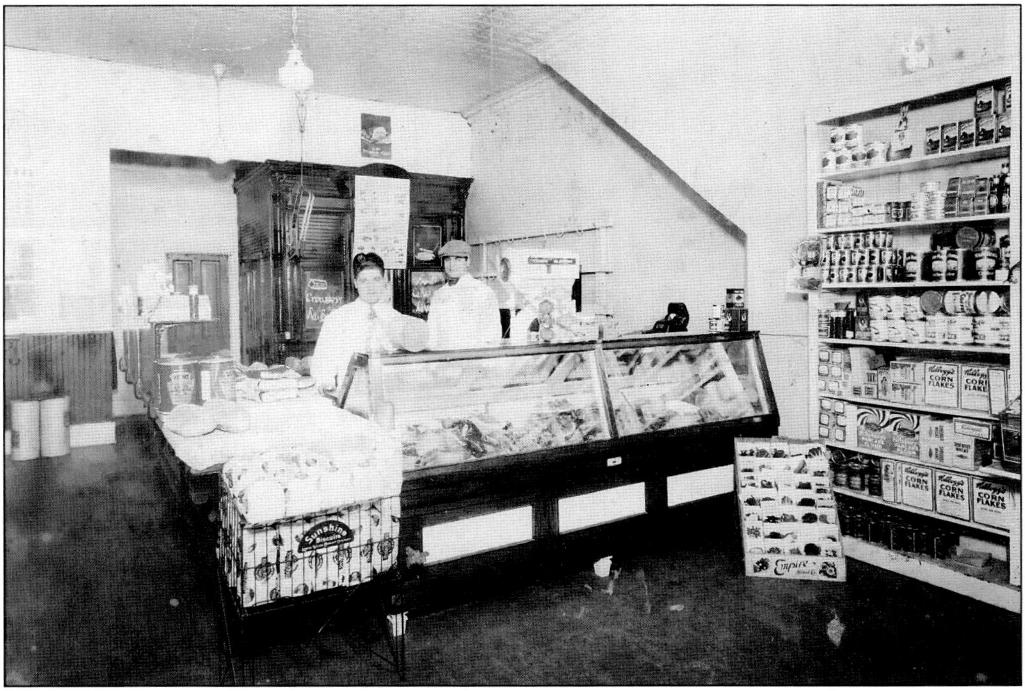

PECORA'S SANITARY MARKET, 1927. This family-run grocery store was located at 195 West Washington Street. Sam Pecora, left, and Frank Pecora, right, are behind the meat counter.

HARRY J. COLLINS, C. 1929. Collins, a city alderman, was an outspoken critic of the Ku Klux Klan movement in Bradford. The KKK burned a cross on Mt. Raub on August 7, 1920, and later that month held a huge rally on the back road to Limestone, with over a thousand attending. Klan activity continued throughout the 1920s, directed mainly at Catholics and Jews.

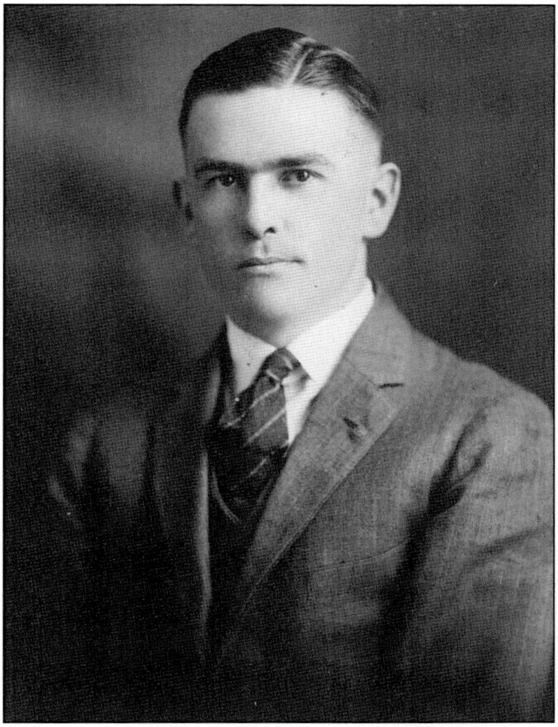

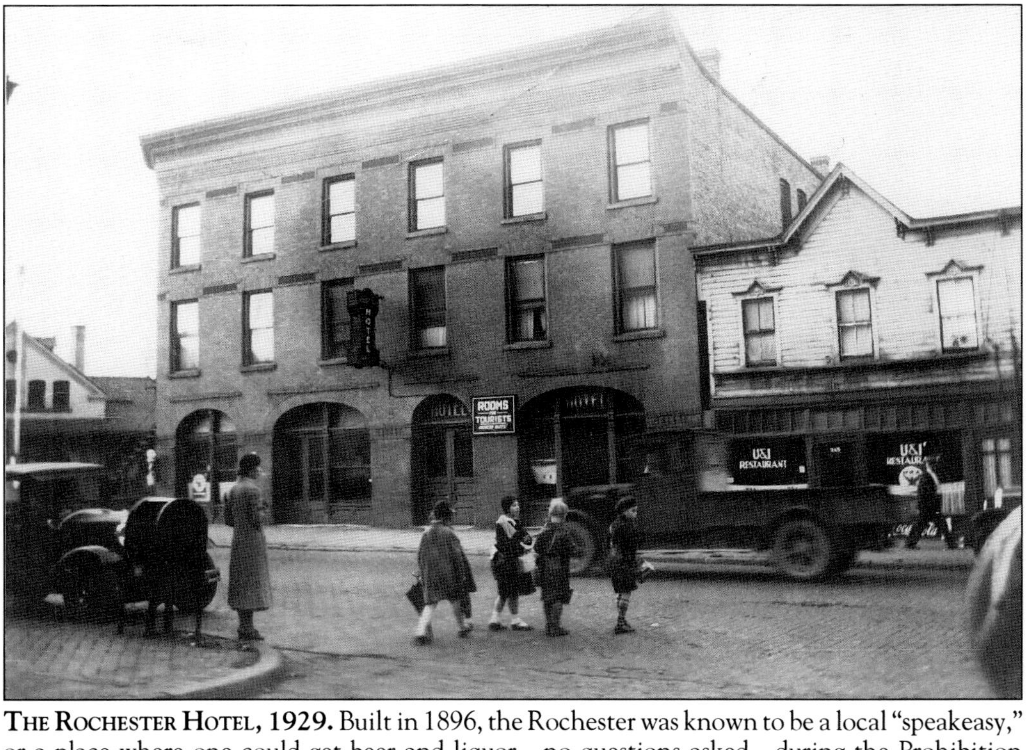

THE ROCHESTER HOTEL, 1929. Built in 1896, the Rochester was known to be a local "speakeasy," or a place where one could get beer and liquor—no questions asked—during the Prohibition years of the 1920s. Today, it is called the Bradford Hotel, and still stands at the foot of Main Street.

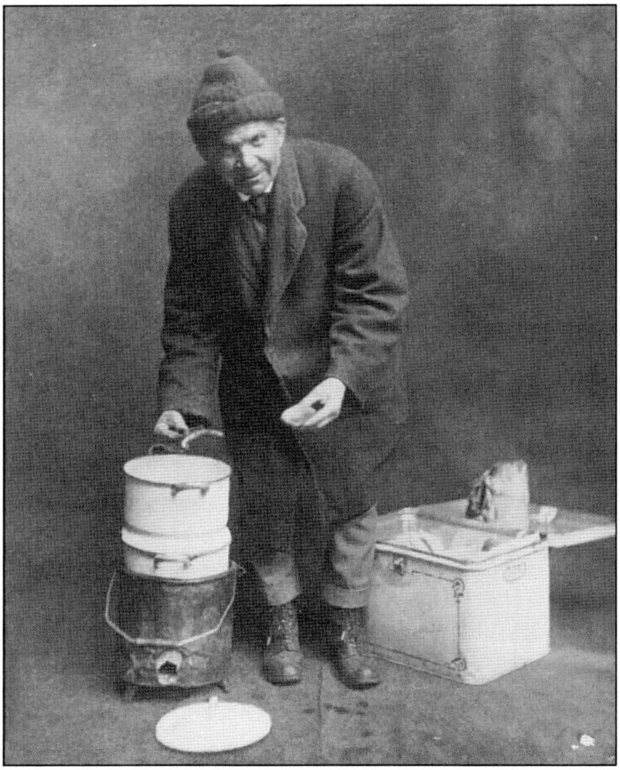

Toots, the Hot Dog Man, c. 1920s. He was known all over Bradford as much for his personality as for his hot dogs, which he sold at ball games and on the street. His real name is unknown, but many people remember the hot dogs, kept warm in a pail of hot water; and buns, kept fresh in a tin bread box.

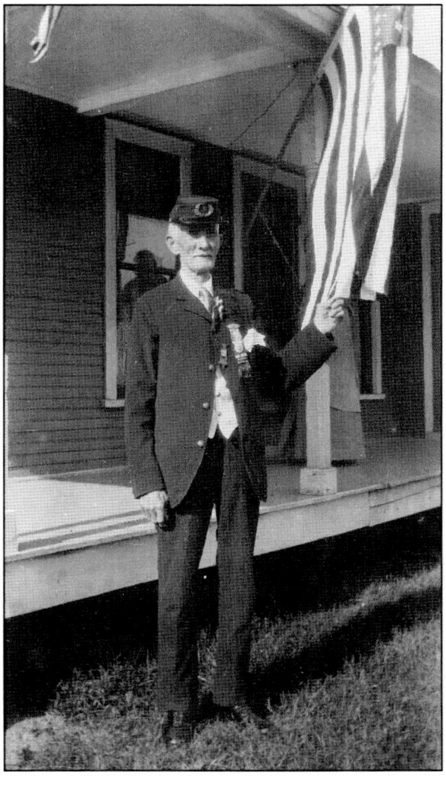

Custer City Resident John Anderson, June 24, 1923. An Irish immigrant, he enlisted at the age of 20 in 1864, serving as a U.S. Marine onboard the *Monitor*, the *Shenandoah*, and the *Idaho* for Union forces. By the 1920s, there were few surviving Civil War veterans in the Bradford area. Anderson, seen here at age 80, died the following year in 1924.

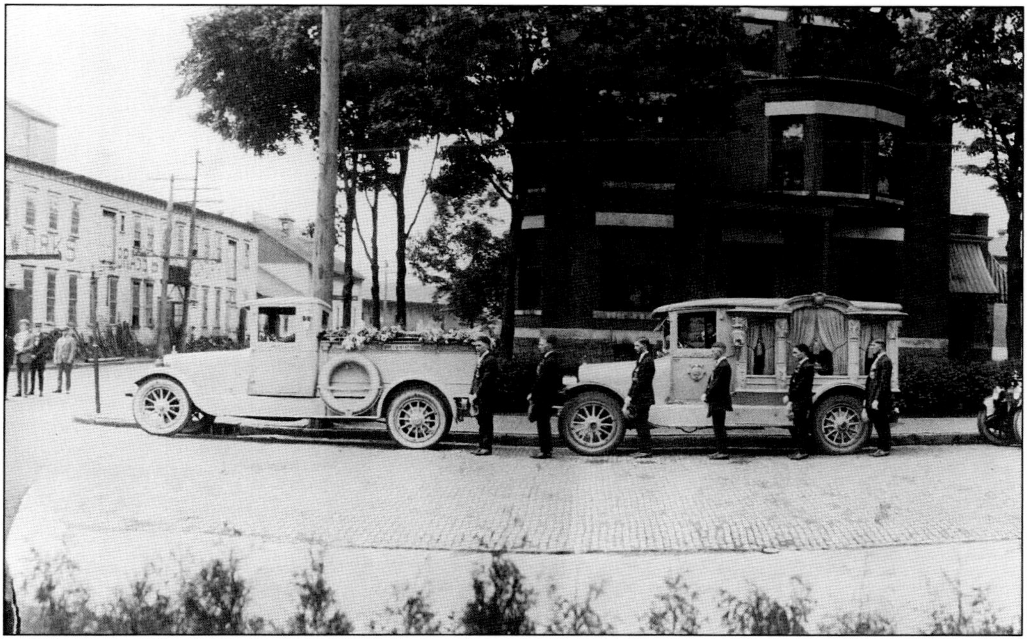

THE FUNERAL OF CLEM PISCATELLI, JULY 1923. Apparently a likable fellow, Piscatelli was only 24 years old when he died. His funeral, seen here as it pauses in front of the St. Bernard's rectory and church on E. Corydon Street, was reported to be one of the largest funerals that Bradford had ever seen. The hearse belonged to Still's Funeral Home.

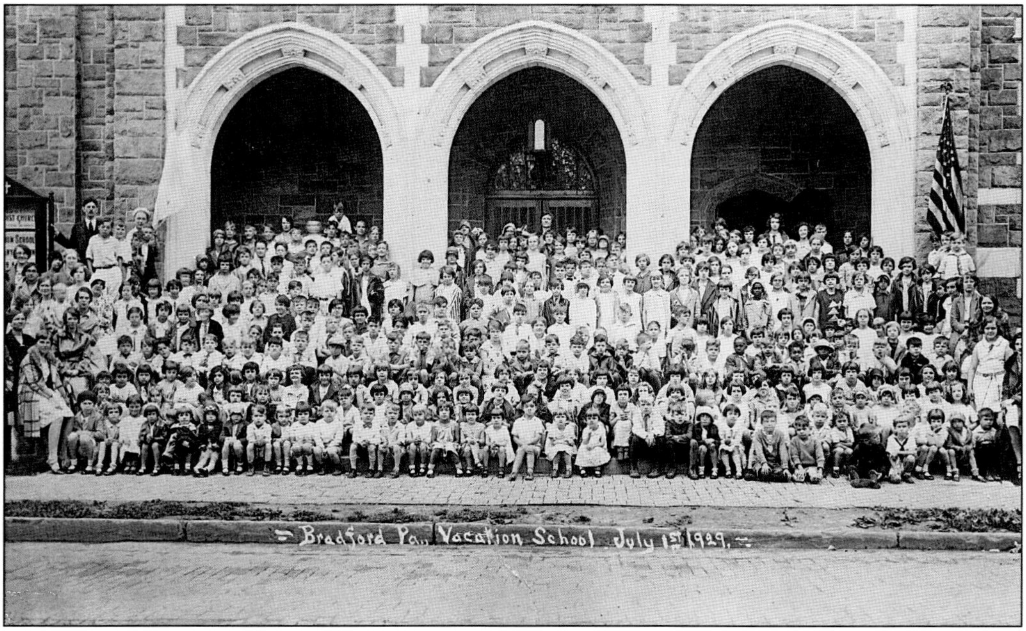

VACATION BIBLE SCHOOL, JULY 1, 1929. These children are gathered in front of the side entrance to the Methodist church.

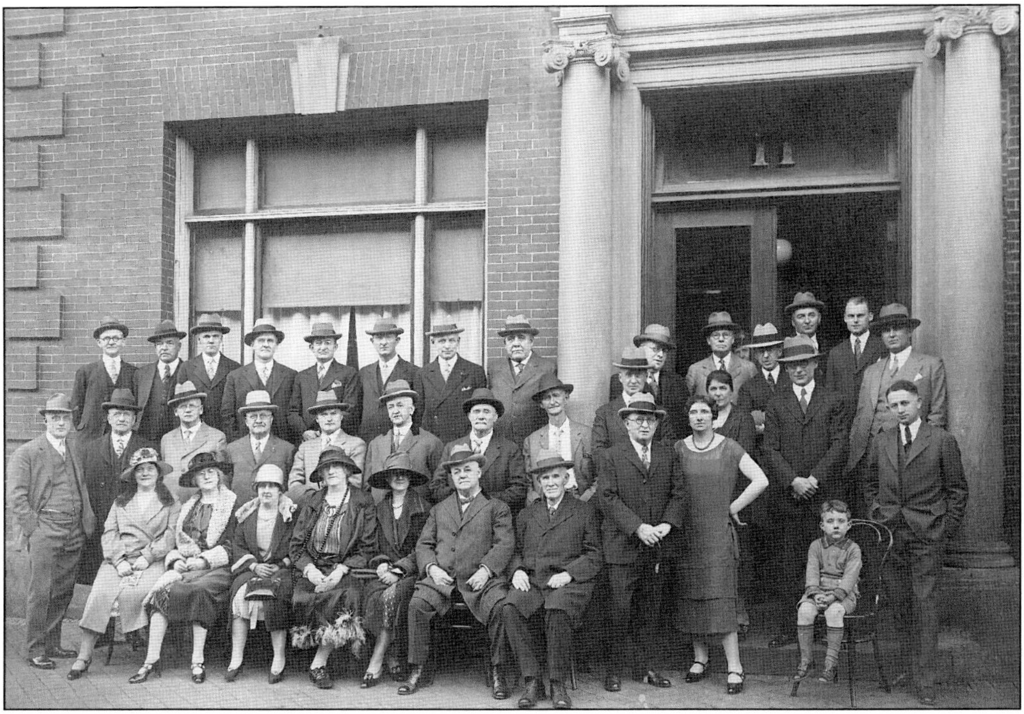

THE BELL TELEPHONE OFFICE, JULY 17, 1926. The employees of the telephone exchange office at 11 Chestnut Street (recently the home of the VFW) gather outside for a photograph commemorating the 50th anniversary of the invention of the telephone. In 1930, a more modern, three-story brick building was built on the corner of Corydon and Congress Streets. Both buildings are still standing.

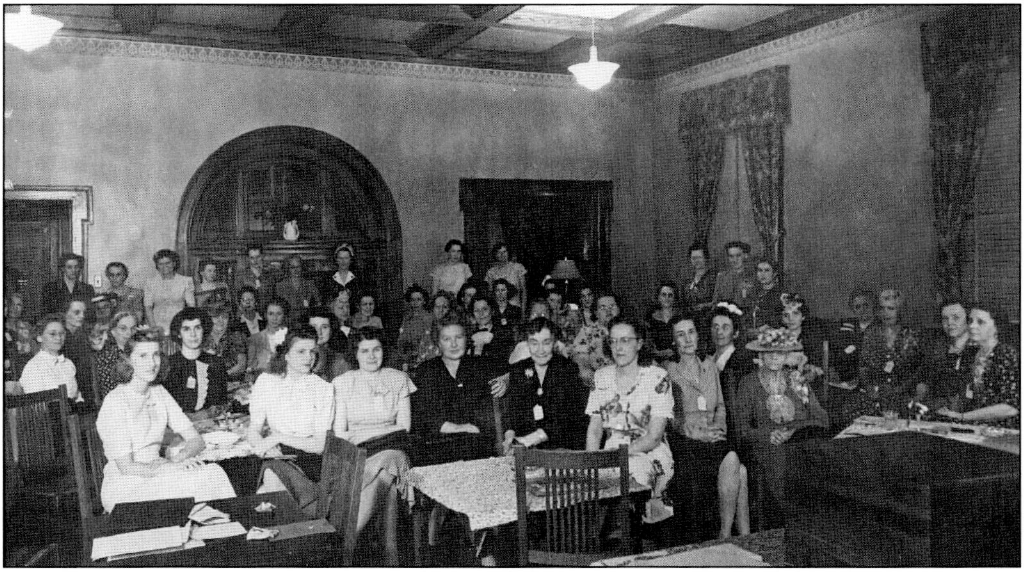

THE AMERICAN ASSOCIATION OF UNIVERSITY WOMEN. The AAUW was formed on April 16, 1921, at the home of Mildred Emery (Harri Emery's sister) on West Corydon Street. There, 20 college women joined together "for the purpose of organizing a college club." Seventy-seven years later, it is still in existence.

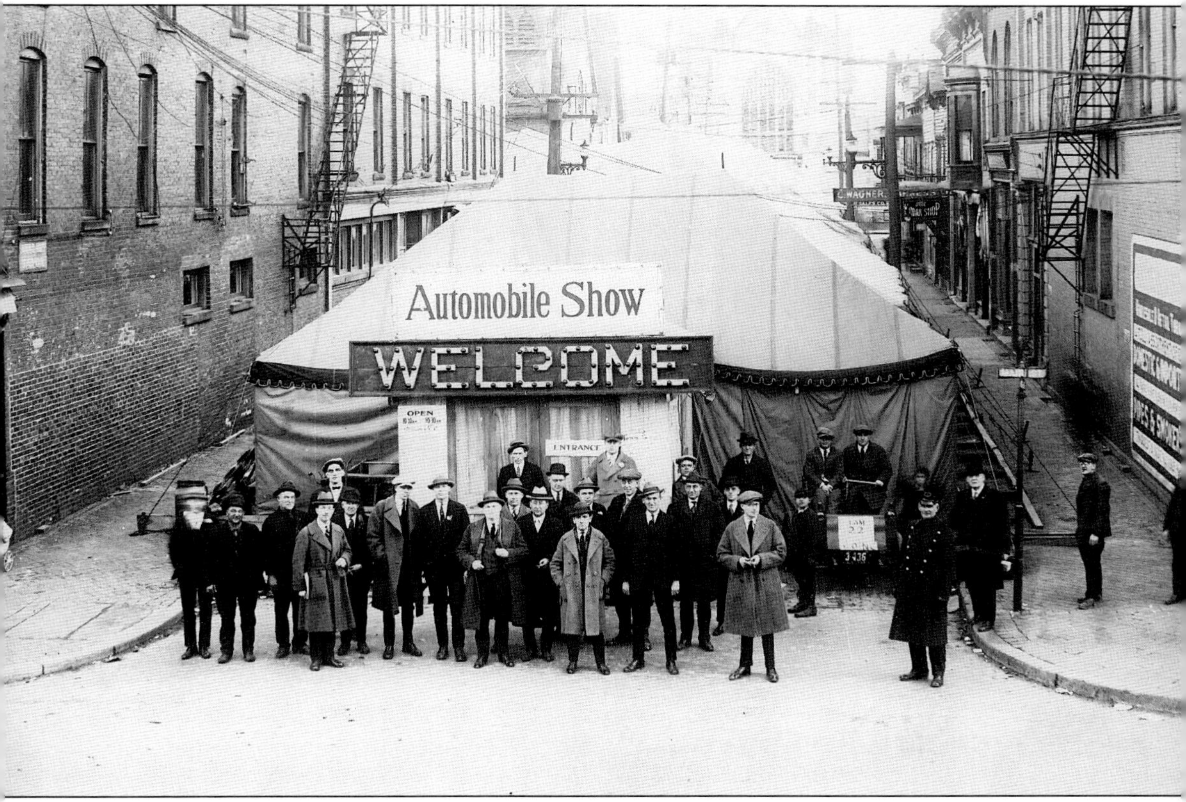

The Automobile Show, Chambers Street, c. 1923. Automobile shows were held each year to introduce new models. This tent was erected that fall. Admission was 35¢. By the 1920s, an automobile could be bought for under $1,000. The Seneca Junction Bridge was dedicated on October 30, 1923, linking the city to the improved road system of New York state. The *Bradford Era* happily reported that "Bradford Breaks Bad Road Bondage Today" as the new bridge opened.

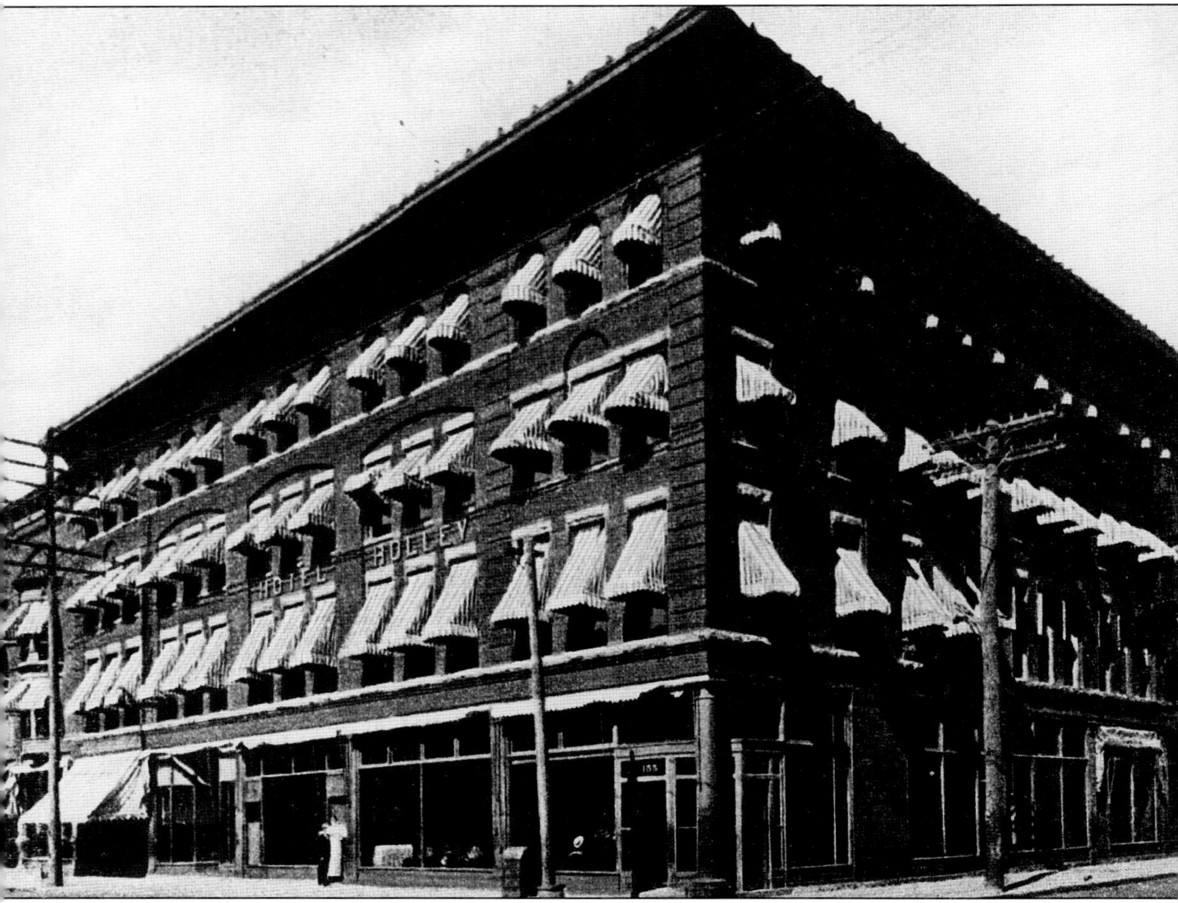

The Corner of Davis and Main Streets, 1922. This corner on Main Street was the scene of a gangster shootout on the afternoon of November 4, 1922, when three men opened fire on each other. Two of the trio were wounded, and the third ran off down the railroad tracks, dropping his gun enroute. Open gunfire was not unusual in the 1920s, as rival gangster mobs tried to gain control of the city.

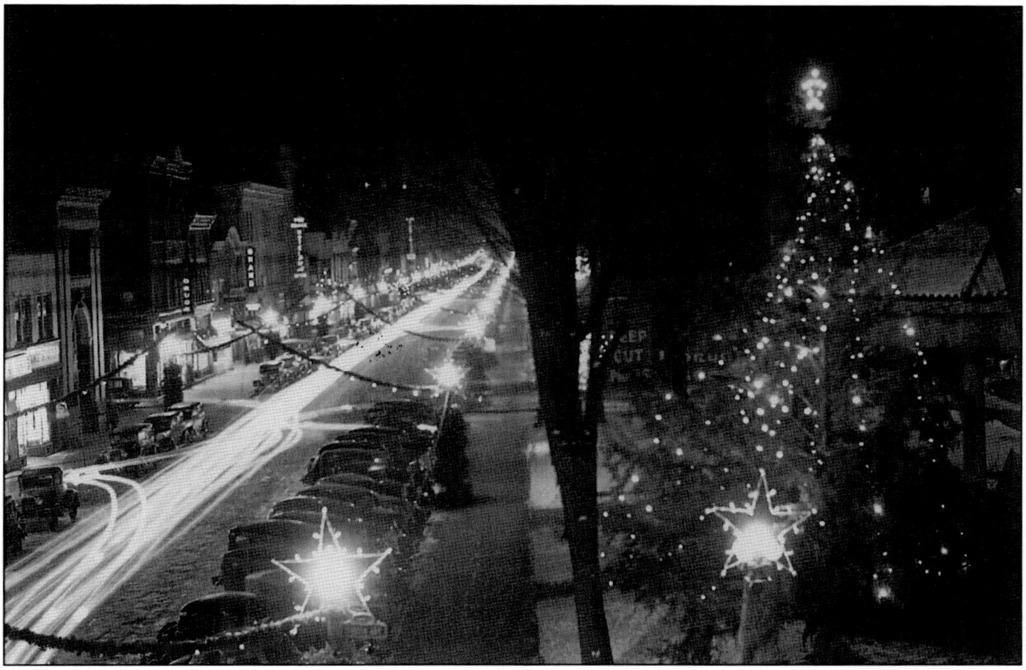

CHRISTMAS, 1928. Taken from an upper floor of the Emery Hotel, the head of Main Street is festive with holiday lights. In the late 1920s, cars were permitted to park on a diagonal near the Public Square—perhaps their owners are at the Grand Theater, a popular movie house, just down the street on the left.

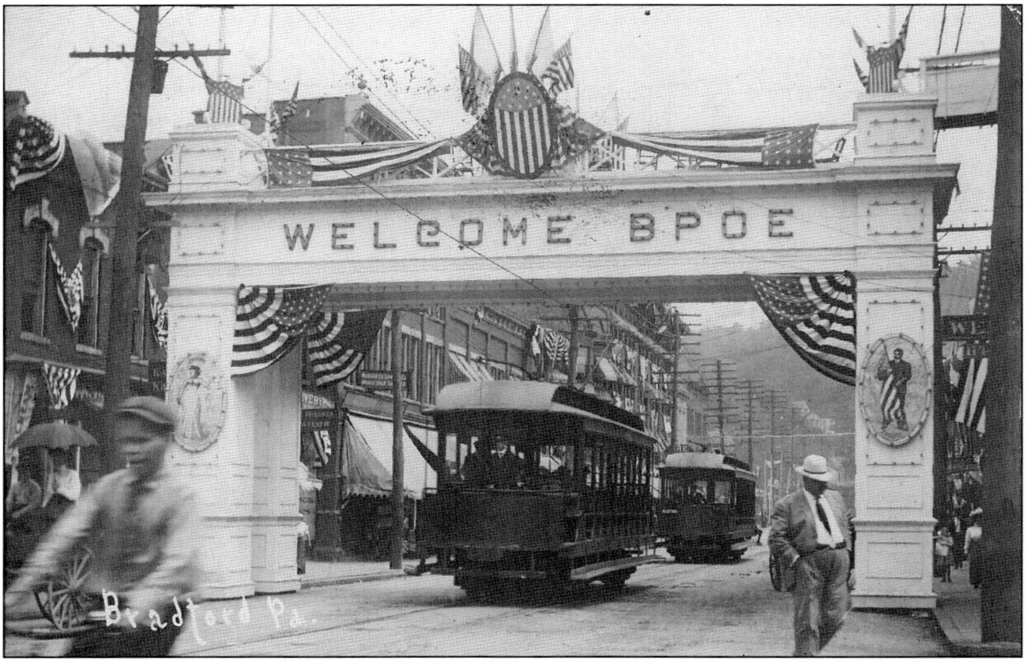

WELCOME BPOE, AUGUST 1909. Using the Old Home Week arch, the Benevolent Protective Order of Elks held their convention that week. Here, two trolleys are about to pass underneath. The arch was dismantled later that fall.

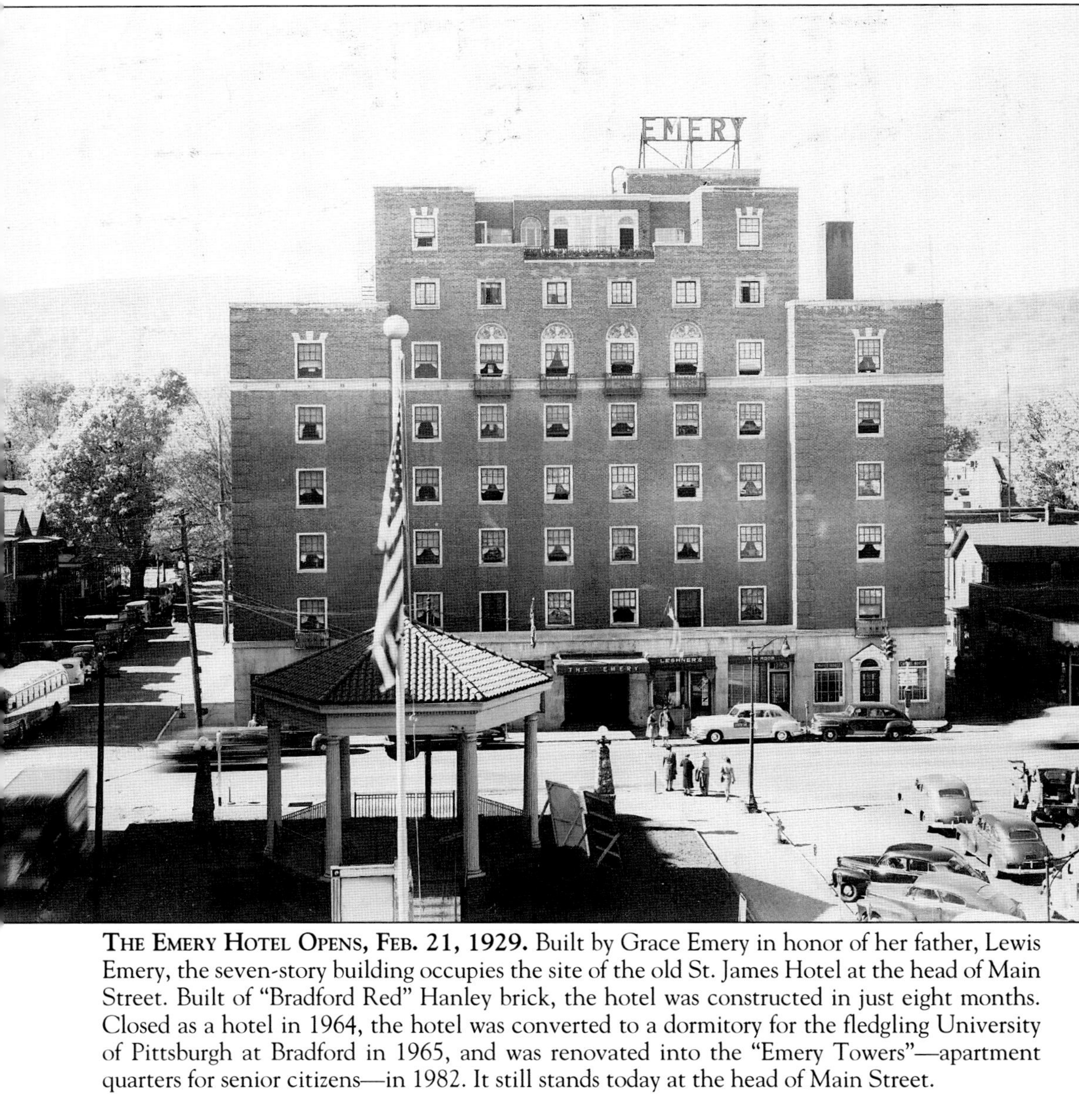

The Emery Hotel Opens, Feb. 21, 1929. Built by Grace Emery in honor of her father, Lewis Emery, the seven-story building occupies the site of the old St. James Hotel at the head of Main Street. Built of "Bradford Red" Hanley brick, the hotel was constructed in just eight months. Closed as a hotel in 1964, the hotel was converted to a dormitory for the fledgling University of Pittsburgh at Bradford in 1965, and was renovated into the "Emery Towers"—apartment quarters for senior citizens—in 1982. It still stands today at the head of Main Street.

Six

Sports—the Games That We Play

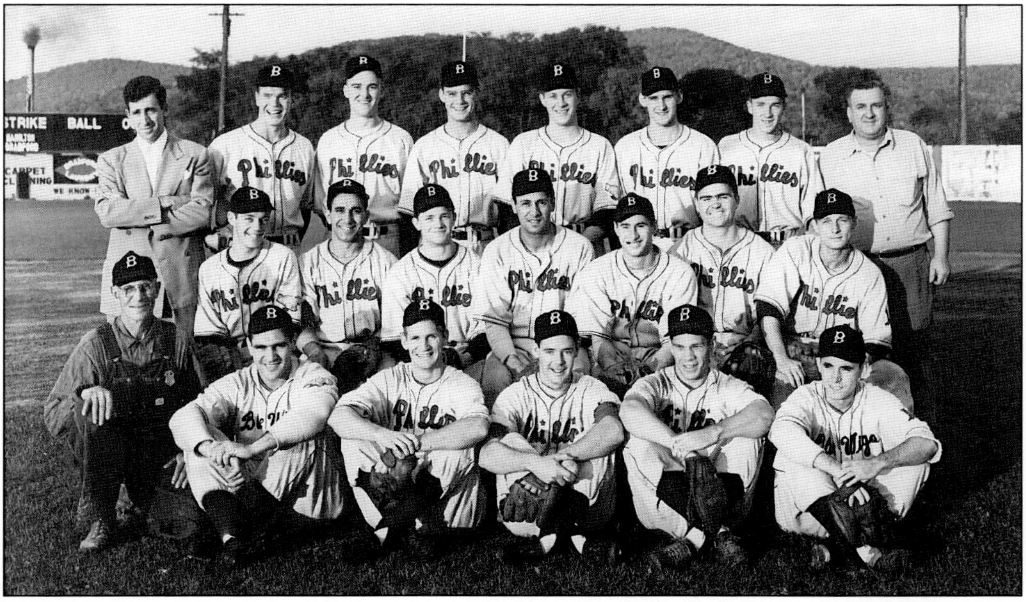

THE BRADFORD PHILLIES, 1949. A farm team of the Philadelphia Phillies, and member of the PONY League (Penna, Ontario, New York), the Phillies won the Governor's Cup championship in 1949. From left to right they are as follows: (front row) "Pop" Bailey (groundskeeper), Chuck Saverine, Jim Deery, Bert Freeman, Bill Spangler, and Jim Reamy; (middle row) Elroy Face, Emil Carlini, Andy Bratkowitz, Danny Carvale (manager), Ed Zeidler, Tom Mankey, and Jack Seltereich; (back row) Fred Tascone (assistant business manager), Jack Schmitt, Stan Edwards, Alex Hoyle, Dan Kubezak, Eddie Urbank, Dick Young, and Bill Bridge (bus driver). The Pony League, organized in 1939, was popular with baseball fans in Bradford and drew huge crowds to the community baseball field.

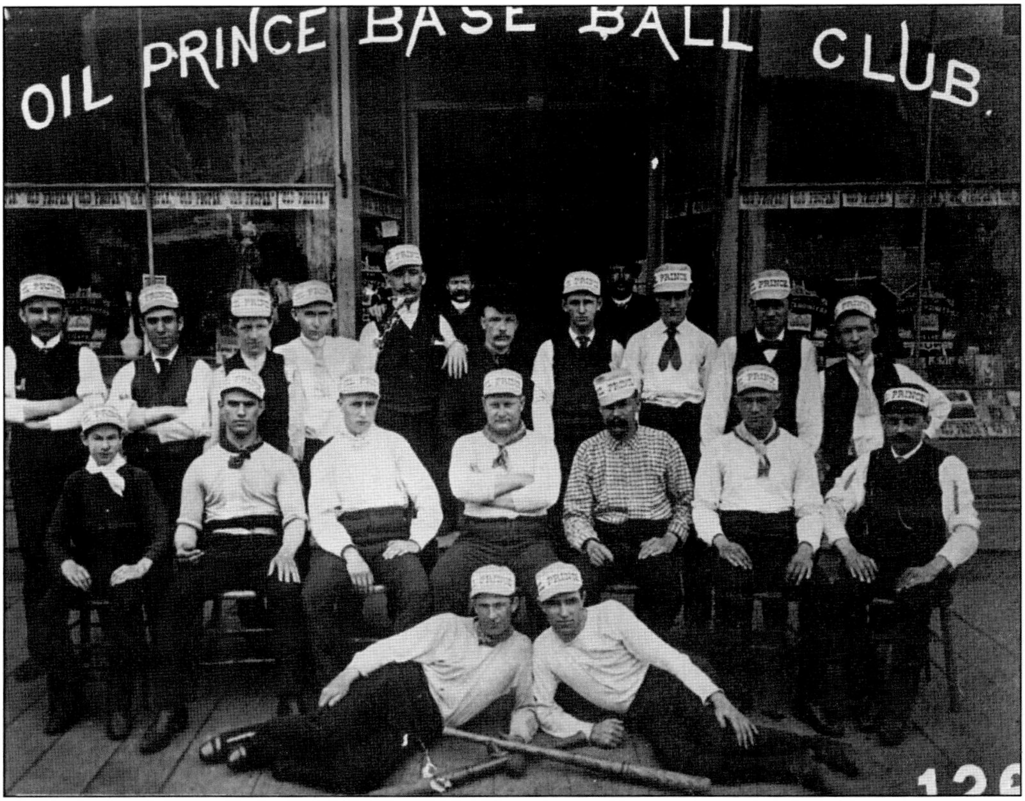

OIL PRINCE CIGARS BASEBALL TEAM, 1890. The Iron and Oil Interstate League would not be formed until February 24, 1898, but inter-city baseball had been played in Bradford for years. These players are employees of a cigar manufacturer on Congress Street.

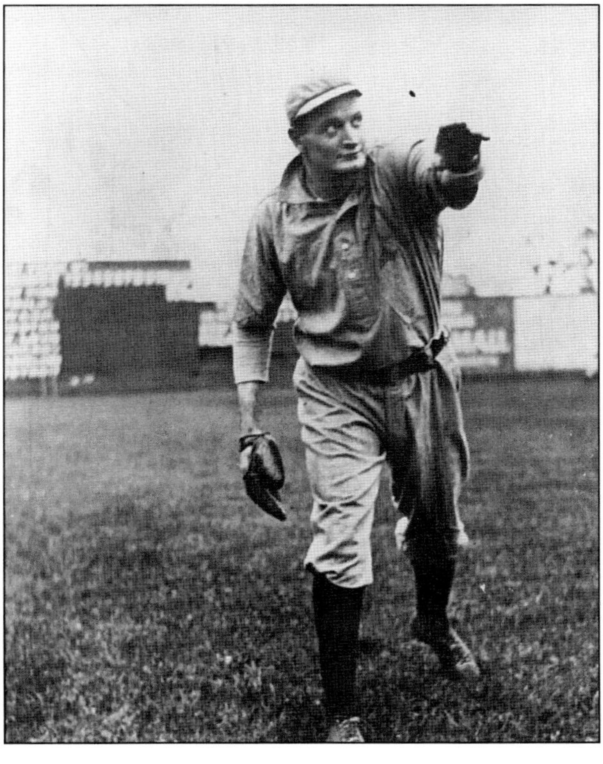

RUBE WADDELL, 1903. "Bradford's Gift to Baseball," this eccentric left-handed pitcher was born on Jackson Avenue in 1876. Waddell played for the Philadelphia Athletics (American League) under Connie Mack and was elected to the Baseball Hall of Fame in 1946, having earned a lifetime record of 191 wins, 141 losses, a 2.16 ERA, and 2,316 strikeouts in 2,961 innings pitched. He died of tuberculosis in 1914.

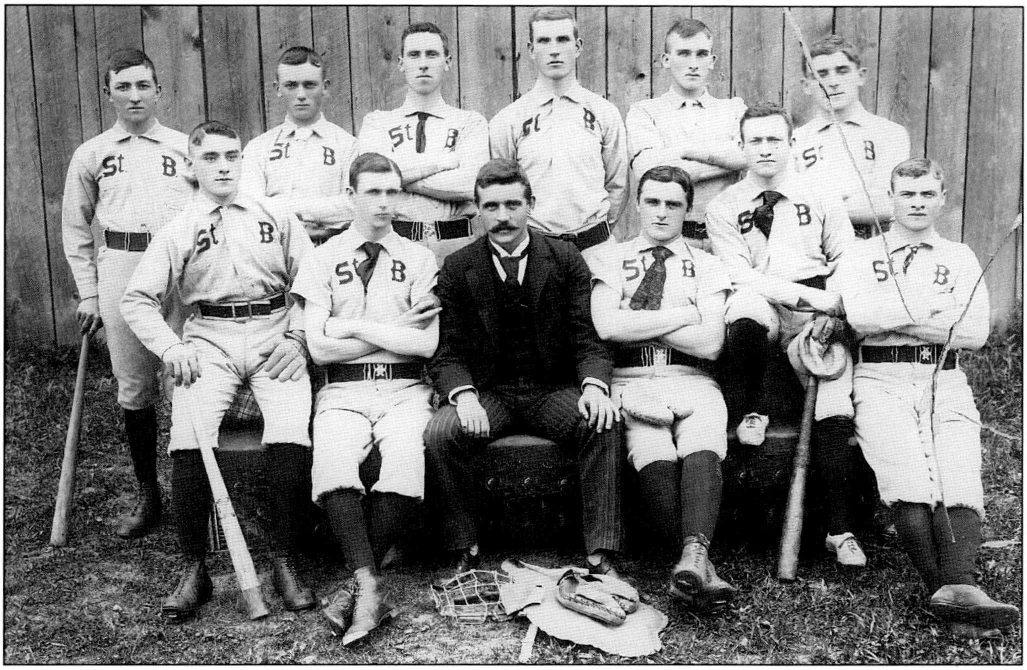

St. Bernard's Baseball Team, 1897. This team had one requirement—all players must be over 17 years of age. They may be young, but they look determined.

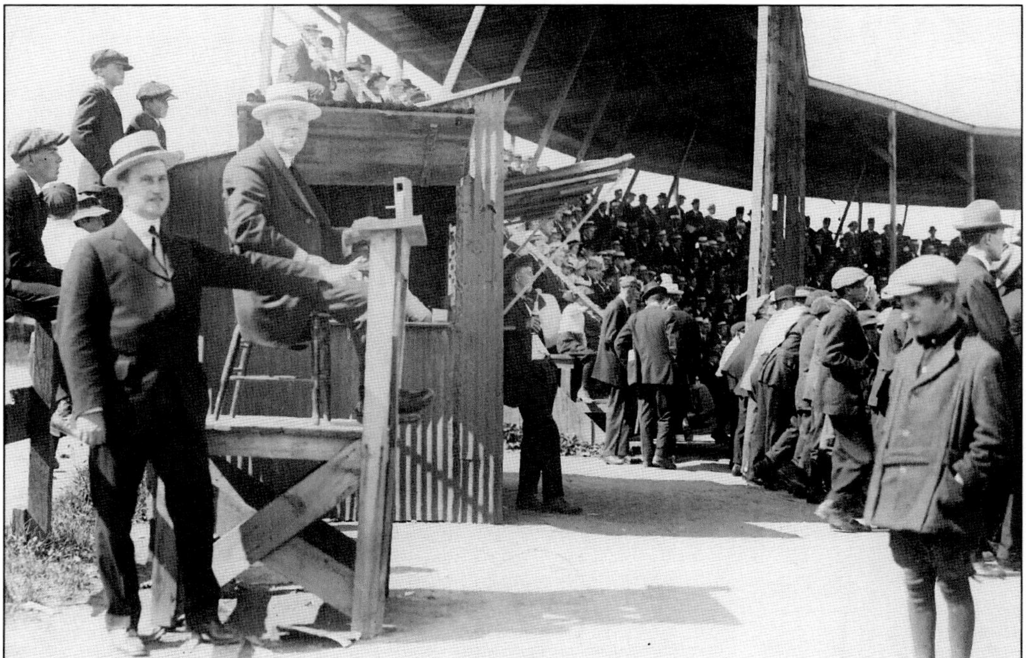

The Community Park Baseball Park, c. 1910. Located near the intersection of Bolivar Drive and Seaward Avenue, the park was the scene of many baseball games. Both Interstate Leagues (1904–1906 and 1914–1916) were played here before the PONY Leagues claimed it as their home park in 1939. Spectators are seated comfortably under the grandstand roof as they watch the action.

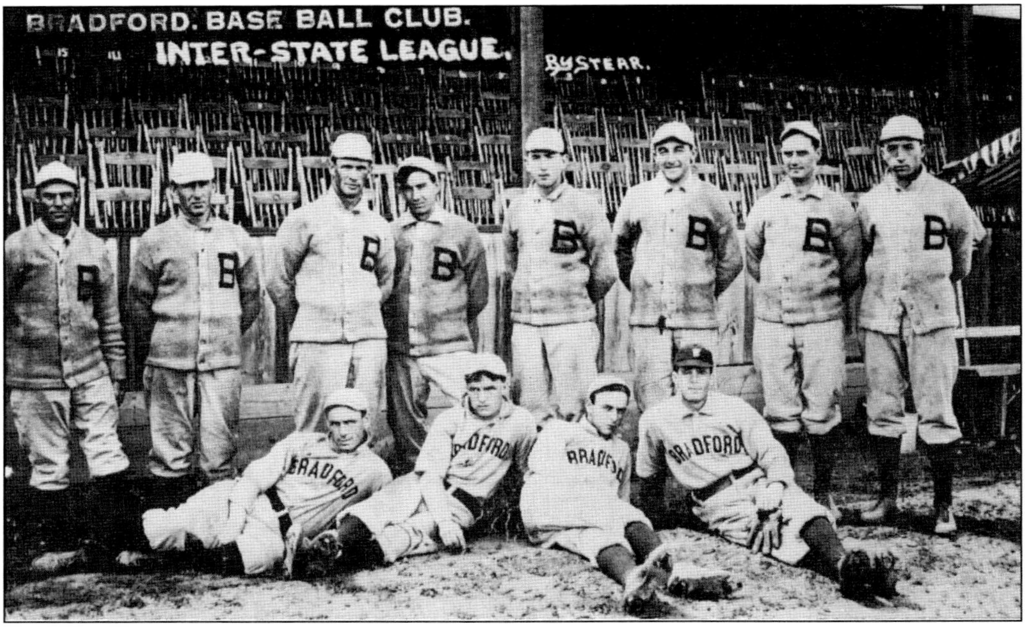

BRADFORD BALL PLAYERS, 1916. These ball players competed in the Interstate League of 1916, and played their games at the community ballpark in Foster Township. Notice the folding chairs in the grandstand instead of benches.

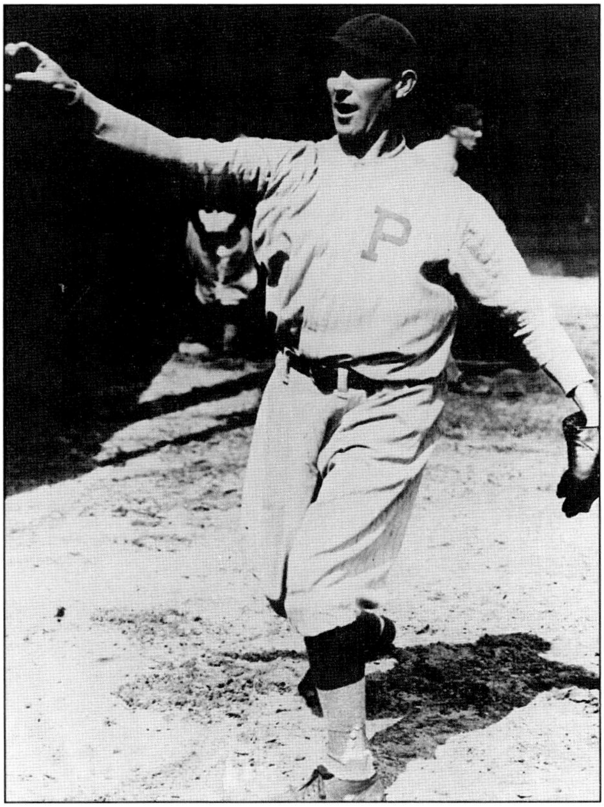

PETE BEHAN, 1921. A ball player in the old Interstate League of 1916, Charles Frederick (Pete) Behan later went on to play for the Philadelphia Phillies from 1921 to 1923. Born in Dallas City in 1887, he was 36 years old when he joined the majors. Following his career, he retired to Bradford, and spent the rest of his life here. He died in 1957, at age 69.

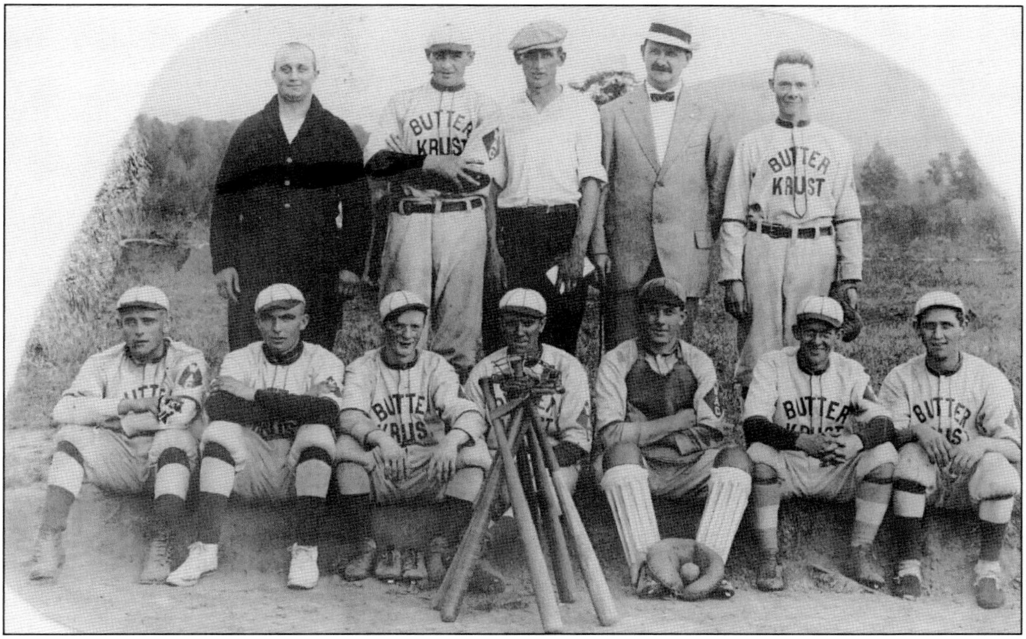

BUTTERKRUST BAKERY BASEBALL TEAM, C. 1930S. Although there was no big league teams playing in Bradford in the years between 1916 and 1939, inter-city ball was competitive. The Butterkrust Bakery players pose for a team picture.

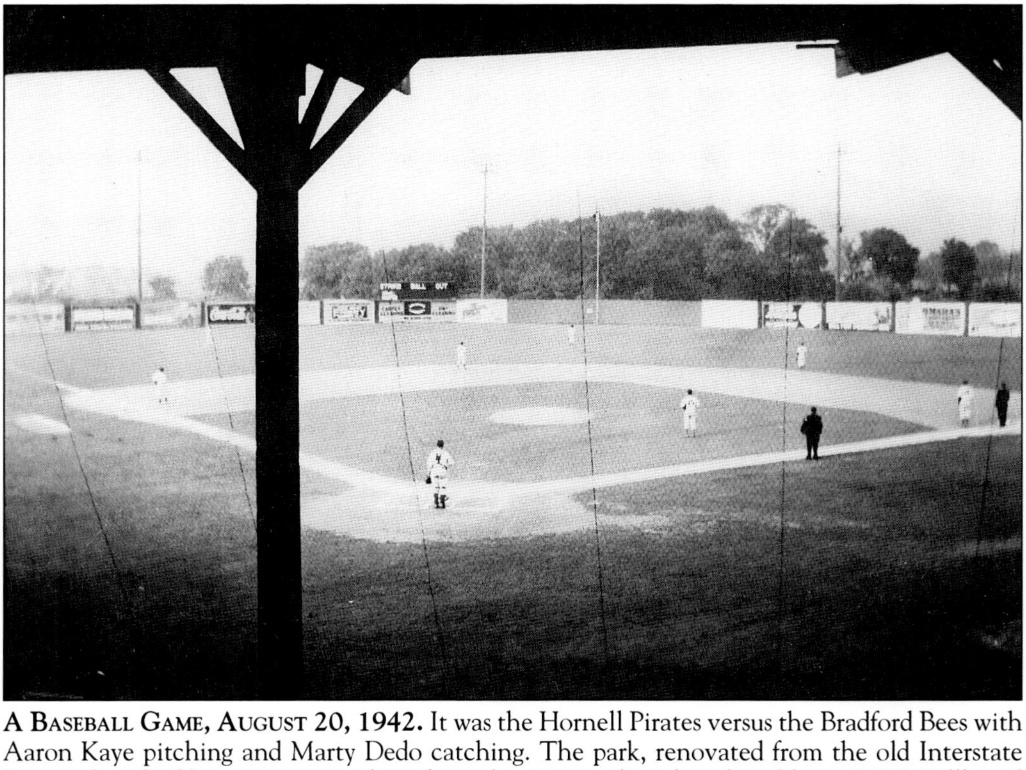

A BASEBALL GAME, AUGUST 20, 1942. It was the Hornell Pirates versus the Bradford Bees with Aaron Kaye pitching and Marty Dedo catching. The park, renovated from the old Interstate League days, had box seats, a grandstand, an electric scoreboard, and could seat 3,500. Billboard signs surrounded the field.

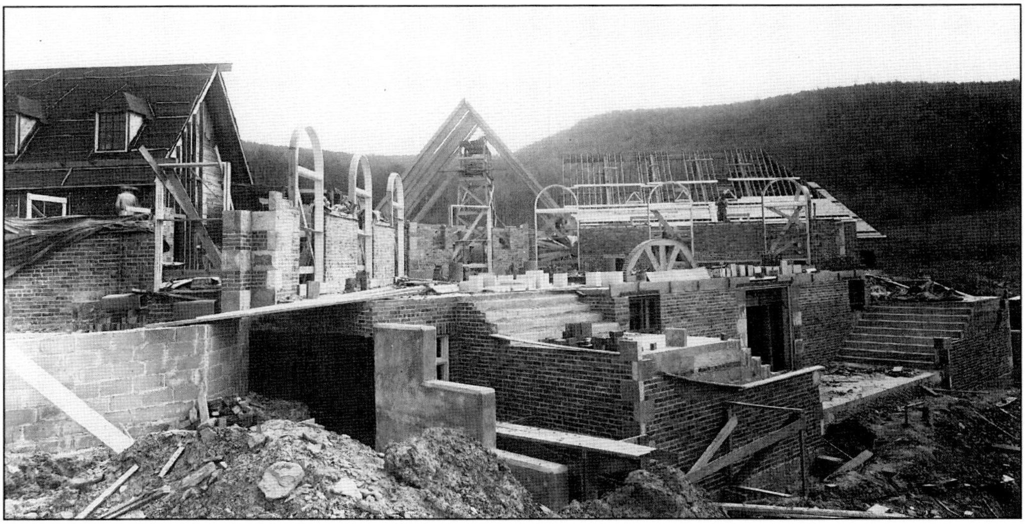

The Pennhills Country Club Under Construction, March 1938. In 1936, an idea grew that would join the North Penn Golf Club with the Country Club of south Bradford. Together they would form the new Pennhills Club, chartered December 6, 1937, featuring a golf course, swimming pool, meeting rooms, a dining room, and club facilities.

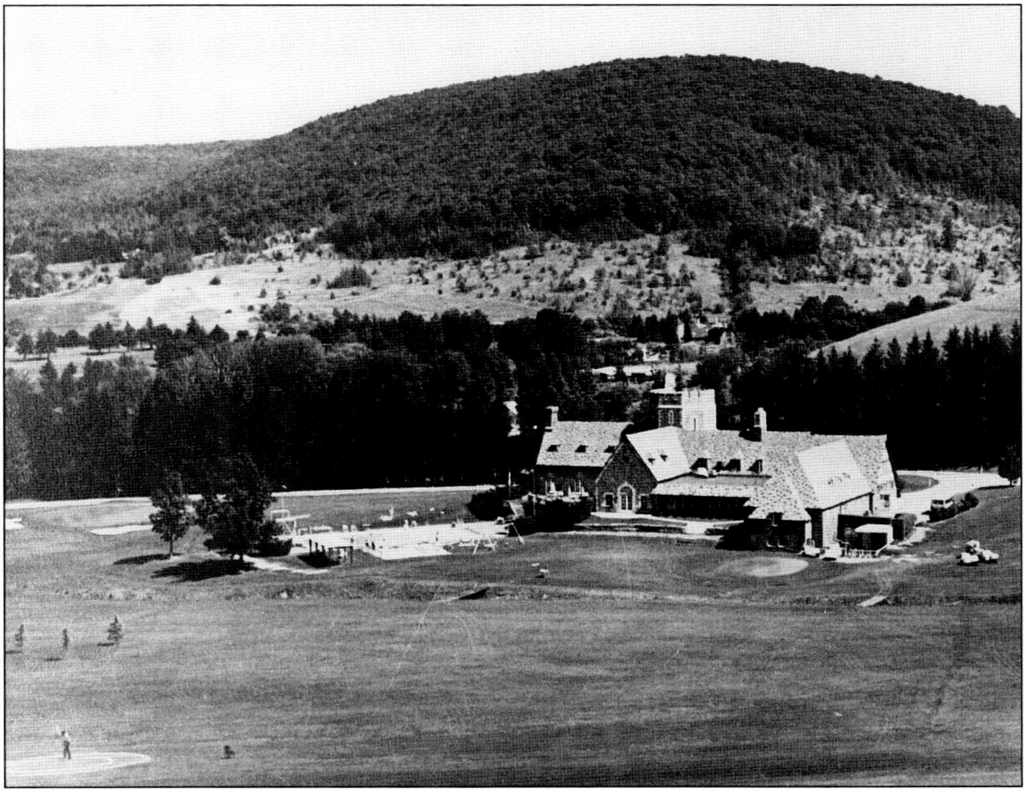

The Pennhills Club. This excellent aerial view shows the completed Pennhills Club on Minard Run. Notice the man at lower left playing golf.

Golf, Anyone? c. 1930. Golf has been popular in Bradford since the 1920s. The North Penn Golf Club was formed in 1922 and the country club on South Avenue (now the Satterwhite home) boasted a nine-hole golf course. This boy is dressed in typical attire for a day "on the links."

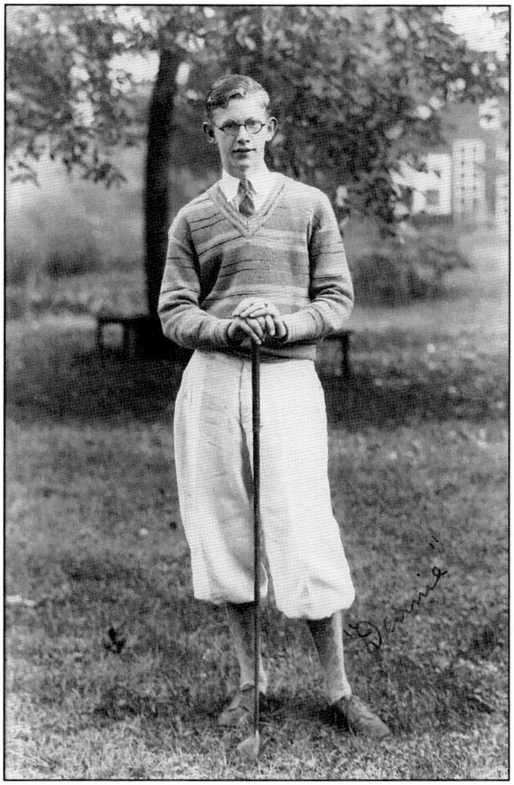

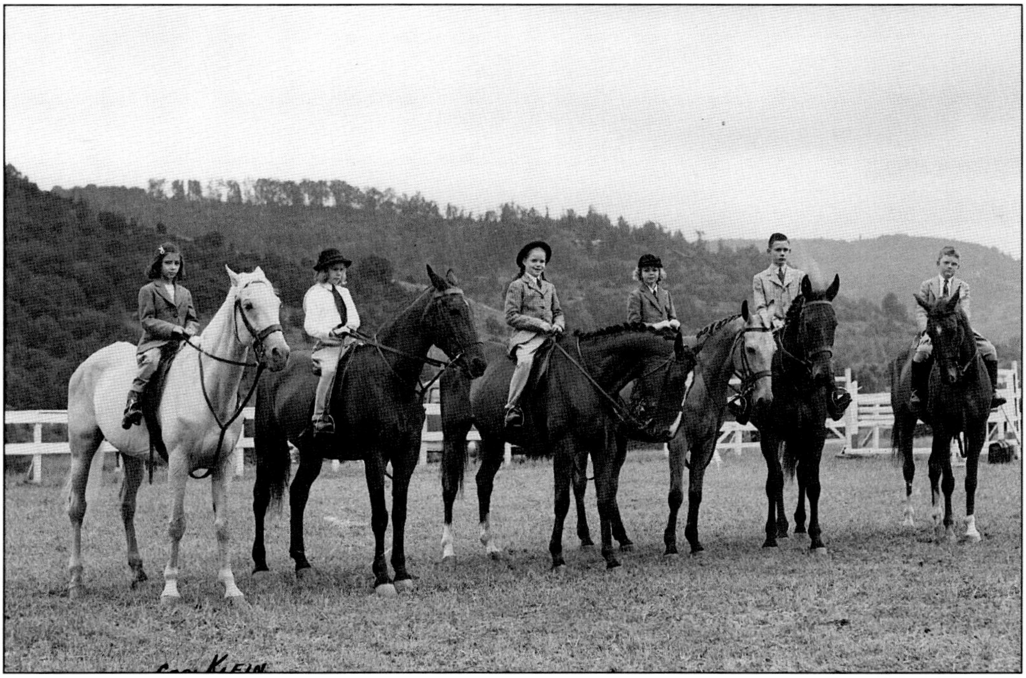

The Valley Hunt Club Riders, c. 1940. Several children proudly show off their mounts. Listed from left to right are Margery Williams, Martha Hamilton, Dion Dana, Nancy Simmons, Bruce Matson, and Peter Brennan.

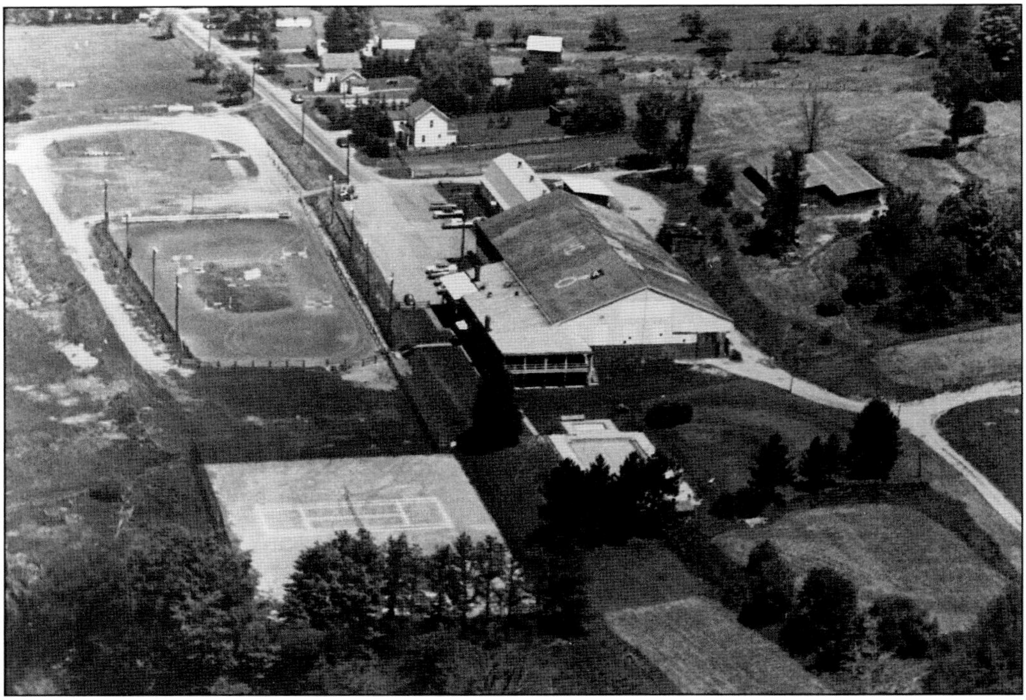

The Valley Hunt Club, Aerial View, c. 1940. It was formed as the Saddle & Bridle Club in 1929 "to provide lawful amusement and recreation of equestrian." The name was changed to the Valley Hunt Club in 1931. The clubhouse and barns were built in 1930 on Haven Street in Lewis Run, and over 7,000 acres of riding trails were available.

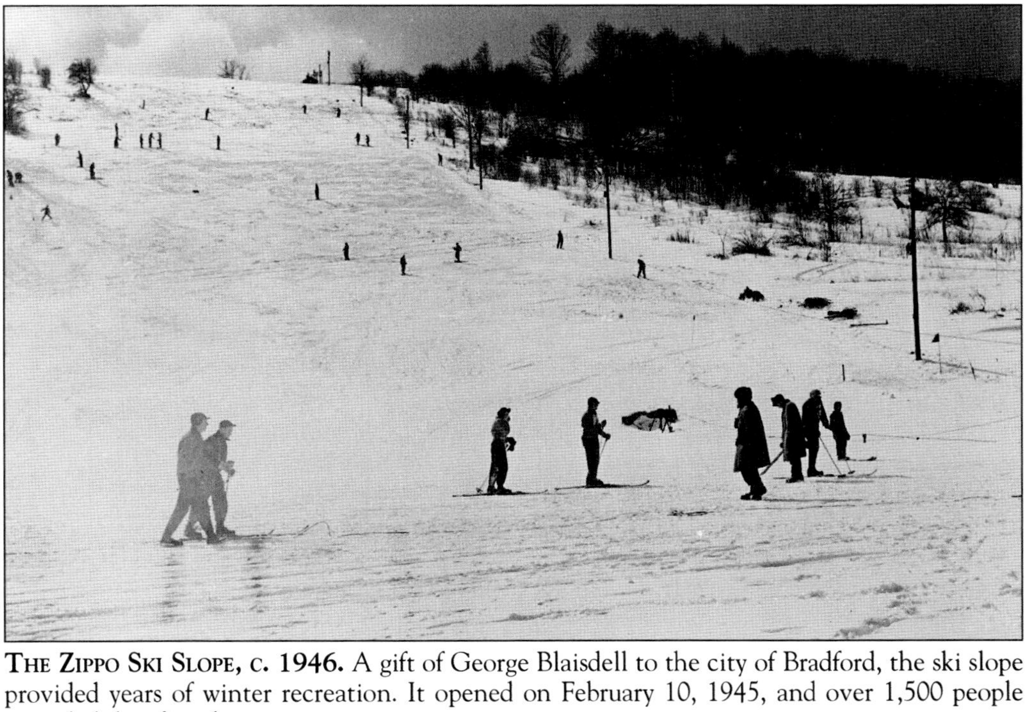

The Zippo Ski Slope, c. 1946. A gift of George Blaisdell to the city of Bradford, the ski slope provided years of winter recreation. It opened on February 10, 1945, and over 1,500 people attended that first day.

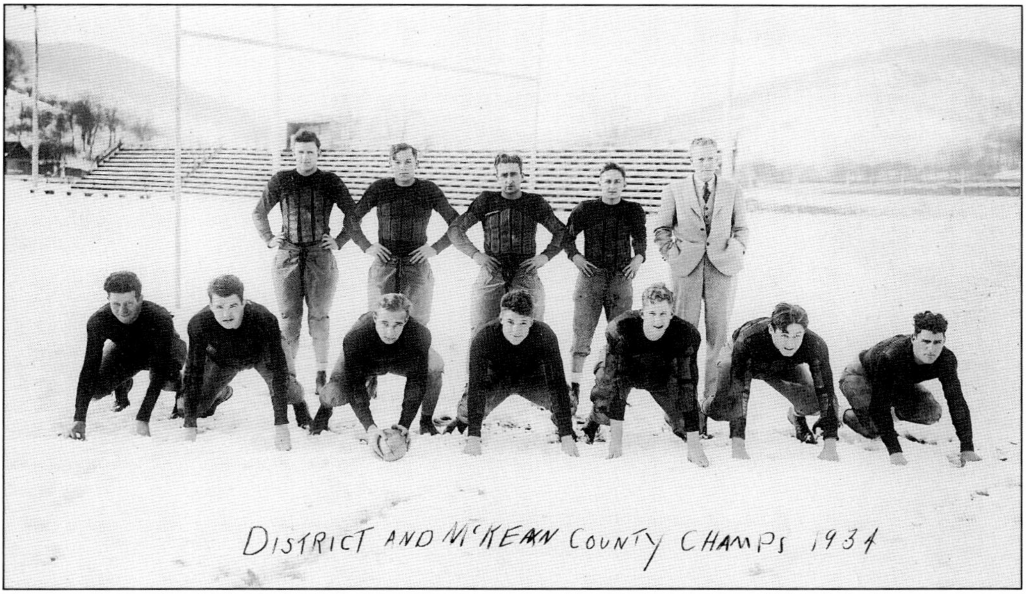

DISTRICT AND McKEAN COUNTY CHAMPS, 1934. A young coach Bob Pflug (just 24 years old) took Bradford High School to an undefeated and untied championship that year. From left to right are as follows: (kneeling) Herbert Baxter, Leo Lyons, Jack Taylor, Blair Phillips, James Nuzzo, James Giest, and Izzy Goodman; (standing) Lawrence Peace, Sam Sylvester, Joe Bizzaro, Homer August, and coach Bob Pflug. Pflug later coached at Princeton University.

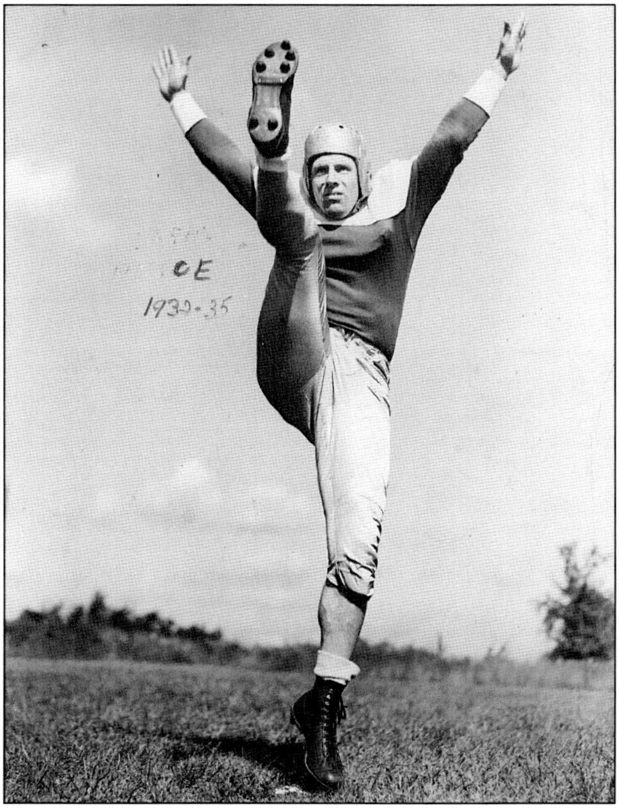

LARRY PEACE, 1934. Co-Captain of the football team, he graduated from Bradford High School in 1936 and attended the University of Pittsburgh.

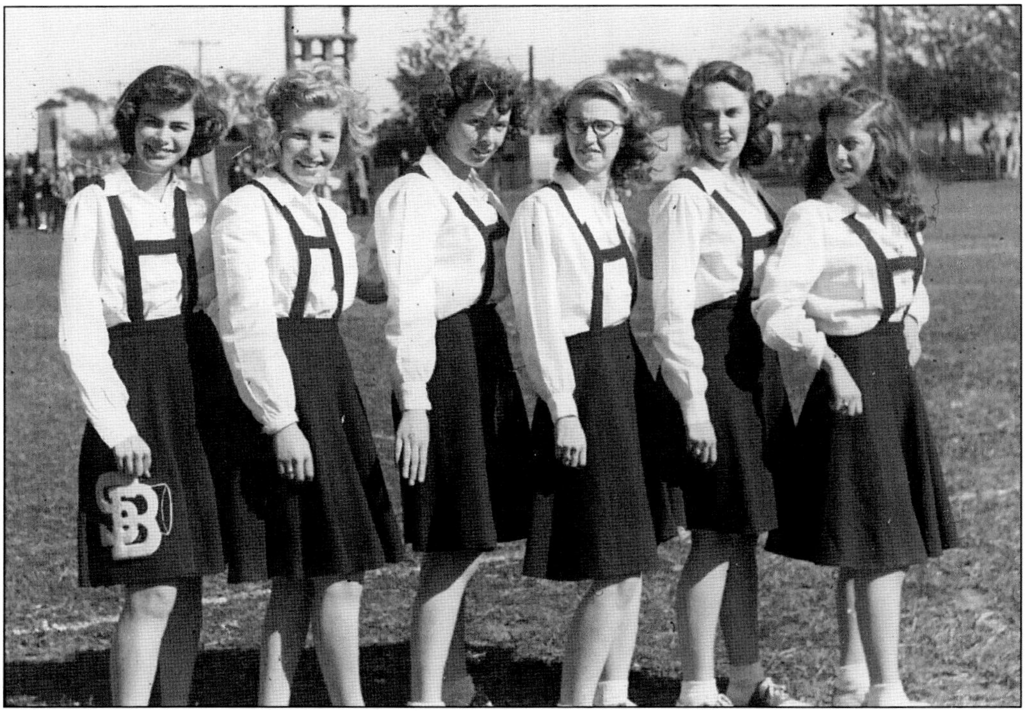

St. Bernard's Cheerleaders, 1948. These girls were the spirit of the Ramblers. Listed from left to right are Martha Whelan, Marjorie Borman, Joan Higie, Barbara Hoop, Joan Shillinger, and Gloria Luciano.

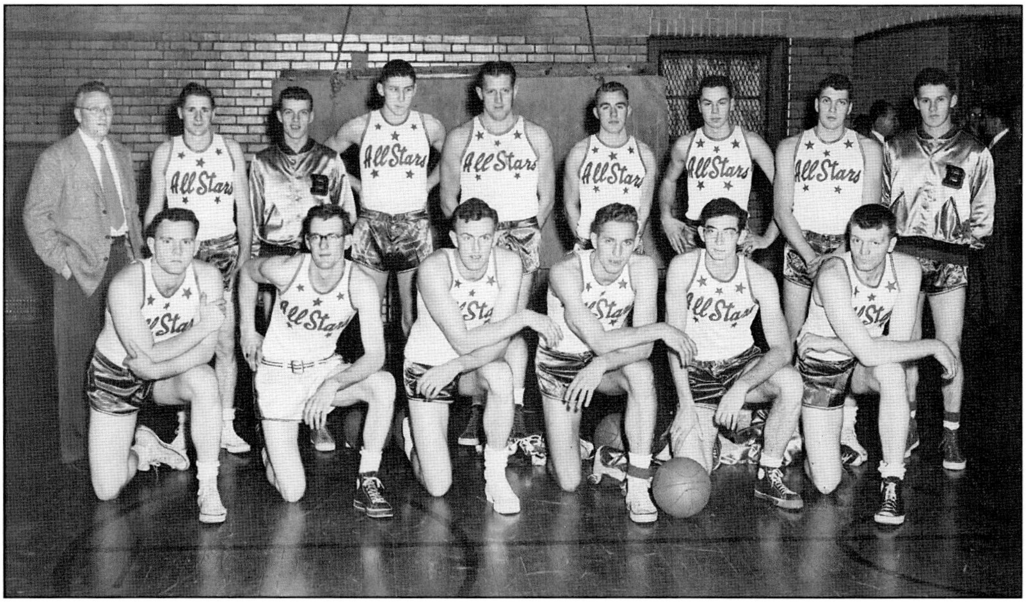

First Annual Polio Benefit Basketball Game, Dec. 23, 1952. Many efforts to combat polio in the days before the Salk vaccine were undertaken. Here, a basketball game sponsored by the *Bradford Journal* was held at School Street Junior High School to raise $1,200 to purchase physiotherapy equipment for the Bradford Hospital. The score? St. Bona—51; Bradford All Stars—49.

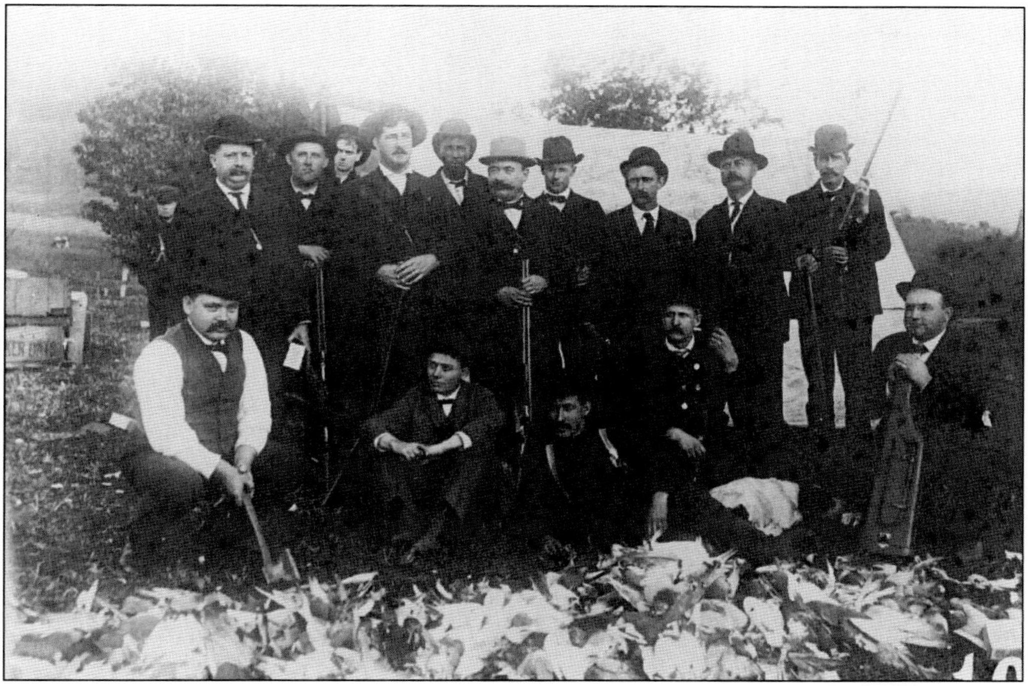

Pigeon Shoot, c. 1883. Company C, 16th Regiment Sharp Shooters, gather for a pigeon shoot near Bradford. The dead pigeons at their feet may have been passenger pigeons, which were still nesting in this area until the late 1880s.

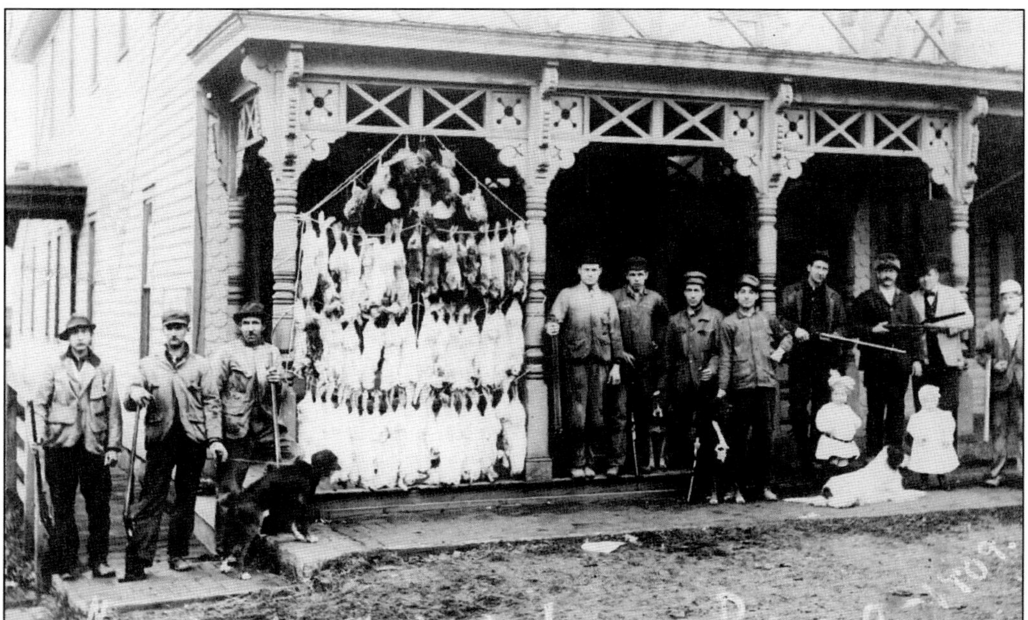

Thanksgiving Day Shoot, November 25, 1909. This hotel in Lewis Run ran a rabbit hunting competition that year, and from the numerous snowshoe hares hanging off the porch, it was successful. The little girls are Irene Cooney, daughter of the hotel owner, and Clara Cannon.

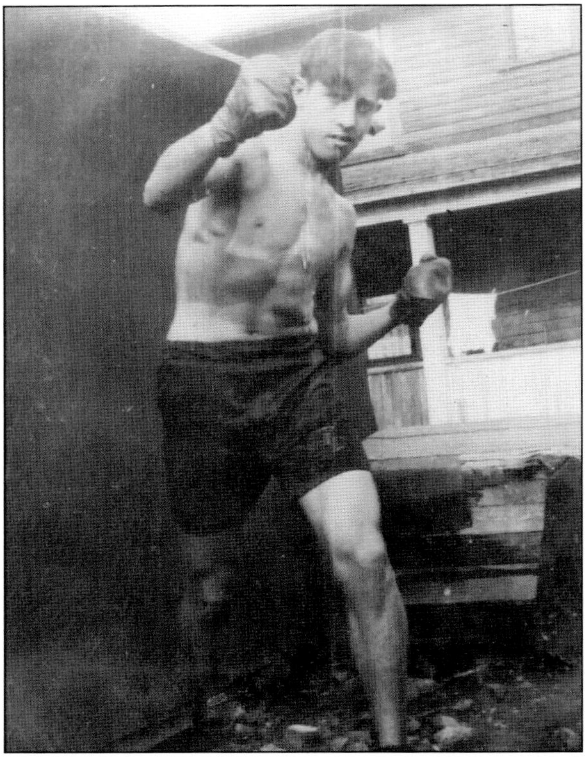

THE PATENT LEATHER KID—TOMMY DARCY, 1926. His ringside name was "The Patent Leather Kid." Tommy Darcy, whose real name is Cardemone, was one of Bradford's young pugilists in the 1920s. He fought in 28 fights; he won 26, lost 2, and was knocked out once. He is seen here at the age of 16. Today he owns Tommy's Barbershop on Mechanic Street.

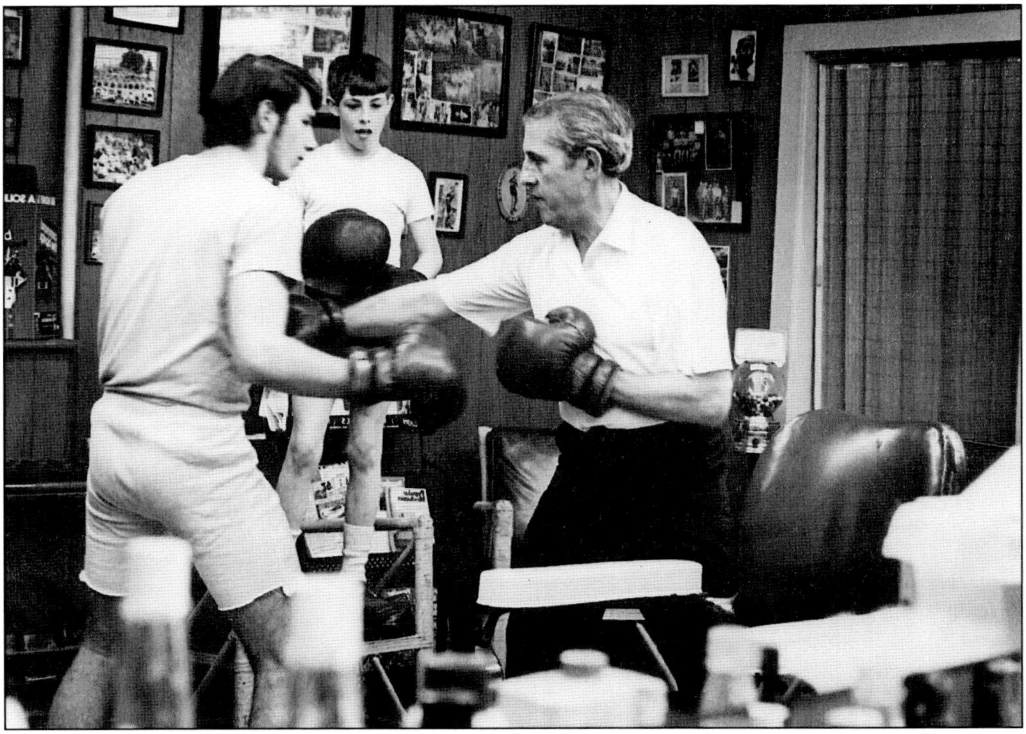

SHOWING 'EM HOW, c. 1970s. Years later, Tommy Cardemone demonstrates his talent to a young customer.

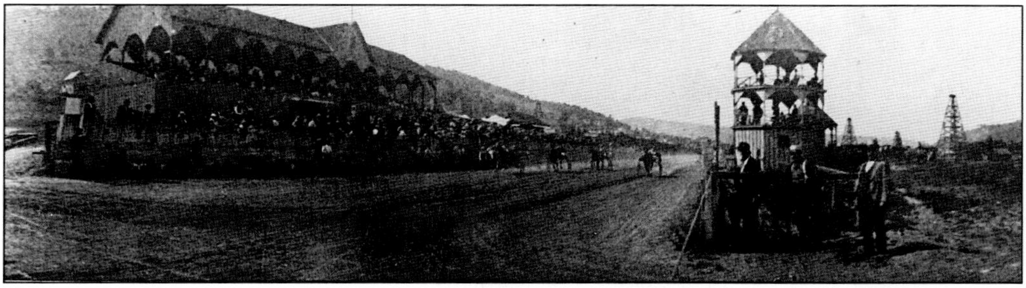

The Driving Park, c. 1880. Later it would become a ball field, and still later the site of the Zippo Manufacturing Plant, but it began as a race track, featuring some of the finest harness racing found on the circuit. Located at the end of Race Street, the Driving Park was in existence as early as 1880 and continued on into this century.

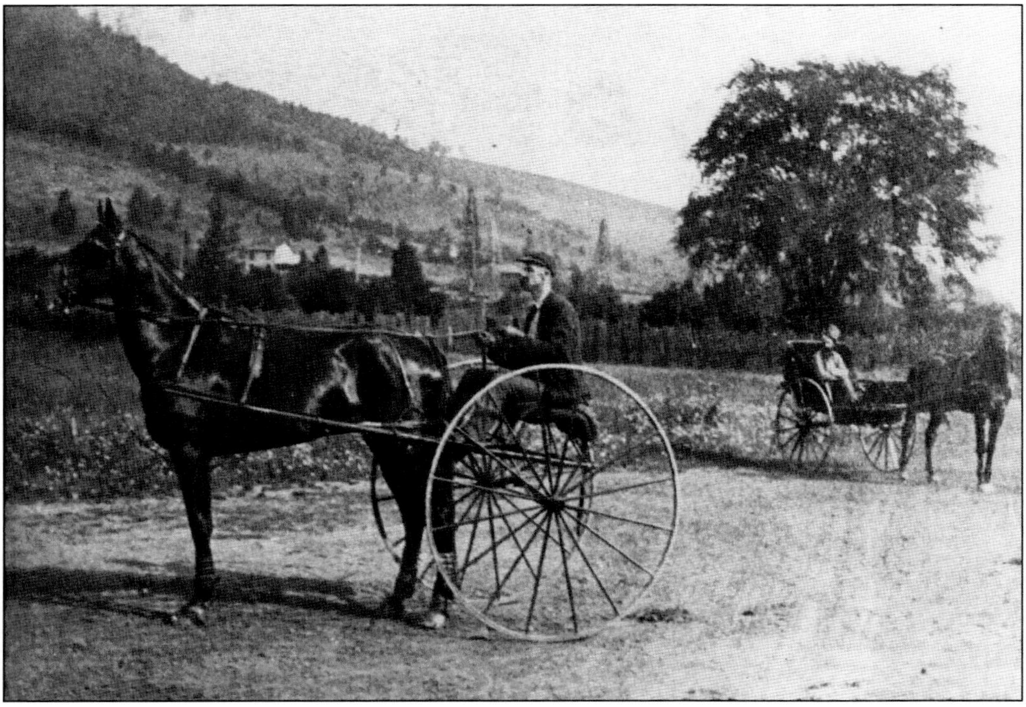

Horses on the Track, c. 1885. On race day, over 30 horses would compete in three heats to determine the winner. Race season lasted from July through late August.

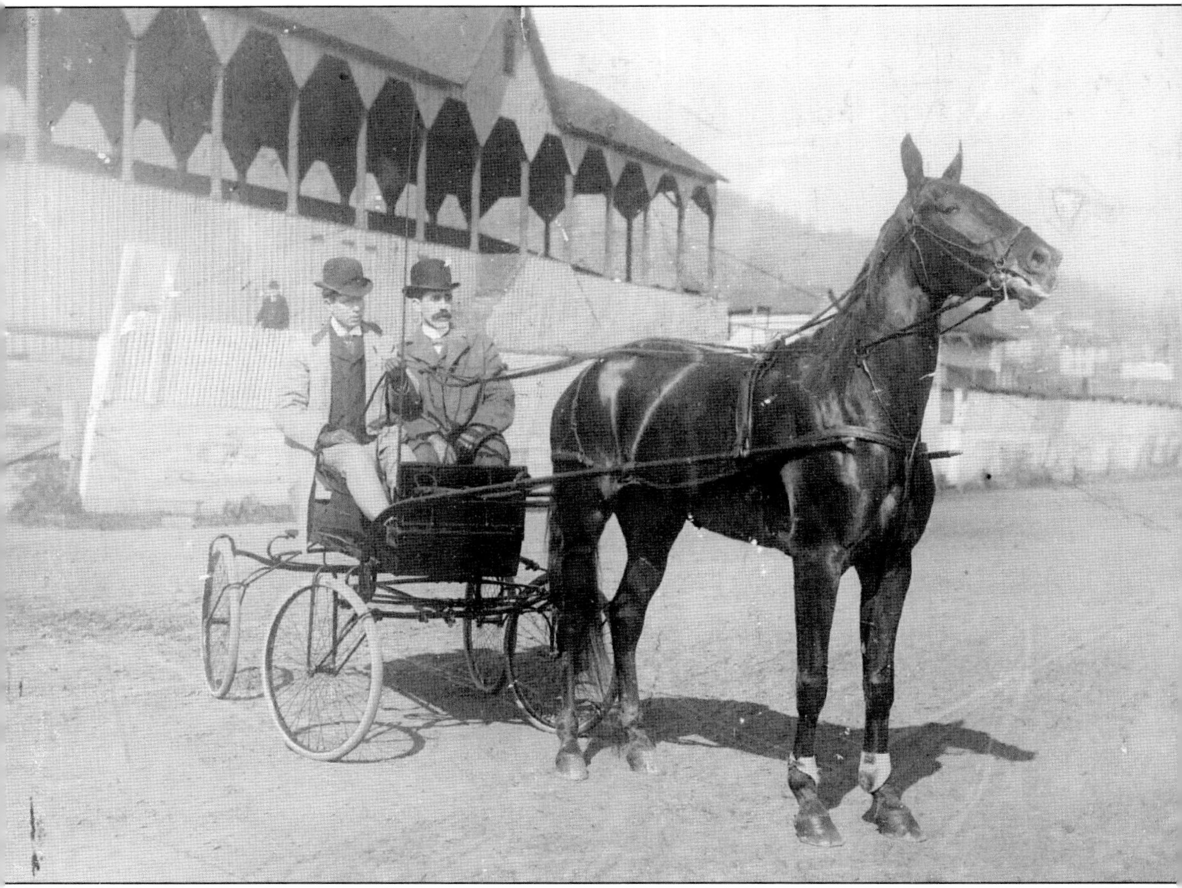

DAVID PHILLIPS AND A.J. SWATHERS AT THE DRIVING PARK, SUMMER 1898. Phillips (at left), a wealthy oil producer, was fond of harness racing, and was one of the original directors of the Bradford Driving Park Association. Here he is seen with his pacer, Miss Jennings. After developing tuberculosis, he traveled to Colorado in hopes of a cure, but died there in 1903, at the age of 28. He was survived by his widow, Bey, and two-year-old son, D. Harvey Phillips.

Seven

Memories Are Made of This

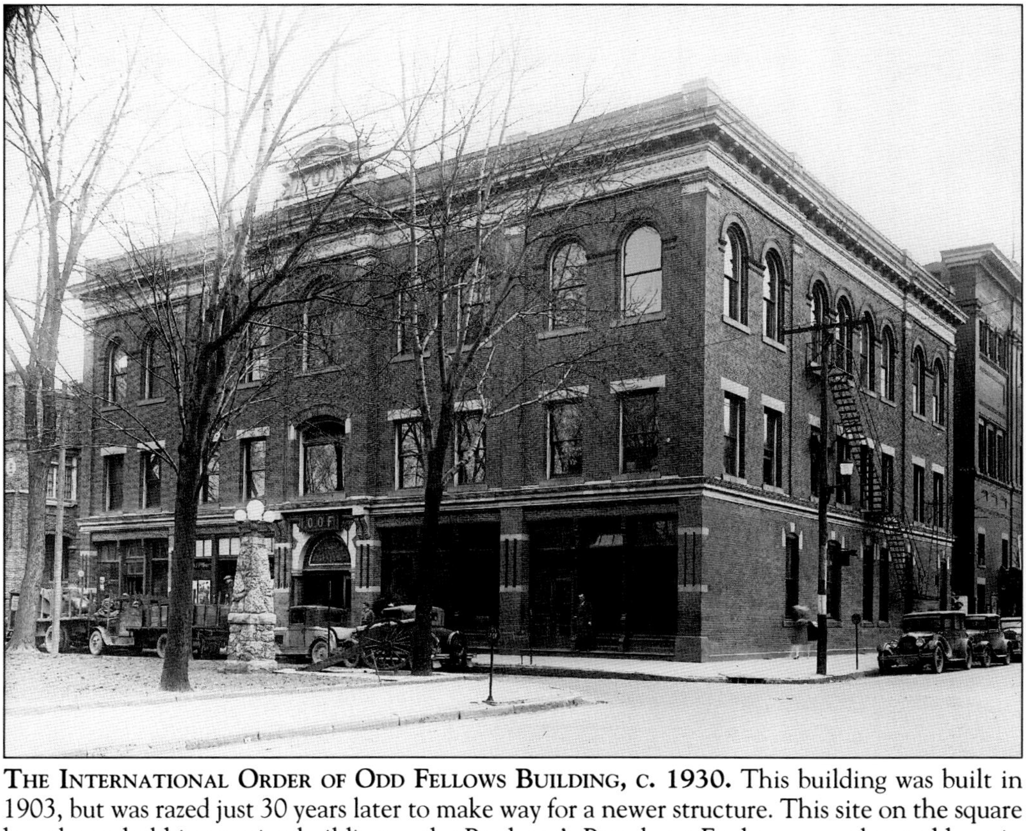

The International Order of Odd Fellows Building, c. 1930. This building was built in 1903, but was razed just 30 years later to make way for a newer structure. This site on the square has always held impressive buildings—the Producer's Petroleum Exchange was located here in the late 1890s (but burned in 1902).

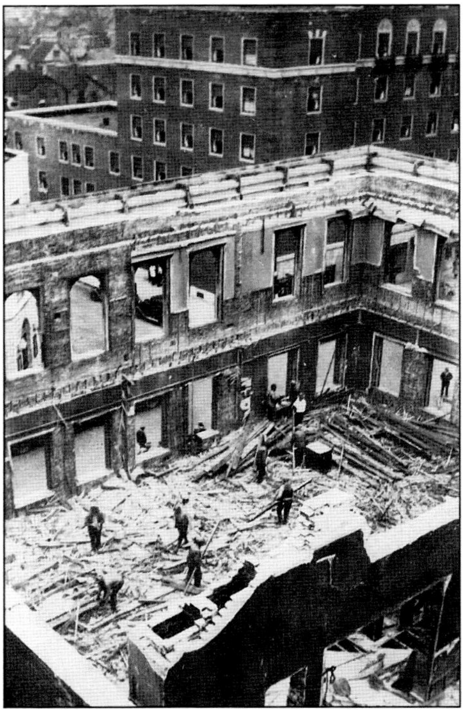

Undergoing Demolition, 1931. The interior of the building was gutted first, then the walls were brought down. The Emery Hotel can be seen in the upper right of the picture.

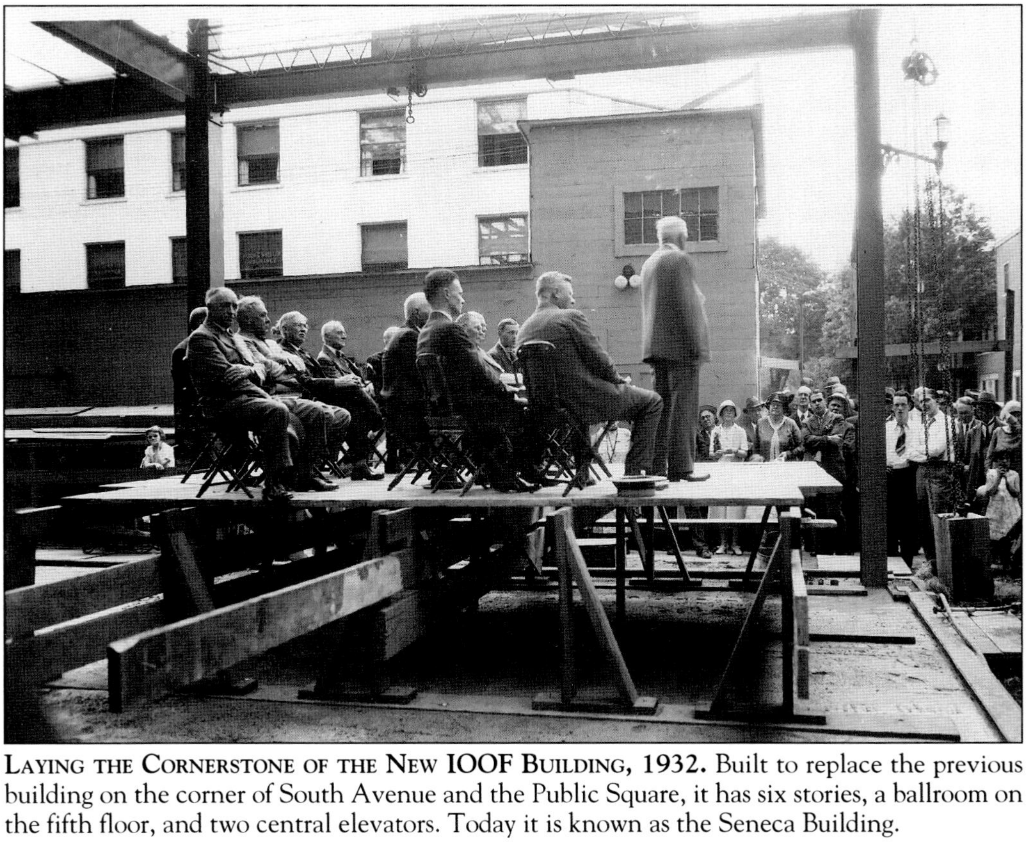

Laying the Cornerstone of the New IOOF Building, 1932. Built to replace the previous building on the corner of South Avenue and the Public Square, it has six stories, a ballroom on the fifth floor, and two central elevators. Today it is known as the Seneca Building.

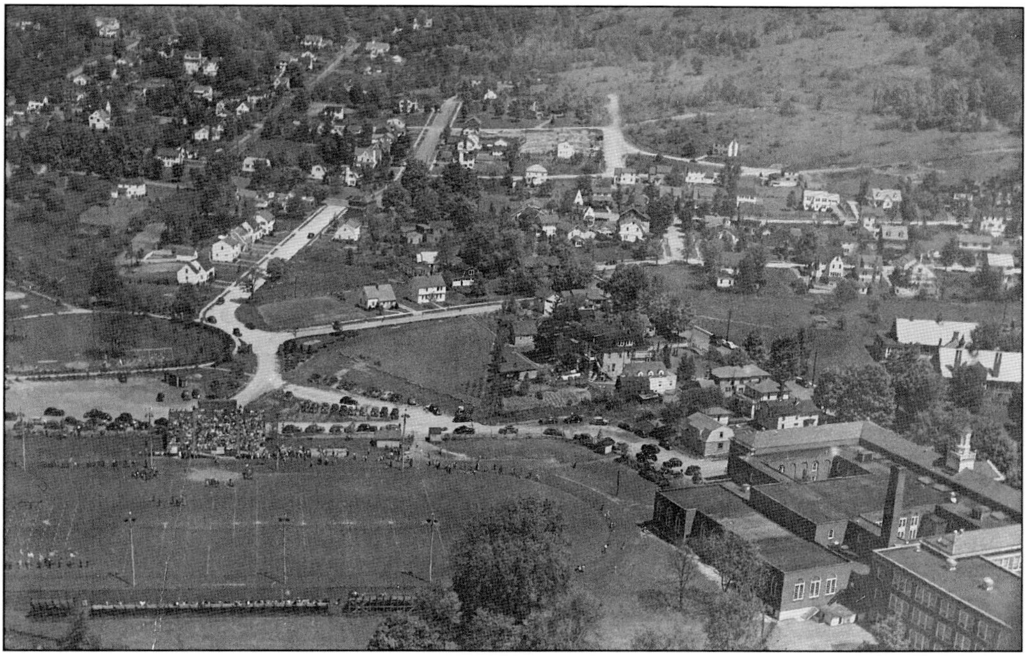

Bradford High School, c. 1930s. This aerial view of the high school shows the new football field and track. Calahan Park, located adjacent to the parking lot, was built in the 1930s.

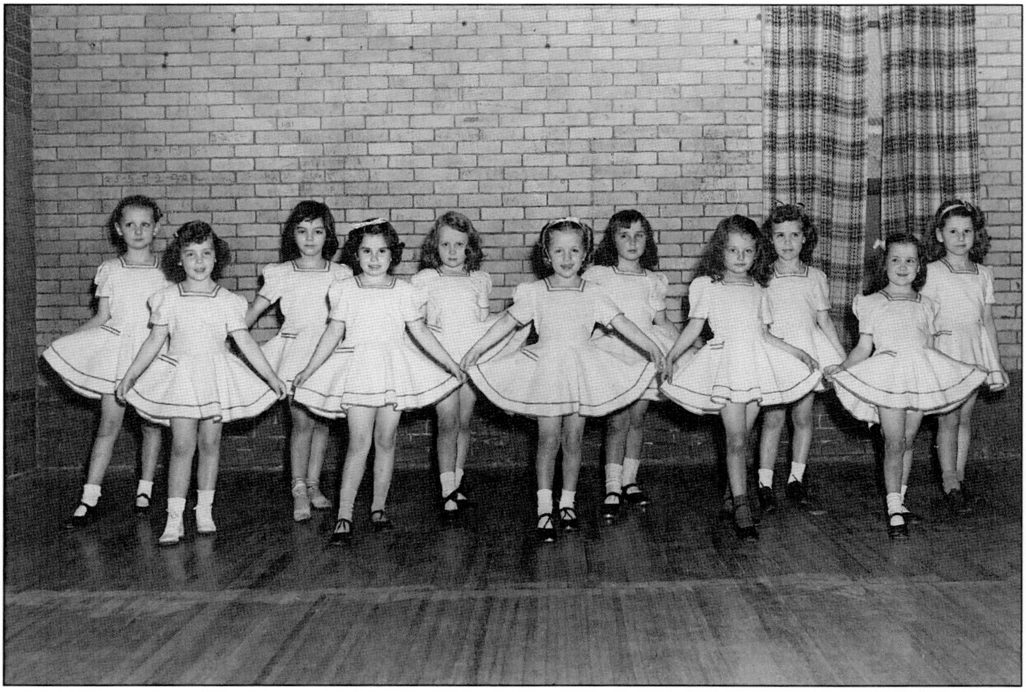

Dance Lessons, c. 1941. Hundreds of children learned to dance at Kreinson's dance class, held from 1932 to 1943 in the basement (the Southern Room) of the old Terminal Building. The School of Dance offered tap, ballet, acrobatic, modern, and ballroom dancing. A musical and dance show was held yearly to showcase the students.

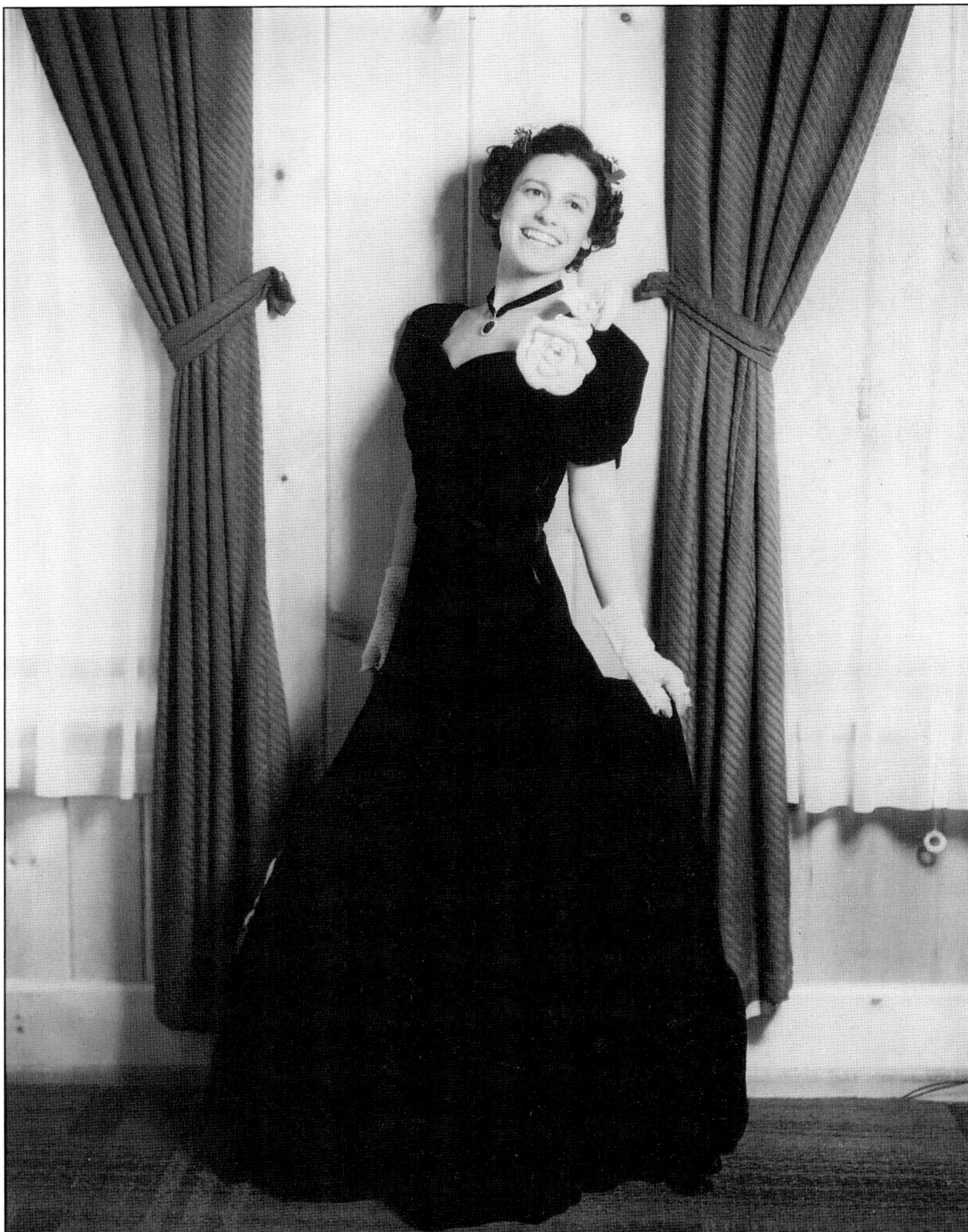

Miriam Kreinson, c. 1930. Kreinson, a Bradford native who had attended some of New York's prominent dance schools, returned in the 1930s to open a dance studio in the city. Dance lessons were available to "children, adults and business girls, as well as boys and young men." Very successful, her dance studio remained in existence until the mid-1940s. Today Miriam Kreinson lives in Las Vegas.

Bradford's Finest, 1936. Lyle Arthur "Art" Dauer was a patrolman on the Bradford Police force. In 1936, all patrolmen earned $145 each month.

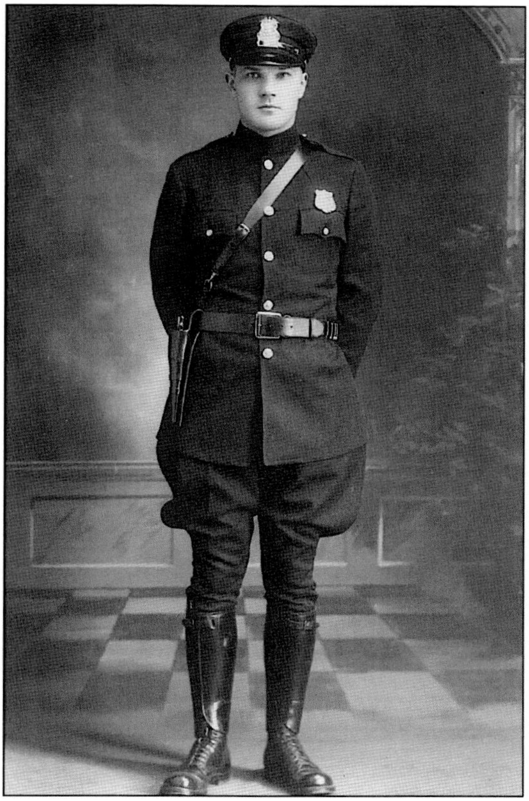

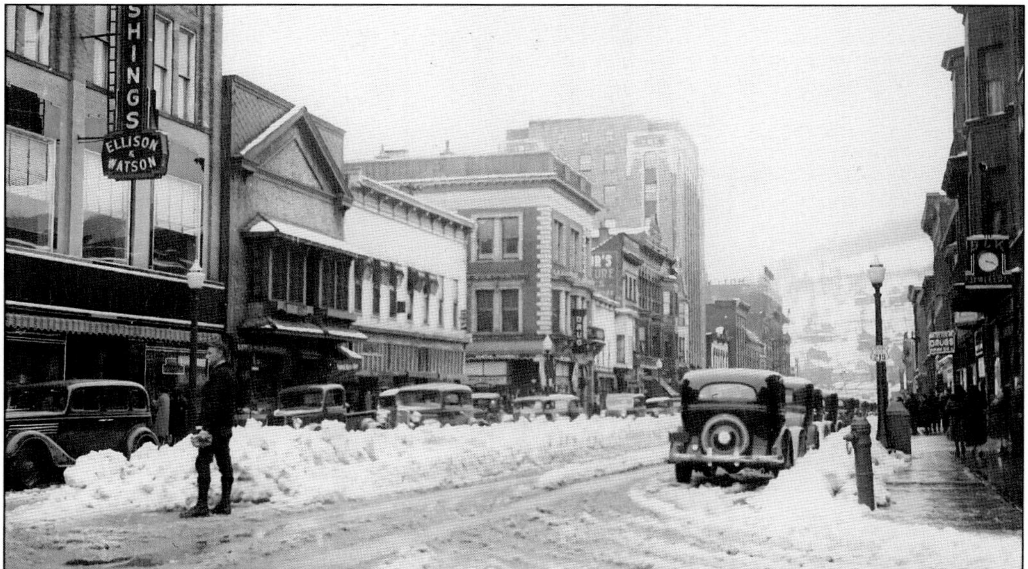

Snow on Main Street, c. 1934. After a heavy snowfall, the snow would be piled in the middle of the street where later it would be removed.

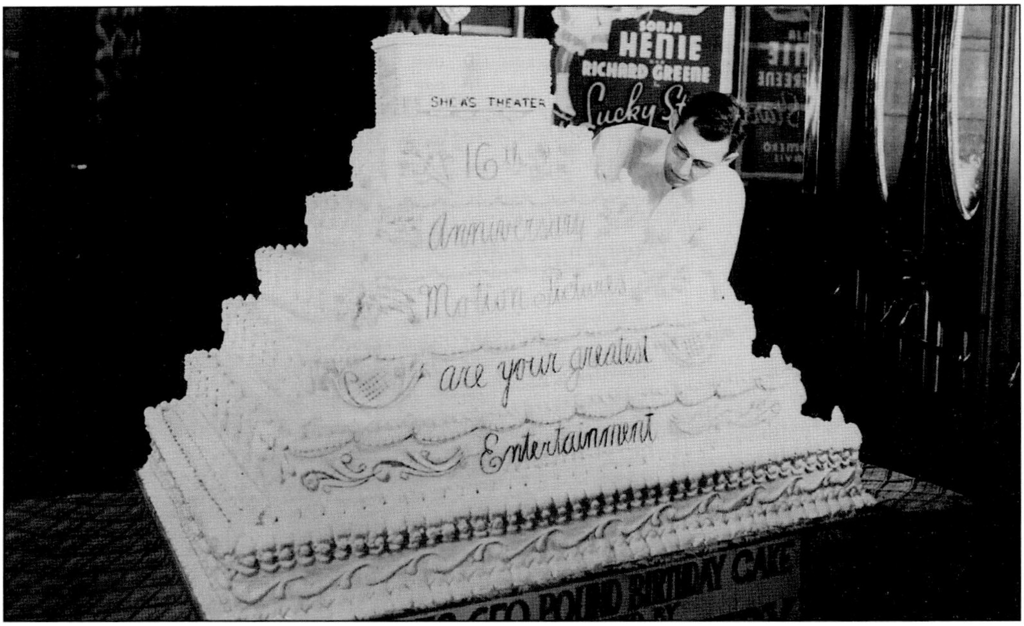

THE SHEA'S THEATER BIRTHDAY CAKE, 1937. In 1921, the Bradford Theater on South Avenue changed owners, becoming part of the Shea Theater line of Buffalo, New York. This cake commemorates its 16th anniversary. Weighing 650 pounds, it was baked and decorated by Ellsworth and Fred Johnson at the Davis Bakery on Mechanic Street. Here, Fred Johnson puts finishing touches on the cake at the theater.

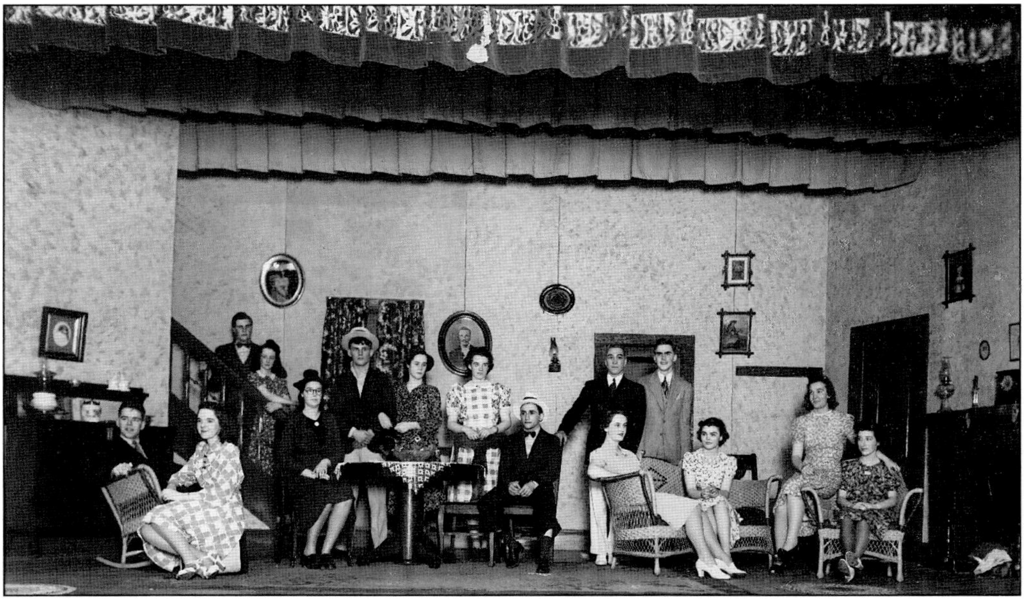

ST. BERNARD'S CLASS PLAY, MAY 17, 1940. A three-act comedy, *New Fires*, was presented by the senior class of St. Bernard's, and received good reviews. Shown here is the cast. Listed from left to right are as follows: (sitting) Walter "Pete" Blaisdell, Peggy Holleran, Jean O'Brien, Francis Gigliotti, Marie Butler, Mary Rita Collins, Eve Janowicz, and Geraldine Rizutti; (standing) Jim White, Joanne Colligan, Francis Barry, Patricia Kopp, Mary Hannon, Dan Rossi, and Tom Parrot.

The Moose Club, c. 1940. Built in 1926, it caught fire at 4:23 a.m. on March 11, 1957, burning for eight hours. The third floor, which had held the largest ballroom in the city, was damaged beyond repair, and was removed during renovation after the fire. The building still stands today on Pine Street.

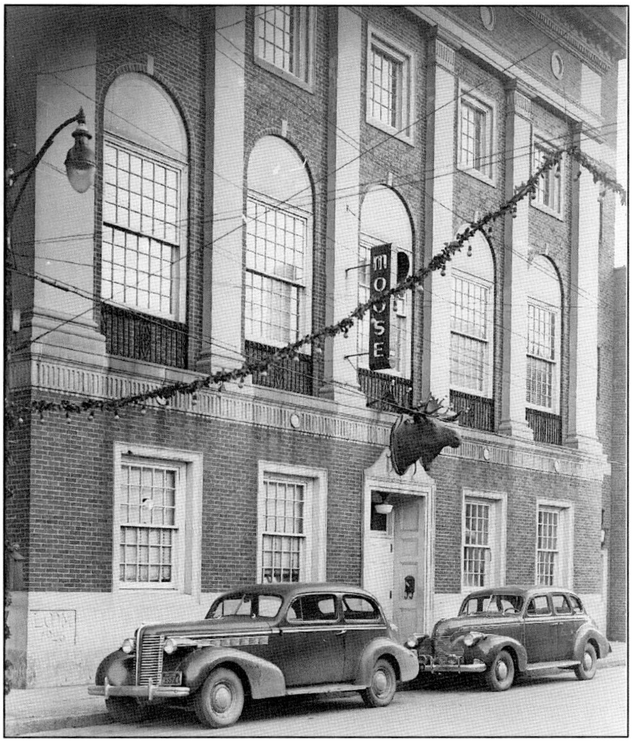

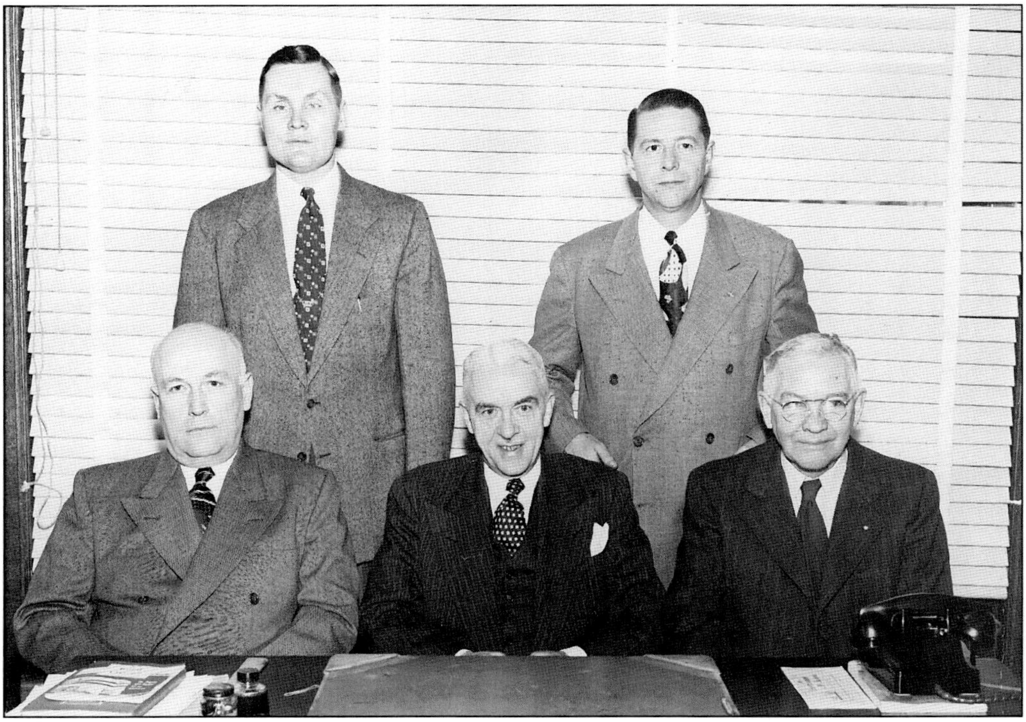

The City Council, c. 1942. These men formed the city government in the early 1940s. Listed from left to right are as follows: (front row) Thomas Coneely, Mayor Hugh Ryan, and Al Mulhaupt; (back row) James Butterworth and Guy Hughey.

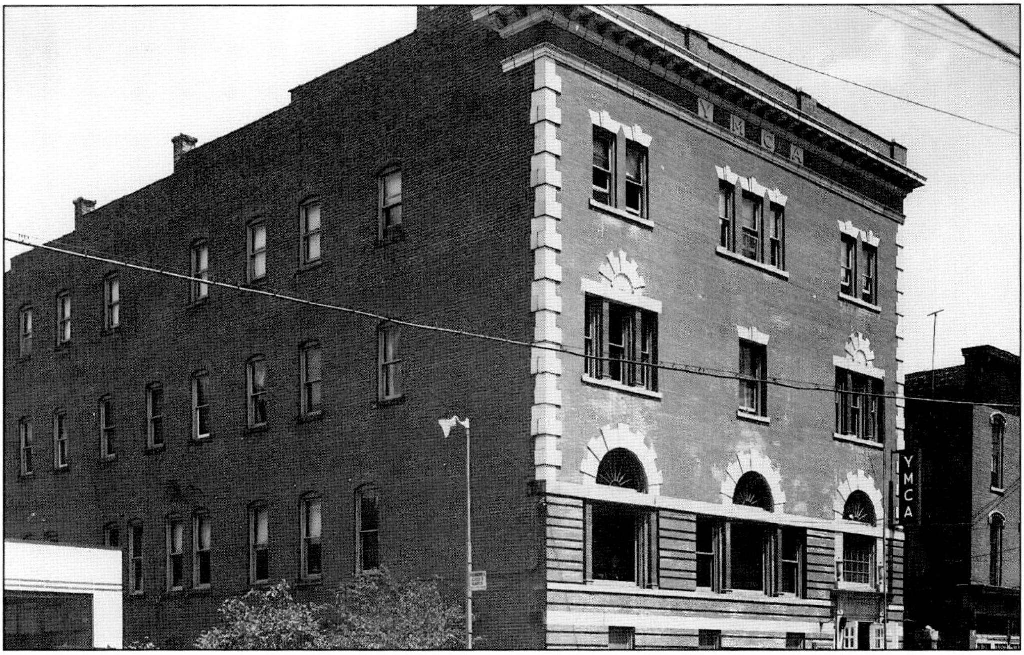

The YMCA, c. 1940. Dedicated June 21, 1908, this is the second building to serve as the YMCA. It contained a reception area, office, gymnasium, 14 resident rooms, Turkish baths, bowling alleys, a game room, parlor, auditorium, kitchen, and dining room; membership stood at 134 adults and 65 junior members. A swimming pool was added in 1927. This building was razed and replaced with the current YMCA in 1967.

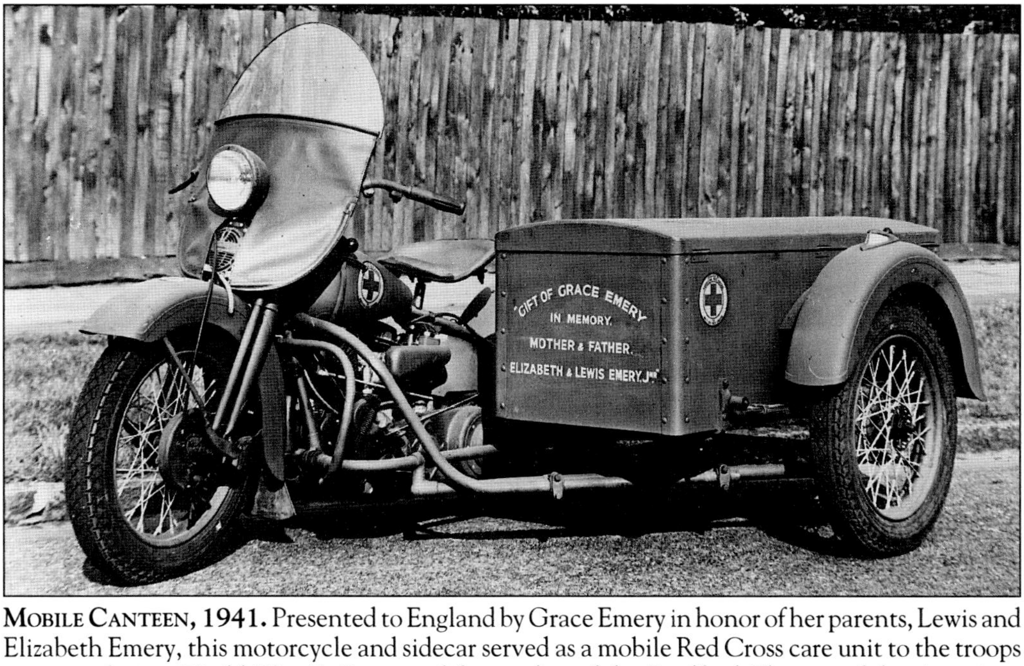

Mobile Canteen, 1941. Presented to England by Grace Emery in honor of her parents, Lewis and Elizabeth Emery, this motorcycle and sidecar served as a mobile Red Cross care unit to the troops overseas during World War II. Emery, a life member of the Bradford Chapter of the American Red Cross, was a generous philanthropist and supported many Bradford organizations.

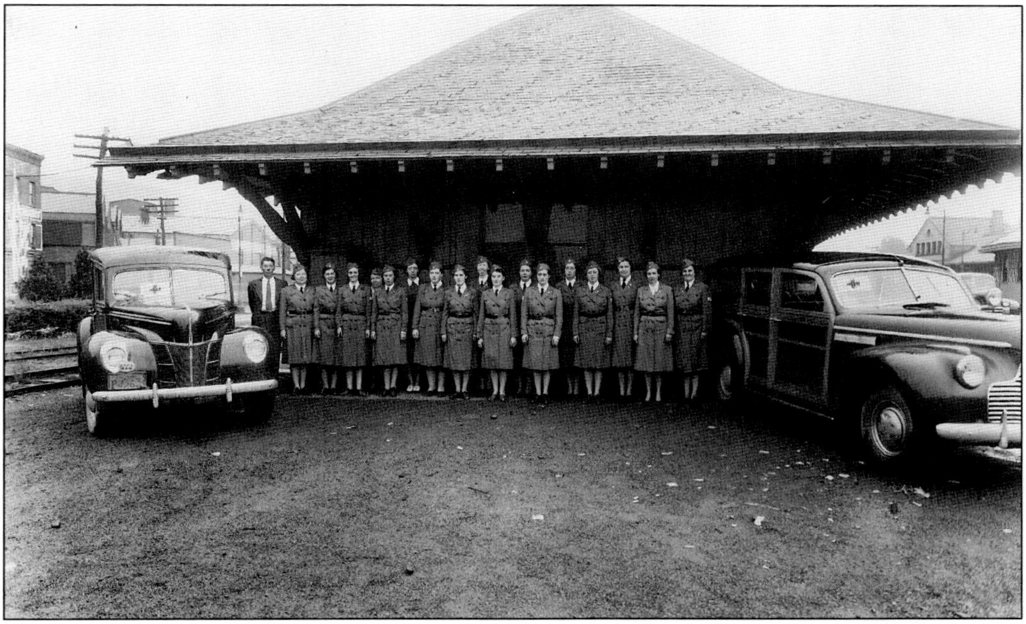

The Bradford Chapter of the American Red Cross, 1943. Formed in April 1917, the Red Cross was ready to serve when needed. These women are part of the Motor Unit, and were trained to drive ambulances and emergency vehicles. Here they are seen standing in front of the Erie station at the foot of Main Street.

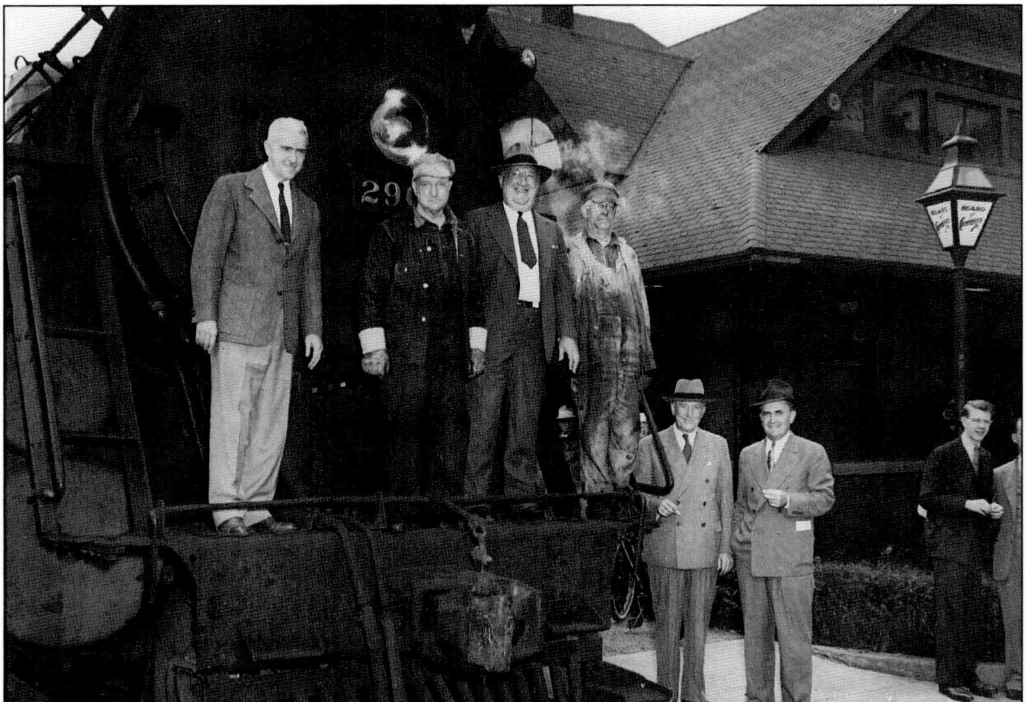

The Dresser Train, 1942. Ten cars on the Erie Railroad took all the Dresser employees to Cleveland, to meet with military officials and to show support for the war effort. Here, Mayor Hugh Ryan, left, and others pose for a picture before departure.

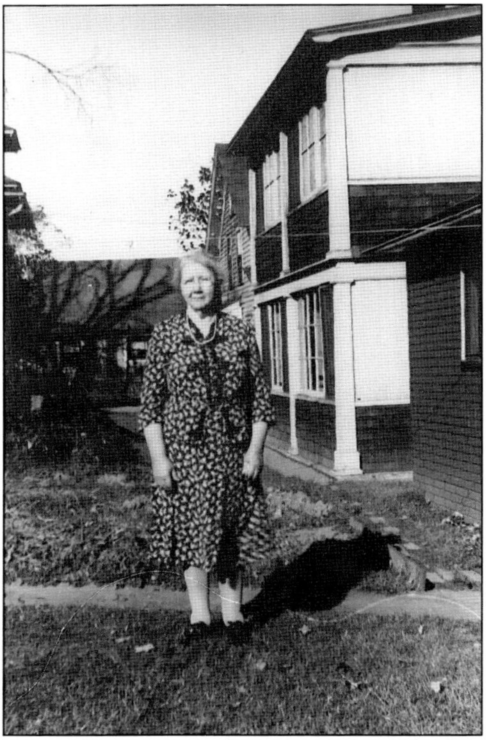

A VICTORY GARDEN, 1942. Like many Bradfordians, Catherine Covley did her part for the war effort by growing a victory garden beside her home on Jefferson Street. Those without garden space could join a community or business-sponsored garden plot—the Kendall Refinery employees, for example, had individual plots for gardens at the Bradford Airport.

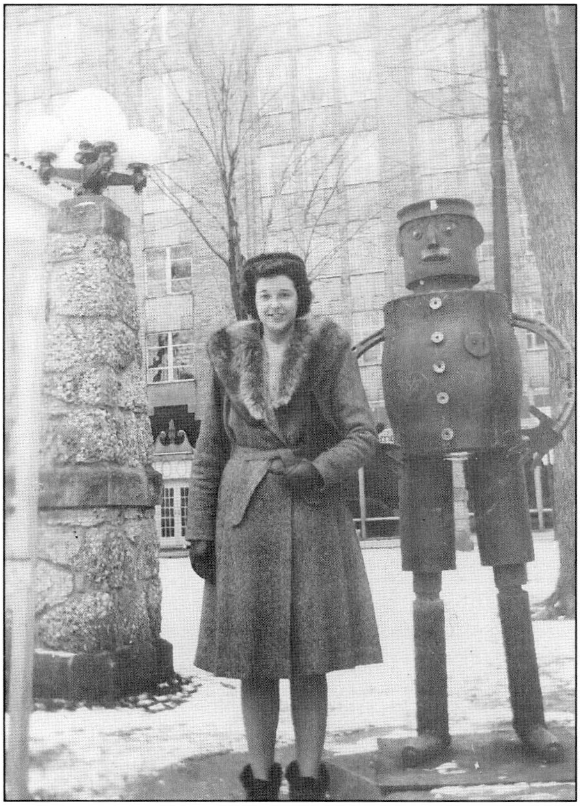

SCRAPMAN IN THE SQUARE, DECEMBER 1943. This "tin man" was erected to promote metal scrap drives during the war and was on display in the Public Square. Many Bradfordians, like Jean O'Brien (shown here), had their picture taken with this man of metal.

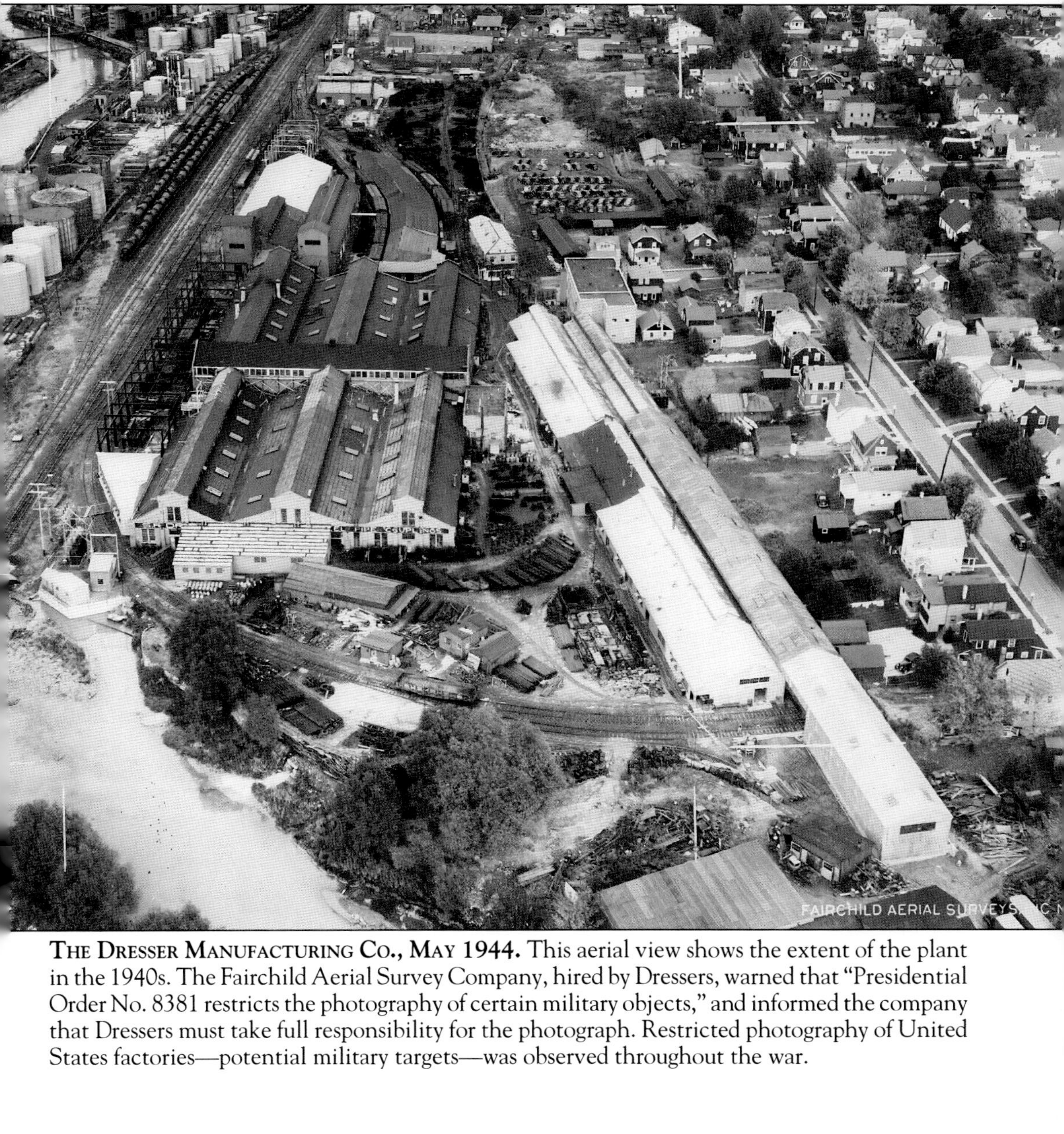

THE DRESSER MANUFACTURING CO., MAY 1944. This aerial view shows the extent of the plant in the 1940s. The Fairchild Aerial Survey Company, hired by Dressers, warned that "Presidential Order No. 8381 restricts the photography of certain military objects," and informed the company that Dressers must take full responsibility for the photograph. Restricted photography of United States factories—potential military targets—was observed throughout the war.

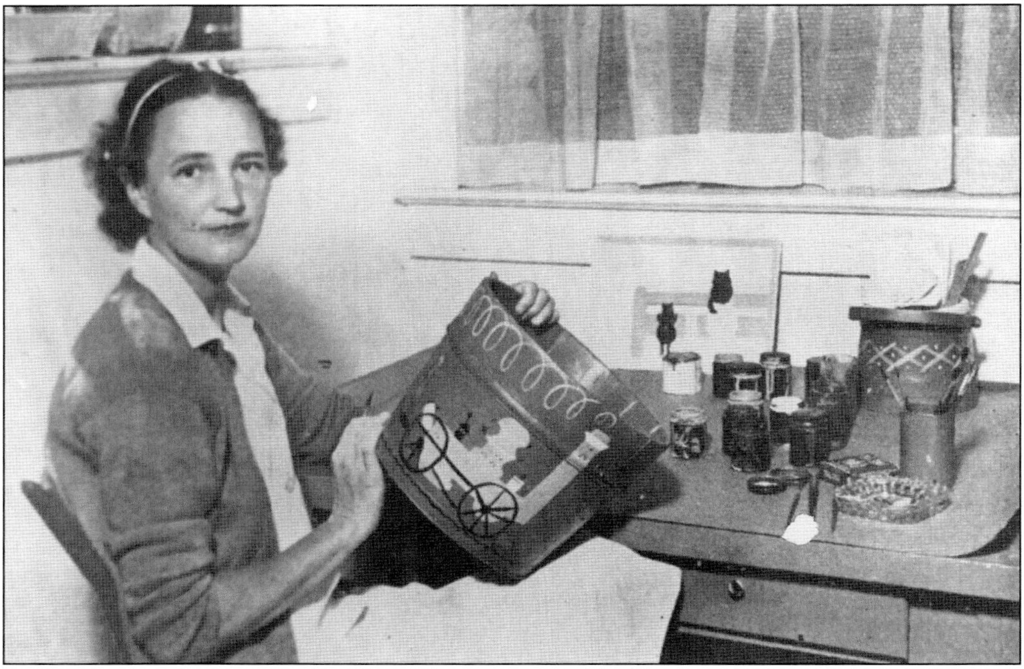

HELEN HUME, 1945. With little more than an old butter tub, a knack for painting, and Vic Moran as the publicity man, Helen Hume built a business that thrived in Bradford for nearly 40 years. She sold the business in 1985, and retired to the home of her son in Wisconsin, dying there in 1993 at the age of 88.

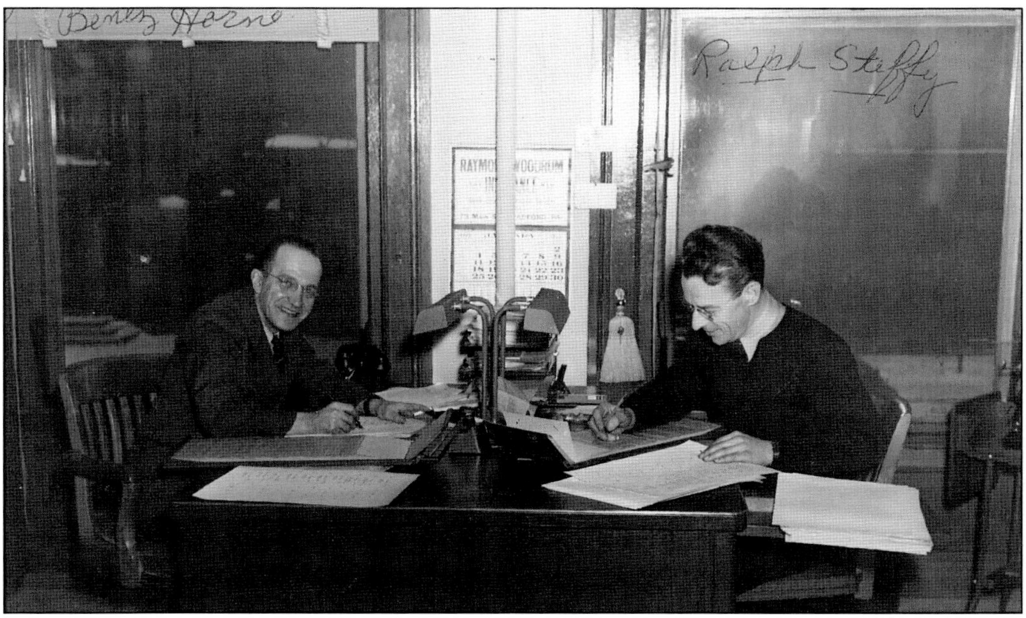

BENTZ HORNE AND RALPH STEFFY, 1943. Both men have been surprised by Chief Edmunds of the Bradford Police Department, testing out the department's new "special speed" camera. Horne, at left, was the assistant city treasurer, and is the father of well-known opera star Marilyn Horne. Bentz Horne died in 1956, at the age of 49.

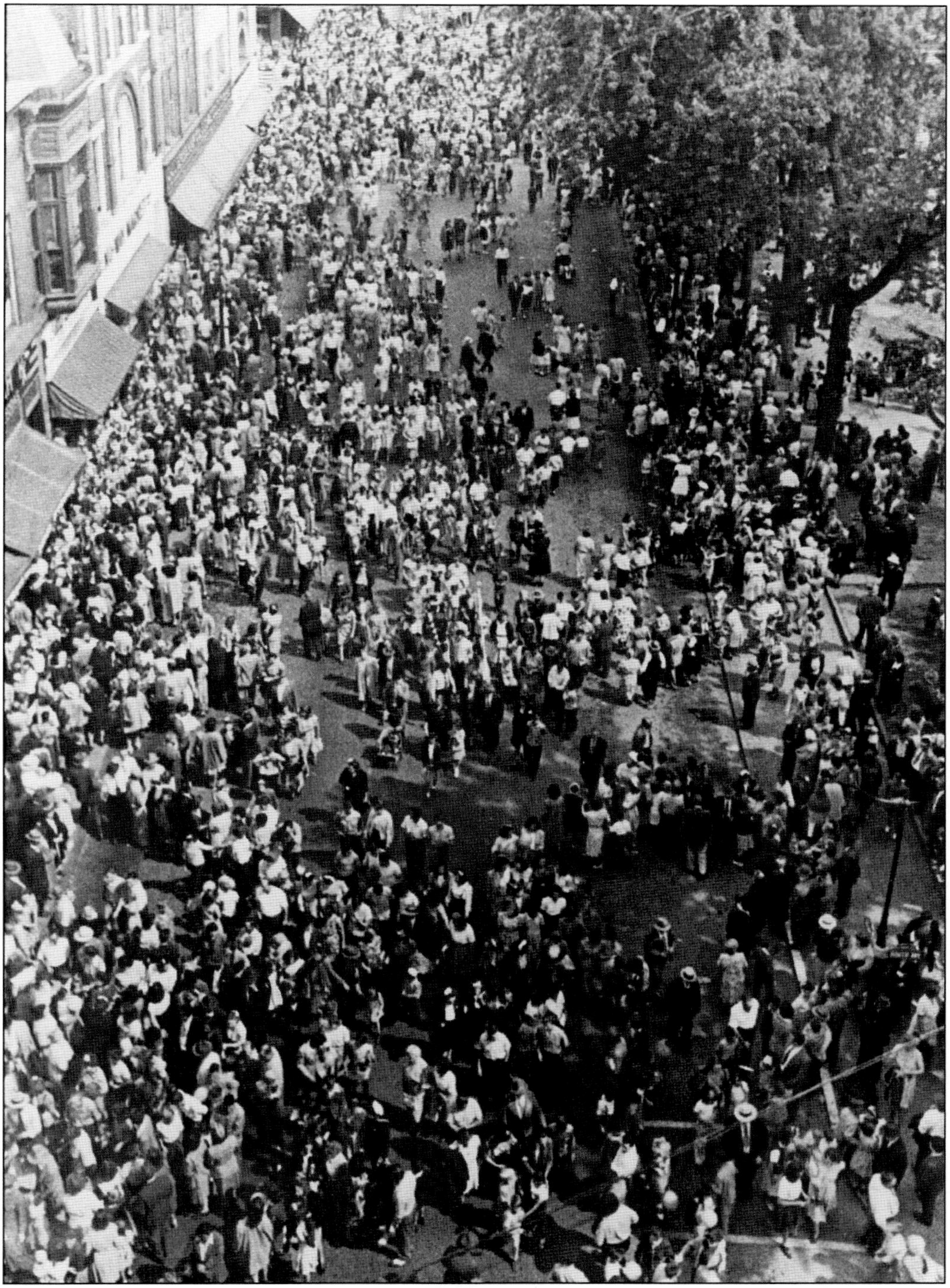

BRADFORD CELEBRATES VJ DAY, SEPT. 3, 1945. Although Japan had surrendered on August 15, the official "VJ" Day was held on Labor Day. Bradford celebrated with a parade, festival, and fireworks. The *Bradford Era* noted that emotions "ran the gamut from gaiety to somber reflection that peace has returned in our time," while Mayor Hugh Ryan declared "The ledger opened at Pearl Harbor has now been balanced and closed."

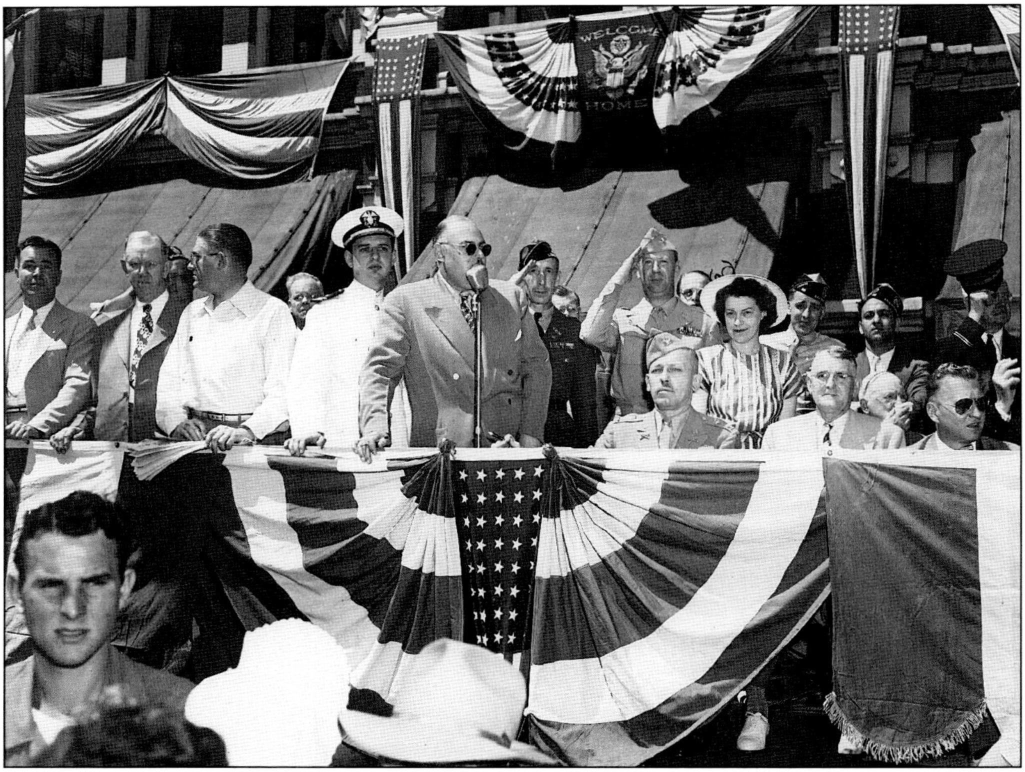

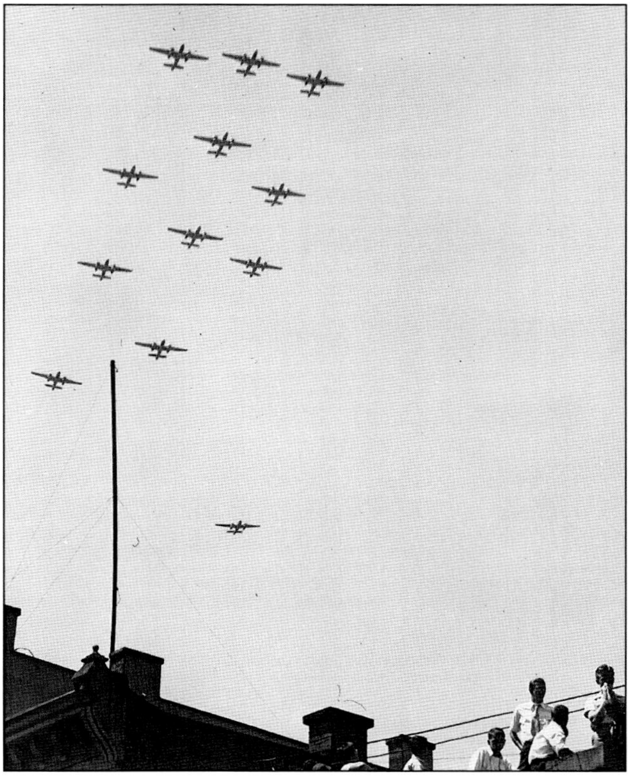

THE REVIEWING STAND, WELCOME HOME PARADE, JULY 4, 1946. Dignitaries and invited guests watched the parade from the reviewing stand near the Bradford National Bank as Parade Marshall James Powell and Brigadier General Fay Upthegrove return the salute of a passing unit. Listed from left to right are Bud Edel, Judge Hubbard, Francis O'Hearn, Navy Lieutenant Jack Still, David Kreinson, Col. Carl Peterson, Mrs. Upthegrove, Glenn Ryan, and John Boylan. Ben Wentworth is in the left foreground.

B-52 BOMBERS OVER BRADFORD, 1946. A featured part of the parade was the fly-by formation of twelve B-52 bombers under the command of Brig. Gen. Fay R. Upthegrove, a former Bradford resident.

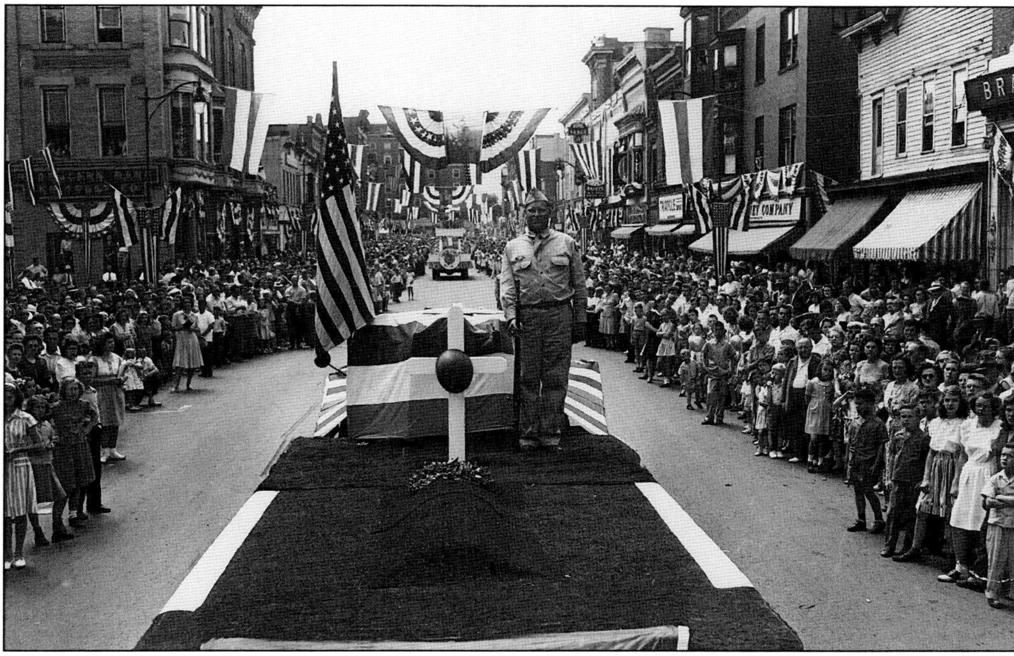

WELCOME BACK HOME. . . AND THANKS, JULY 4, 1946. The war was over, and the largest parade in Bradford's history—over 3 miles long, with 25,000 spectators—was held on July 4, 1946, in honor of the returning veterans. This float, near the end of the parade, honored the graves of unknown soldiers.

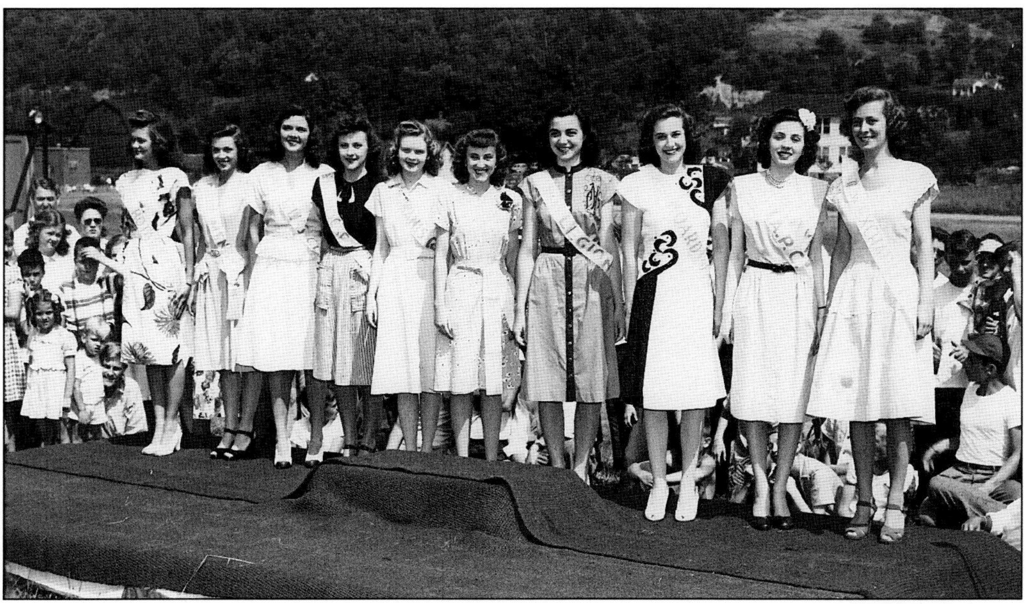

MISS BRADFORD CONTESTANTS, JULY 6, 1946. These girls vied for the title of Miss Bradford on parade day. Listed from left to right are Miss Rotary Club, Patricia Hanes; Miss Y-Men's Club, Marguerite Stengel; Miss Elks, Jean Hokanson; Miss Moose Club, Mary Ann Mecanko; Miss Kiwanis, Winnie Ward; Miss VFW, Patricia Ledden; Miss American Legion, Ruth Ann Podlas; Miss AmVet, Dorothy Rowand; Miss IAPC, Theresa Monago; and Miss Exchange Club, Anna Strand. Dorothy Roward, third from right, was the winner.

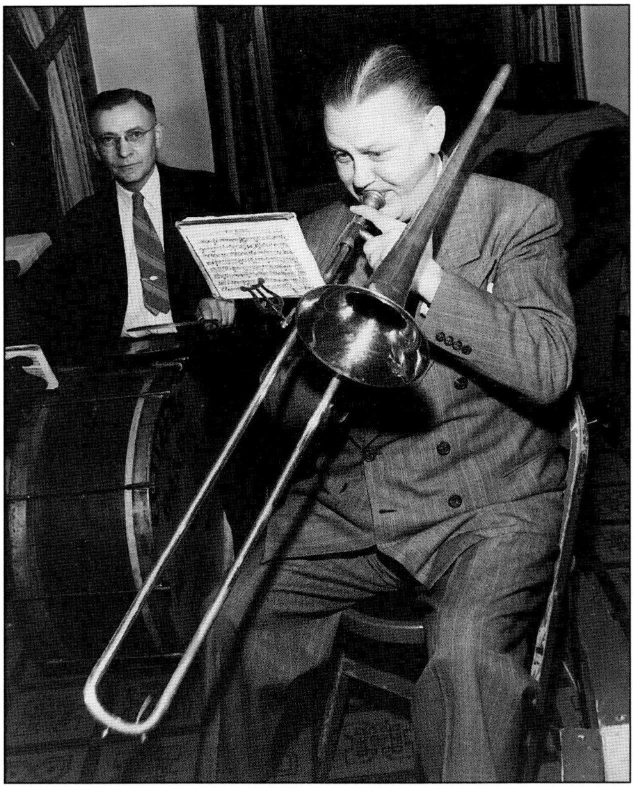

Hoyt Meredith, 1945. Meredith was the owner of the Brook Club, and a member of the Circus of the Saints & Sinners of Bradford. Here, he tries his hand at the trombone during a get-together.

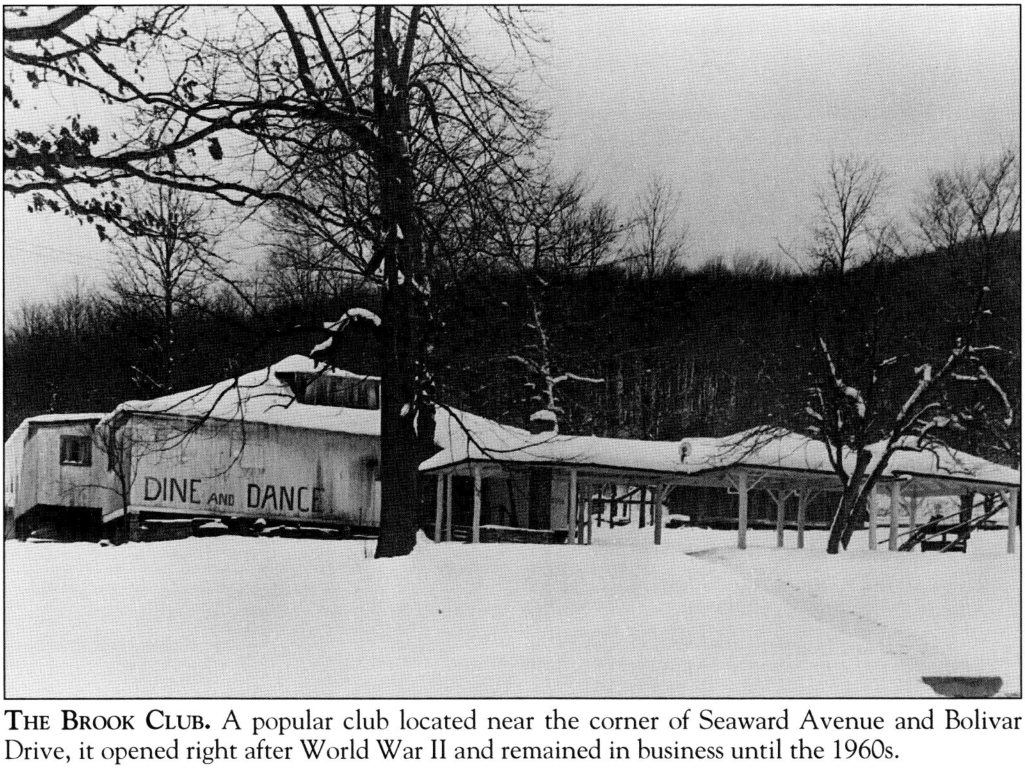

The Brook Club. A popular club located near the corner of Seaward Avenue and Bolivar Drive, it opened right after World War II and remained in business until the 1960s.

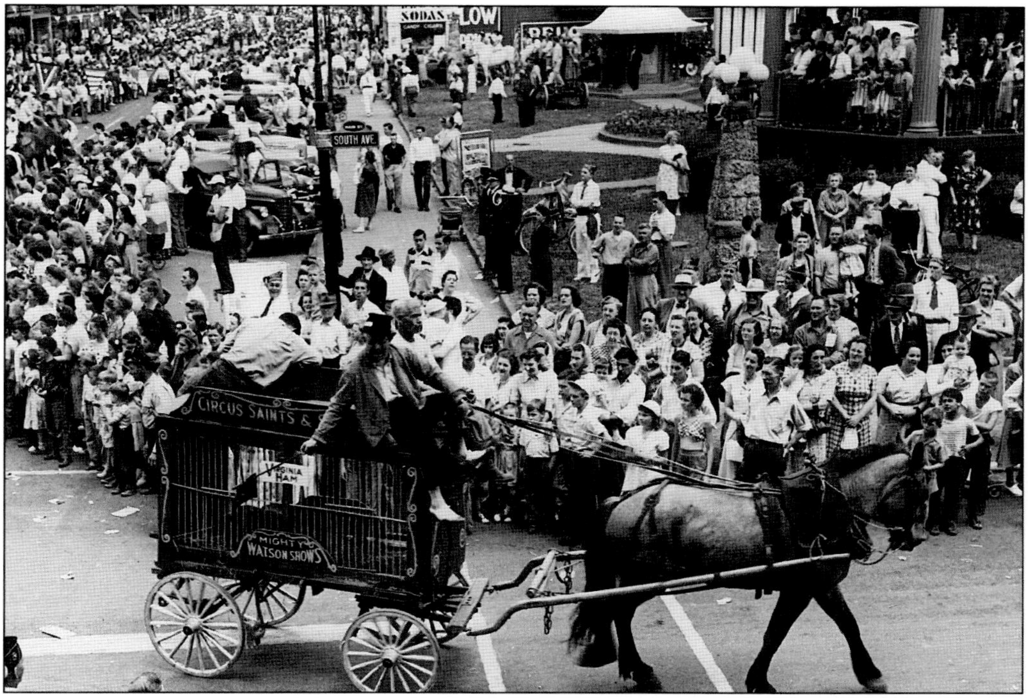

CIRCUS OF THE SAINTS AND SINNERS PARADE, 1949. Members of this unique club always seemed to be having fun. The National Convention came to Bradford in 1949. This photograph shows just a portion of the parade as they come around the square.

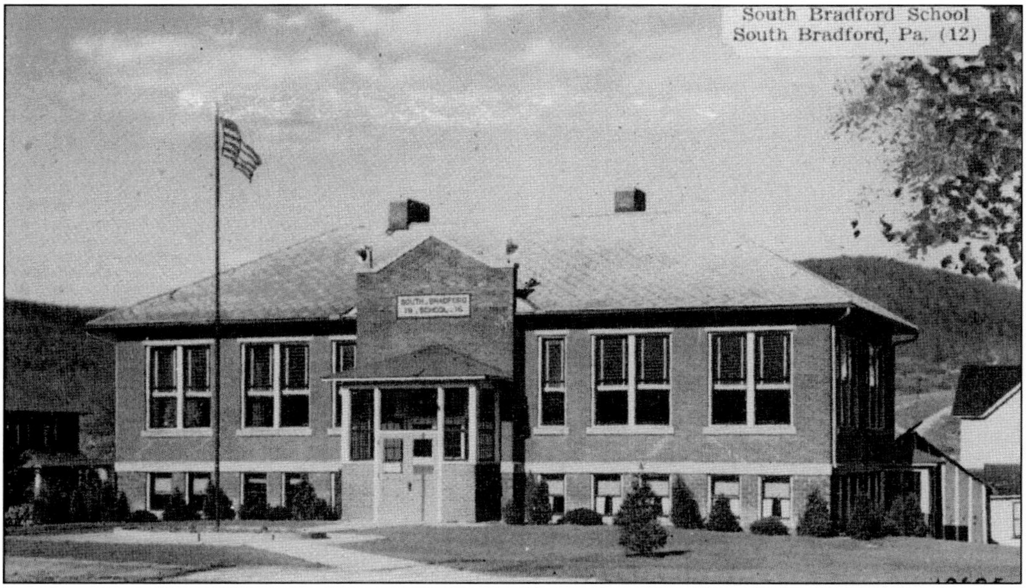

THE SOUTH BRADFORD SCHOOL, C. 1949. Located where the South Bradford Fruit Market now stands, the 34-year-old school was destroyed by fire on January 29, 1950. All 55 children, well rehearsed in fire drill procedure, escaped safely moments before the school exploded into a mass of flames. Hundreds of people raced to the scene, including frantic parents, who heard the news on WESB's radio broadcast. The children were sent to the Custer City School for the remainder of the school term.

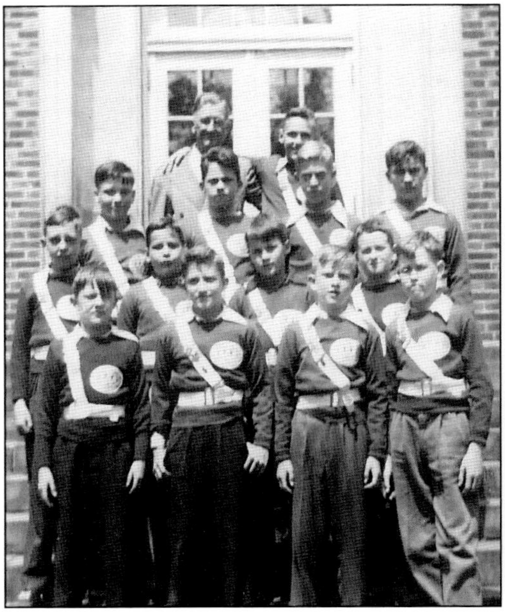

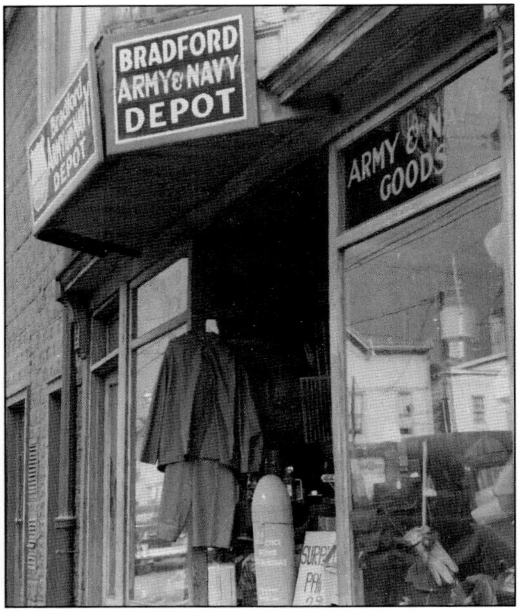

Left: **School Patrol Boys, 1948.** These boys are standing in front of Third Ward School. The man in the rear is Harry Garvin, who organized the McKean County Motor Club (now the AAA) in 1929, and instituted the School Boy Patrols in 1930. Each year the boys were rewarded with a trip to Washington D.C.
Right: **The Army and Navy Depot, c. 1950s.** This store, which sold surplus army and navy supplies, was in operation as early as 1921, and remained in operation for 50 years. Run by Russian-born Robert Galle (1892–1987), it was located at 5 West Washington Street and sold a wide variety of items, including this "practice bomb."

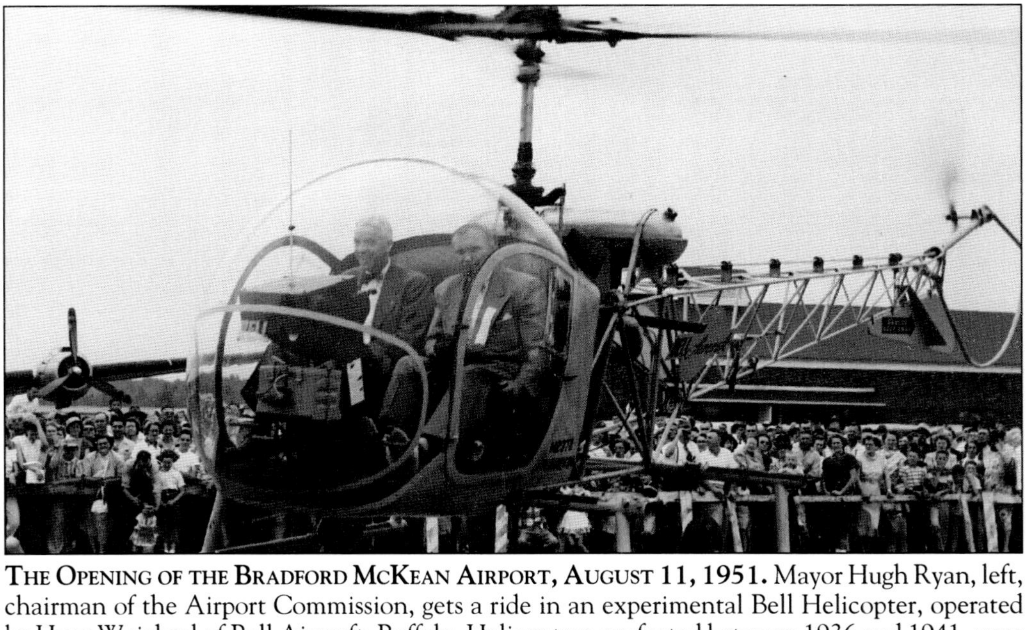

The Opening of the Bradford McKean Airport, August 11, 1951. Mayor Hugh Ryan, left, chairman of the Airport Commission, gets a ride in an experimental Bell Helicopter, operated by Hans Weichsel of Bell Aircraft, Buffalo. Helicopters, perfected between 1936 and 1941, were just beginning to be widely used as a means of transportation. At this time helicopters were an unusual sight in the Bradford area.

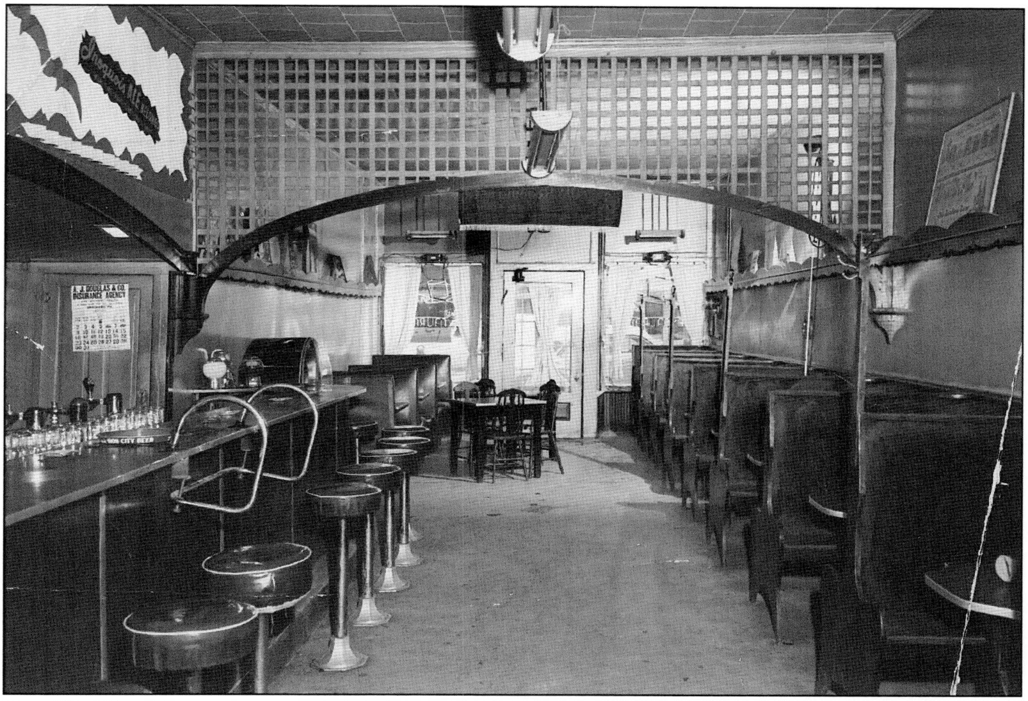

THE HI HAT RESTAURANT, 1948. Located on Mechanic Street, the 'Hi Hat,' owned by Nuzio Carducci and Frank Pazzelli, was a popular spot for a late meal after a night at Shea's Theater.

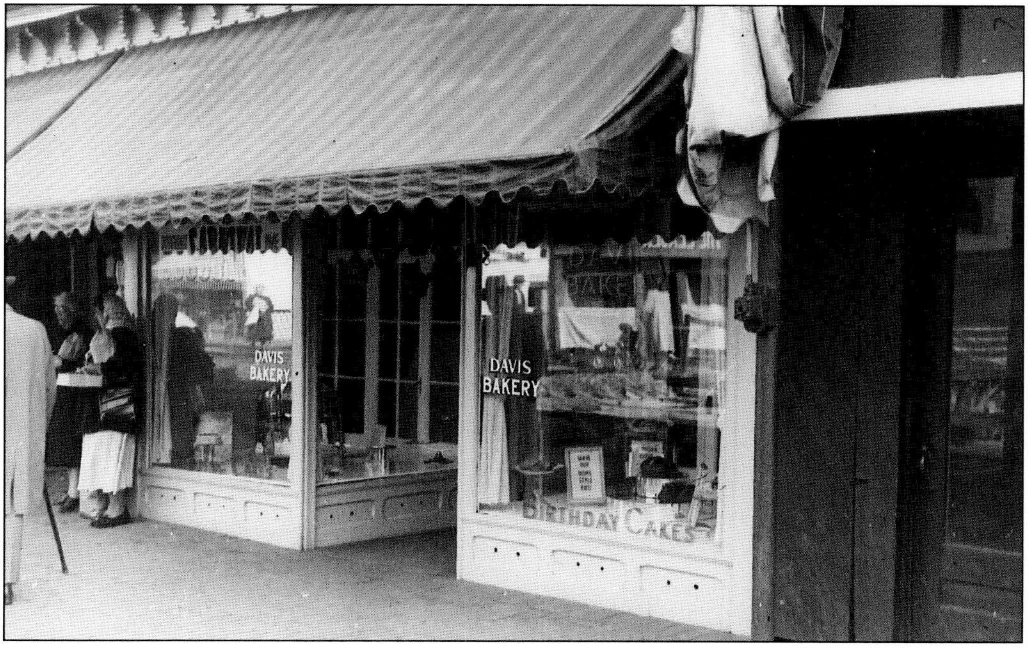

THE DAVIS BAKERY, OCTOBER, 1949. Located on Mechanic Street, the bakery sold a wide variety of cakes, cookies, pies, and pastries. Managed by Fred Johnson since 1928 (he became the owner in 1932) for over 50 years, it is fondly remembered by many, especially children—who always got a free cookie! The bakery was sold in 1981 and today is known as the John Williams Pastry Shoppe.

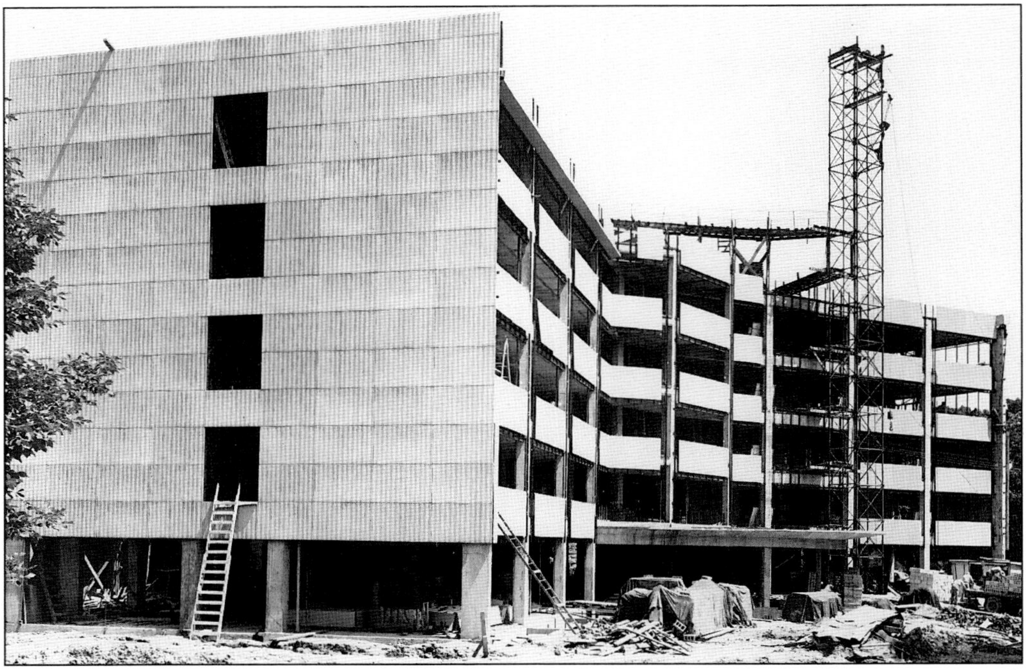

THE BRADFORD HOSPITAL UNDER CONSTRUCTION, JULY 7, 1950. The construction took two years, but when finished the new $1,800,000 five-story fireproof hospital could claim the distinction of being the first aluminum-clad hospital in the world. It officially opened on May 12, 1951, with Mayor Hugh Ryan cutting the ribbon.

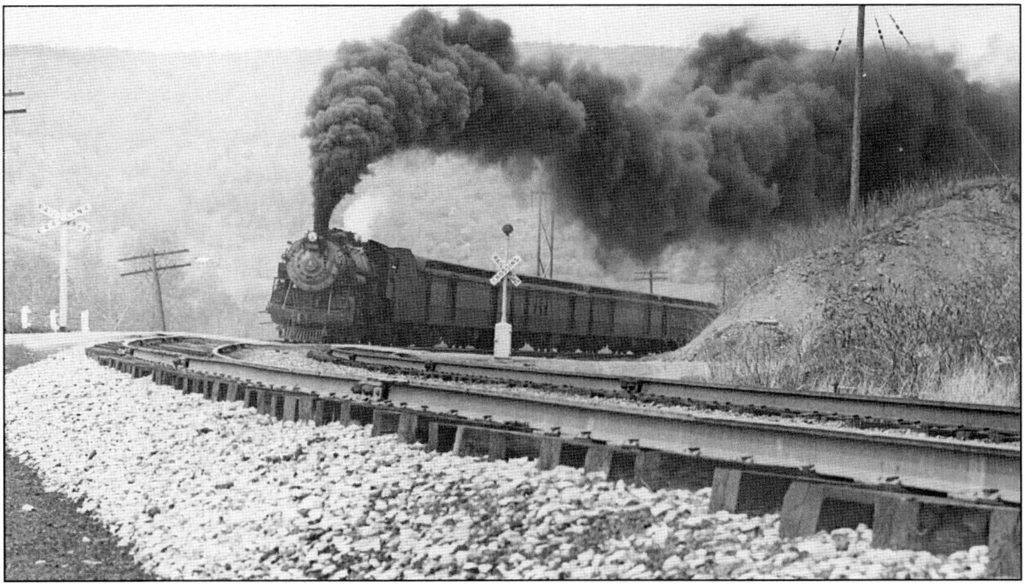

THE LAST STEAM TRAIN OUT OF BRADFORD, 1955. It was the passing of an era at 2:10 p.m., May 4, when the 144-ton Baltimore & Ohio Railroad steam locomotive chugged out of Bradford on its last scheduled run. It was the last regular train—freight or passenger—to be hauled by a steam locomotive. Dr. Matthew A. McGrail of Bradford, a railroad surgeon for both the B & O and the Erie Railroads and a railroad buff, was on hand to fire the engine for the last time. Beginning May 5, diesel locomotives were used exclusively.